C# and .NET Core Test-Driven Development

Dive into TDD to create flexible, maintainable, and production-ready .NET Core applications

Ayobami Adewole

BIRMINGHAM - MUMBAI

C# and .NET Core Test-Driven Development

Commissioning Editor: Merint Mathew
Acquisition Editor: Chaitanya Nair
Content Development Editor: Priyanka Sawant
Technical Editor: Ruvika Rao
Copy Editor: Safis Editing
Project Coordinator: Vaidehi Sawant
Proofreader: Safis Editing
Indexer: Rekha Nair
Graphics: Jason Monteiro
Production Coordinator: Deepika Naik

First published: May 2018

Production reference: 1160518

Published by Packt Publishing Ltd.
Livery Place
35 Livery Street
Birmingham
B3 2PB, UK.

ISBN 978-1-78829-248-1

www.packtpub.com

To my mother, Modupe Adewole, and my father, Adegoke Adewole, for believing in me and buying me my first computer. Also, to my siblings and partner for their love and support.

`mapt.io`

Mapt is an online digital library that gives you full access to over 5,000 books and videos, as well as industry leading tools to help you plan your personal development and advance your career. For more information, please visit our website.

Why subscribe?

- Spend less time learning and more time coding with practical eBooks and Videos from over 4,000 industry professionals

- Improve your learning with Skill Plans built especially for you

- Get a free eBook or video every month

- Mapt is fully searchable

- Copy and paste, print, and bookmark content

PacktPub.com

Did you know that Packt offers eBook versions of every book published, with PDF and ePub files available? You can upgrade to the eBook version at `www.PacktPub.com` and as a print book customer, you are entitled to a discount on the eBook copy. Get in touch with us at `service@packtpub.com` for more details.

At `www.PacktPub.com`, you can also read a collection of free technical articles, sign up for a range of free newsletters, and receive exclusive discounts and offers on Packt books and eBooks.

Contributors

About the author

Ayobami Adewole comes from Ibadan city in Nigeria. He is very passionate about computers and what they can be programmed to do. He is an ardent lover of the .NET stack of technologies and has developed several cutting-edge enterprise applications using the platform.

He offers consultancy services on VoIP and Unified Communication technologies, Customer Relationship Management Systems, Business Process Automation, Enterprise Application Development, and Quality Assurance.

I would like to specially thank Chaitanya Nair, Priyanka Sawant, Ruvika Rao, and the other staff at Packt for their dedication, patience, and support throughout the course of writing the book. I would also like to thank Gaurav Aroraa for taking the time to review the book.

Special thanks to my parents, siblings, and partner for their unwavering support while I was writing the book.

About the reviewer

Gaurav Aroraa has an MPhil in computer science. He is a Microsoft MVP, lifetime member of Computer Society of India (CSI), advisory member of IndiaMentor, certified as a Scrum trainer/coach, XEN for ITIL-F, and APMG for PRINCE-F and PRINCE-P. He is an open source developer, contributor to TechNet Wiki, and the founder of Ovatic Systems Private Limited. During his 20 year career, he has mentored thousands of students and industry professionals. In addition to this, he's written 100+ white papers for research scholars and various universities across the globe.

> *I'd like to thank my wife, Shuby Arora, and my angel daughter, Aarchi Arora, as well as the team at Packt.*

Packt is searching for authors like you

If you're interested in becoming an author for Packt, please visit `authors.packtpub.com` and apply today. We have worked with thousands of developers and tech professionals, just like you, to help them share their insight with the global tech community. You can make a general application, apply for a specific hot topic that we are recruiting an author for, or submit your own idea.

Table of Contents

Preface

How do you verify that your cross-platform .NET Core application will work wherever it is deployed? As your business, team, and the technical environment evolves, can your code evolve with it? You can simplify your code base, make finding and fixing bugs trivial, and ensure your code does what you think it does by following the principles of test-driven development.

This book guides developers through the process of creating robust, production-ready C# 7 and .NET Core applications by establishing a professional test-driven development process. To do this, you will begin by learning the stages of the TDD life cycle, some best practices, and some anti-patterns.

After covering the basics of TDD in the first chapter, you will get right into creating a sample ASP.NET Core MVC application. You will learn how to write testable code with SOLID principles, and set up dependency injection.

Next, you will learn how to create unit tests using the xUnit.net testing framework, and how to use its attributes and assertions. Once you have the basics in place, you will learn how to create data-driven unit tests and how to mock dependencies in your code.

At the end of this book, you will wrap up by creating a healthy continuous integration process, using GitHub, TeamCity, VSTS, and Cake. Finally, you will modify the Continuous Integration build to test, version, and package a sample application.

Who this book is for

This book is for .NET developers who would like to build quality, flexible, easy-to-maintain, and efficient enterprise applications by implementing the principles of test-driven development.

What this book covers

Chapter 1, *Exploring Test-Driven Development*, introduces you to how you can improve your coding habits and code by learning and following the proven principles of test-driven development.

Chapter 2, *Getting Started with .NET Core,* introduces you to the super-cool new cross-platform capabilities of .NET Core and C# 7. You will learn by doing as we create an ASP.NET MVC application on Ubuntu Linux with test-driven development principles.

Chapter 3, *Writing Testable Code,* demonstrates that, in order to reap the benefits of a test-driven development cycle, you must write code that is testable. In this chapter, we will discuss the SOLID principles for creating testable code and learn how to set up our .NET core application for dependency injection.

Chapter 4, *.NET Core Unit Testing,* presents the unit testing frameworks available for .NET Core and C#. We will use the xUnit framework to create a shared test context of setup and teardown code. You will also understand how to create basic unit tests and prove the results of your unit tests with xUnit assertions.

Chapter 5, *Data-Driven Unit Tests,* presents concepts that allow you to test your code over a variety of inputs by running over a set of data, either inline or from a data source. In this chapter, we will create data-driven unit tests or theories in xUnit.

Chapter 6, *Mocking Dependencies,* explains that mock objects are simulated objects that mimic the behavior of real objects. In this chapter, you will learn how to use the Moq framework to isolate the class you're testing from its dependencies using mock objects created with Moq.

Chapter 7, *Continuous Integration and Project Hosting,* focuses on the goal of the test-driven development cycle of quickly providing feedback on code quality. A continuous integration process extends this feedback cycle to uncovering code integration issues. In this chapter, you will begin creating a continuous integration process that can provide rapid feedback on code quality and integration issues across a development team.

Chapter 8, *Creating Continuous Integration Build Processes,* explains that a great continuous integration process brings together many different steps into an easily repeatable process. In this chapter, you will configure TeamCity and VSTS to use a cross-platform build automation system called Cake to clean, build, restore package dependencies and test your solution.

Chapter 9, *Testing and Packaging the Application,* teaches you to modify the Cake build script to run your suite of xUnit tests. You will finish up the process by versioning and packaging an application for distribution on the various platforms that .NET Core supports.

To get the most out of this book

C# programming and working knowledge of Microsoft Visual Studio is assumed.

Download the example code files

You can download the example code files for this book from your account at
`www.packtpub.com`. If you purchased this book elsewhere, you can visit
`www.packtpub.com/support` and register to have the files emailed directly to you.

You can download the code files by following these steps:

1. Log in or register at `www.packtpub.com`.
2. Select the **SUPPORT** tab.
3. Click on **Code Downloads & Errata**.
4. Enter the name of the book in the **Search** box and follow the onscreen
   instructions.

Once the file is downloaded, please make sure that you unzip or extract the folder using the
latest version of:

- WinRAR/7-Zip for Windows
- Zipeg/iZip/UnRarX for Mac
- 7-Zip/PeaZip for Linux

The code bundle for the book is also hosted on GitHub at `https://github.com/
PacktPublishing/CSharp-and-.NET-Core-Test-Driven-Development`. In case there's an
update to the code, it will be updated on the existing GitHub repository.

We also have other code bundles from our rich catalog of books and videos available
at `https://github.com/PacktPublishing/`. Check them out!

Download the color images

We also provide a PDF file that has color images of the screenshots/diagrams used in this
book. You can download it here: `https://www.packtpub.com/sites/default/files/
downloads/CSharpanddotNETTestDrivenDevelopment_ColorImages.pdf`.

Conventions used

There are a number of text conventions used throughout this book.

`CodeInText`: Indicates code words in text, database table names, folder names, filenames, file extensions, pathnames, dummy URLs, user input, and Twitter handles. Here is an example: "For the test to pass, you have to implement the production code iteratively. When the following `IsServerOnline` method is implemented, the `Test_IsServerOnline_ShouldReturnTrue` test method is expected to pass."

A block of code is set as follows:

```
[Fact]
public void Test_IsServerOnline_ShouldReturnTrue()
{
    bool isOnline=IsServerOnline();
    Assert.True(isOnline);
}
```

Any command-line input or output is written as follows:

```
sudo apt-get update
sudo apt-get install dotnet-sdk-2.0.0
```

Bold: Indicates a new term, an important word, or words that you see onscreen. For example, words in menus or dialog boxes appear in the text like this. Here is an example: "Visual Studio Code will attempt to download the required dependencies for the Linux platform, **Omnisharp for Linux** and **.NET Core Debugger**."

 Warnings or important notes appear like this.

 Tips and tricks appear like this.

Get in touch

Feedback from our readers is always welcome.

General feedback: Email `feedback@packtpub.com` and mention the book title in the subject of your message. If you have questions about any aspect of this book, please email us at `questions@packtpub.com`.

Errata: Although we have taken every care to ensure the accuracy of our content, mistakes do happen. If you have found a mistake in this book, we would be grateful if you would report this to us. Please visit `www.packtpub.com/submit-errata`, selecting your book, clicking on the Errata Submission Form link, and entering the details.

Piracy: If you come across any illegal copies of our works in any form on the Internet, we would be grateful if you would provide us with the location address or website name. Please contact us at `copyright@packtpub.com` with a link to the material.

If you are interested in becoming an author: If there is a topic that you have expertise in and you are interested in either writing or contributing to a book, please visit `authors.packtpub.com`.

Reviews

Please leave a review. Once you have read and used this book, why not leave a review on the site that you purchased it from? Potential readers can then see and use your unbiased opinion to make purchase decisions, we at Packt can understand what you think about our products, and our authors can see your feedback on their book. Thank you!

For more information about Packt, please visit `packtpub.com`.

1
Exploring Test-Driven Development

In order to craft robust, maintainable, and scalable software applications, software development teams and stakeholders must make certain important decisions early in the software development process. These decision makers must adopt the software industry's tested and proven best practices and standards throughout the different stages of software development.

The quality of software projects can quickly degrade when developers build the code base using development approaches, coding styles, and practices that automatically make source code rigid and difficult to maintain. This chapter points out the habits and practices that result in writing bad code and should therefore be avoided. The programming habits, development styles, and approaches that should be learned to facilitate writing clean and maintainable code are explained.

In this chapter, we will cover the following topics:

- Difficulty in maintaining code
- How bad code gets that way
- What we can do to prevent bad code
- The principles of test-driven development
- The test-driven development cycle

Difficulty in maintaining code

There are two types of code—good code and bad code. The syntax of both types of code may be correct when compiled and running the code can give the expected results. However, bad code leads to serious issues when it comes to extending or even making little changes to the code, due to the way it was written.

When programmers write code using unprofessional approaches and styles, this often results in bad code. Also, the use of unreadable coding styles or formats as well as not properly and effectively testing code are all precursors to bad code. Code can be written poorly when programmers sacrifice professionalism in order to meet approaching deadlines and project milestones.

I have come across a few software projects that rapidly become legacy software projects that are abandoned because of incessant production bugs and the inability to incorporate change requests from users easily. This is because these software applications were deployed into production with a severe accumulation of technical debts through bad code written by software developers as a result of making poor design and development decisions and using programming styles known to cause future maintenance problems.

Source code elements—methods, classes, comments, and other artifacts—should be easy to read, understand, debug, refactor, and extend if required by another developer other than the original developer; otherwise, bad code has already been written.

You know you have bad code when, extending or adding new features, you break the existing working features. This can also happen when there are portions of code that cannot be decoded or any changes to them will bring the system to a halt. Another reason for bad code is usually because of nonadherence to object-oriented and **Don't Repeat Yourself (DRY)** principles or wrong use of the principles.

 DRY is an important principle in programming, which aims at breaking down a system into small components. These components can easily be managed, maintained, and reused in order to avoid writing duplicate code and having different parts of code performing the same function.

How does bad code appear?

Bad code doesn't just appear in a code base; programmers write bad code. Most of the time, bad code can be written because of any of the following reasons:

- Use of wrong approaches by developers when writing code that is often attributed to tight coupling of components
- Faulty program designs
- Bad naming conventions for program elements and objects

- Writing code that is not readable as well as having a code base without proper test cases, thus causing difficulty when there is a need to maintain the code base

Tight coupling

Most legacy software applications are known to be tightly coupled, with little or no flexibility and modularity. Tightly coupled software components lead to a rigid code base which can be difficult to modify, extend, and maintain. As most software applications evolve over time, big maintenance issues are created when components of applications are tightly coupled. This is due to the changes in requirements, user's business processes, and operations.

Third-party libraries and frameworks reduce development time and allow developers to concentrate on implementing users' business logic and requirements without having to waste valuable productive time reinventing the wheel through implementing common or mundane tasks. However, at times, developers tightly couple the applications with third-party libraries and frameworks, creating maintenance bottlenecks that require great efforts to fix when the need arises to replace a referenced library or framework.

The following code snippet shows an example of tight coupling with a third-party smpp library:

```
public void SendSMS()
{
    SmppManager smppManager= new SmppManager();
    smppManager.SendMessage("0802312345","Hello", "John");
}

public class SmppManager
{
    private string sourceAddress;
    private SmppClient smppClient;

    public SmppManager()
    {
        smppClient = new SmppClient();
        smppClient.Start();
    }
    public void SendMessage(string recipient, string message, string
senderName)
    {
        // send message using referenced library
    }
}
```

Code smell

Code smell is a term that was first used by *Kent Beck*, which indicates deeper issues in the source code. Code smell in a code base can come from having replications in the source code, use of inconsistent or vague naming conventions and coding styles, creating methods with a long list of parameters, and having monster methods and classes, that is methods or classes that know and do too much thereby violating the single responsibility principle. The list goes on and on.

A common code smell in the source code is when a developer creates two or more methods that perform the same action with little or no variation or with program details or facts that ought to be implemented in a single point replicated in several methods or classes, leading to a code base that is not easy to maintain.

The following two ASP.NET MVC action methods have lines of code that create a strongly-typed list of strings of years and months. These lines of code, that could easily have been refactored into a third method and called by both methods, have been replicated in these two methods:

```
[HttpGet]
public ActionResult GetAllTransactions()
{
    List<string> years = new List<string>();
    for (int i = DateTime.Now.Year; i >= 2015; i--)
        years.Add(i.ToString());
    List<string> months = new List<string>();
    for (int j = 1; j <= 12; j++)
        months.Add(j.ToString());
    ViewBag.Transactions= GetTransactions(years,months);
     return View();
}


[HttpGet]
public ActionResult SearchTransactions()
{
    List<string> years = new List<string>();
    for (int i = DateTime.Now.Year; i >= 2015; i--)
        years.Add(i.ToString());
    List<string> months = new List<string>();
    for (int j = 1; j <= 12; j++)
        months.Add(j.ToString());
    ViewBag.Years = years;
    ViewBag.Months = months;
    return View();
```

```
}
```

Another common code smell occurs when developers create methods with a long list of parameters, as in the following method:

```
public void ProcessTransaction(string  username, string password, float
transactionAmount, string transactionType, DateTime time, bool canProcess,
bool retryOnfailure)
{
    //Do something
}
```

Bad or broken designs

Quite often, the structure or design and patterns used in implementing an application can result in bad code, most especially when object-oriented programming principles or design patterns are wrongly used. A common anti-pattern is **spaghetti coding**. It is common among developers with little grasp of object-orientation and this involves creating a code base with unclear structures, little or no reusability, and no relationships between objects and components. This leads to applications that are difficult to maintain and extend.

There is a common practice among inexperienced developers, which is the unnecessary or inappropriate use of design patterns in solving application complexity. The design patterns when used incorrectly can give a code base bad structure and design. The use of design patterns should simplify complexity and create readable and maintainable solutions to software problems. When a pattern is causing a readability issue and overtly adding complexity to a program, it is worth reconsidering whether to use the pattern at all, as the pattern is being misused.

For example, a singleton pattern is used to create a single instance to a resource. The design of a singleton class should have a private constructor with no arguments, a static variable with reference to the single instance of the resource, and a managed public means of referencing the static variable. A singleton pattern can simplify the access to a single-shared resource but can also cause a lot of problems when not implemented with thread safety in mind. Two or more threads can access the `if (smtpGateway==null)` line at the same time, which can create multiple instances of the resource if the line is evaluated to `true`, as with the implementation shown in the following code:

```
public class SMTPGateway
{
    private static SMTPGateway smtpGateway=null;

    private SMTPGateway()
```

```
        {
        }

    public static SMTPGateway SMTPGatewayObject
    {
        get
        {
            if (smtpGateway==null)
            {
                smtpGateway = new SMTPGateway();
            }
            return smtpGateway;
        }
    }
}
```

Naming the program elements

Meaningful and descriptive element naming can greatly improve the source code's readability. It allows easy comprehension of the logical flow of the program. It is amazing how software developers still give names to program elements that are too short or not descriptive enough, such as giving a variable a letter name or using acronyms for variable naming.

Generic or elusive names for elements lead to ambiguity. For example, having a method name as `Extract()` or `Calculate()` at first glance results in subjective interpretations. The same is applicable to using vague names for variables. For example:

```
int x2;

string xxya;
```

While program element naming in itself is an art, names are to be selected to define the purposes as well as succinctly describe the elements and ensure that the chosen names comply with the standards and rules of the programming language being used.

More information on acceptable naming guidelines and conventions is available at: `https://docs.microsoft.com/en-us/dotnet/standard/design-guidelines/naming-guidelines`.

Source code readability

A good code base can be easily distinguished from a bad one by how quickly a new team member or even the programmer can easily understand it after leaving it for a few years. Quite often, because of tight schedules and approaching deadlines, software development teams tend to compromise and sacrifice professionalism to meet deadlines, by not following the recommended best practices and standards. This often leads them to produce code that is not readable.

The following code snippet will perform what it is intended to do, although it contains elements written using terrible naming conventions and this affects the code's readability:

```
public void updatetableloginentries()
{
    com.Connection = conn;
    SqlParameter par1 = new SqlParameter();
    par1.ParameterName = "@username";
    par1.Value = main.username;
    com.Parameters.Add(par1);
    SqlParameter par2 = new SqlParameter();
    par2.ParameterName = "@date";
    par2.Value = main.date;
    com.Parameters.Add(par2);
    SqlParameter par3 = new SqlParameter();
    par3.ParameterName = "@logintime";
    par3.Value = main.logintime;
    com.Parameters.Add(par3);
    SqlParameter par4 = new SqlParameter();
    par4.ParameterName = "@logouttime";
    par4.Value = DateTime.Now.ToShortTimeString(); ;
    com.Parameters.Add(par4);
    com.CommandType = CommandType.Text;
    com.CommandText = "update loginentries set logouttime=@logouttime where
username=@username and date=@date and logintime=@logintime";
    openconn();
    com.ExecuteNonQuery();
    closeconn();
}
```

Poor source code documentation

Code can be easily understood when written using the programming language's coding style and convention while avoiding the bad code pitfalls discussed earlier. However, source code documentation is very valuable and its importance in software projects cannot be overemphasized. Brief and meaningful documentation of classes and methods can give developers a quick insight into their internal structures and operations.

Understanding a complex or poorly written class becomes a nightmare when there is no proper documentation in place. When the original programmer that wrote the code is no longer around to provide clarifications, valuable productive time can be lost trying to understand how the class or method is implemented.

Non-tested code

Though many articles have been written and discussions have been initiated at various developers' conferences on different types of testing—test-driven development, behavior-driven development, and acceptance test-driven development—it is very concerning that there are developers that continuously develop and ship software applications that are not thoroughly tested or tested at all.

Shipping applications that are poorly tested can have catastrophic consequences and maintenance problems. Notable is **NASA's Mars Climate Orbiter** launched on **December 11, 1998** that failed just as the orbiter approached Mars, due to a software error caused by an error in conversion where the orbiter's program code was calculating a metric in pounds instead of newtons. A simple unit testing of the particular module responsible for calculating the metrics could have detected the error and maybe prevented the failure.

Also, according to the *State of Test-First Methodologies 2016 Report*, a survey of the adoption of test-first methodologies of more than 200 software organizations from 15 different countries, conducted by a testing services company named **QASymphony**, revealed that nearly half of the survey respondents had not implemented a test-first methodology in the applications they had developed.

What we can do to prevent bad code

Writing clean code requires a conscious effort of maintaining professionalism and following best industry standards throughout the stages of the software development process. Bad code should be avoided right from the onset of software project development, because the accumulation of bad debt through bad code can slow down software project completion and create future issues after the software has been deployed to production.

To avoid bad code, you have to be lazy, as the general saying goes that lazy programmers are the best and smartest programmers because they hate repetitive tasks, such as having to go back to fix issues that could have been prevented. Try to use programming styles and approaches that avoid writing bad code, to avoid having to rewrite your code in order to fix avoidable issues, bugs, or to pay technical debts.

Loose coupling

Loose coupling is the direct opposite of tight coupling. This is a good object-oriented programming practice of separation of concerns by allowing components to have little or no information of the internal workings and implementation of other components. Communication is done through interfaces. This approach allows for an easy substitution of components without many changes to the entire code base. The sample code in the *Tight coupling* section can be refactored to allow loose coupling:

```
//The dependency injection would be done using Ninject
public ISmppManager smppManager { get; private set; }

public void SendSMS()
{
    smppManager.SendMessage("0802312345","Hello", "John");
}

public class SmppManager
{
    private string sourceAddress;
    private SmppClient smppClient;

    public SmppManager()
    {
        smppClient = new SmppClient();
        smppClient.Start();
    }
    public void SendMessage(string recipient, string message, string
senderName)
```

```
        {
            // send message using referenced library
        }
}
public interface ISmppManager
{
    void SendMessage(string recipient, string message, string senderName);
}
```

Sound architecture and design

Bad code can be avoided through the use of a good development architecture and design strategy. This will ensure that development teams and organizations have a high-level architecture, strategy, practices, guidelines, and governance plans that team members must follow to prevent cutting corners and avoiding bad code throughout the development process.

Through continuous learning and improvement, software development team members can develop thick skins towards writing bad code. The sample code snippet in the *Bad or broken designs* section can be refactored to be thread-safe and avoid thread-related issues, as shown in the following code:

```
public class SMTPGateway
{
    private static SMTPGateway smtpGateway=null;
    private static object lockObject= new object();

    private SMTPGateway()
    {
    }

    public static SMTPGateway SMTPGatewayObject
    {
        get
        {
            lock (lockObject)
            {
                if (smtpGateway==null)
                {
                    smtpGateway = new SMTPGateway();
                }
            }
            return smtpGateway;
        }
    }
```

```
}
```

Preventing and detecting code smell

Programming styles and coding formats that result in code smell should be avoided. By adequately paying attention to the details, bad code pointers discussed in the *Code smell* section should be avoided. The replicated lines of code in the two methods of the source code mentioned in the *Code smell* section can be refactored to a third method. This avoids replication of code and allows for easy modifications:

```
[HttpGet]
public ActionResult GetAllTransactions()
{
    var yearsAndMonths=GetYearsAndMonths();
    ViewBag.Transactions=
GetTransactions(yearsAndMonths.Item1,yearsAndMonths.Item2);
    return View();
}

[HttpGet]
public ActionResult SearchTransactions()
{
    var yearsAndMonths=GetYearsAndMonths();
    ViewBag.Years = yearsAndMonths.Item1;
    ViewBag.Months = yearsAndMonths.Item2;
    return View();
}

private (List<string>, List<string>) GetYearsAndMonths(){
    List<string> years = new List<string>();
    for (int i = DateTime.Now.Year; i >= 2015; i--)
        years.Add(i.ToString());
    List<string> months = new List<string>();
    for (int j = 1; j <= 12; j++)
        months.Add(j.ToString());
    return (years,months);
}
```

Also, the method with a long list of parameters in the *Code smell* section can be refactored to use C# **Plain Old CLR Object (POCO)** for clarity and reusability:

```
public void ProcessTransaction(Transaction transaction)
{
    //Do something
}
```

```
public class Transaction
{
    public string  Username{get;set;}
    public string Password{get;set;}
    public float TransactionAmount{get;set;}
    public string TransactionType{get;set;}
    public DateTime Time{get;set;}
    public bool CanProcess{get;set;}
    public bool RetryOnfailure{get;set;}
}
```

Development teams should have guidelines, principles, and coding conventions and standards developed jointly by the team members and should be constantly updated and refined. These, when used effectively, will prevent code smell in the software code base and allow for the easy identification of potential bad code by team members.

C# coding conventions

Using the guidelines in C# coding conventions facilitates the mastery of writing clean, readable, easy to modify, and maintainable code. Use variable names that are descriptive and represent what they are used for, as shown in the following code:

```
int accountNumber;

string firstName;
```

Also, having more than one statement or declaration on a line clogs readability. Comments should be on a new line and not at the end of the code. You can read more about C# coding conventions at: https://docs.microsoft.com/en-us/dotnet/csharp/programming-guide/inside-a-program/coding-conventions.

Succinct and proper documentation

You should always try to write self-documenting code. This can be achieved through good programming style. Write code in such a manner that your classes, methods, and other objects are self-documenting. A new developer should be able to pick your code and not have to be stressed out before understanding what the code does and its internal structure.

Coding elements should be descriptive and meaningful to provide an insight to the reader. In situations where you have to document a method or class to provide further clarity, adopt the **Keep It Simple Short (KISS)** approach, briefly stating the reasons for a certain decision. Check the following code snippet; nobody wants to have to read two pages of documentation for a class containing 200 lines of code:

```
///
/// This class uses SHA1 algorithm for encryption with randomly generated
salt for uniqueness
///
public class AESEncryptor
{
    //Code goes here
}
```

 KISS also known as **Keep it Simple, Stupid**, is a design principle that states that most systems work at their best when they are kept simple rather than making them unnecessarily complex. The principle aims at aiding programmers to keep the code simple as much as possible, to ensure that code can be easily maintained in the future.

Why test-driven development?

Each time I enter a discussion with folks not practicing test-driven development, they mostly have one thing in common, which is that it consumes time and resources and it does not really give a return on investment. I usually reply to them by asking which is better, detecting bugs and potential bottlenecks and fixing them while the application is being developed or hotfixing bugs when the application is in production? Test-driven development will save you a lot of problems and ensure you produce robust and issue-free applications.

Building for longevity

To avoid future problems resulting from issues when making modifications to a system in production as a result of changes in user requirements, as well as bugs which get exposed because of inherent bad code in a code base and accumulated technical debt, you need to have the mindset of developing with the future in mind and embracing changes.

Use flexible patterns and always employ good object-oriented development and design principles when writing code. The requirements of most software projects change over their life cycles. It is wrong to assume that a component or part might not change, so try and put a mechanism in place to allow the application to be graceful and accept future changes.

The principles of test-driven development

Test-driven development (TDD) is an iterative agile development technique that emphasizes test-first development, which implies that you write a test before you write production-ready code to make the test pass. The TDD technique focuses on writing clean and quality code by ensuring that the code passes the earlier written tests by continuously refactoring the code.

TDD, being a test-first development approach, places greater emphasis on building well-tested software applications. This allows developers to write code in relation to solving the tasks defined in the tests after a thorough thought process. It is a common practice in TDD that the development process begins with writing the tests code before the actual application code is written.

TDD introduces an entirely new development paradigm and shifts your mindset to begin thinking about testing your code right before you even start writing the code. This contrasts with the traditional development technique of deferring code testing to the later stage of the development cycle, an approach known as **test last development (TLD)**.

TDD has been discussed at several conferences and hackathons. Many technology advocates and bloggers have blogged about TDD, its principles, and its benefits. At the same time, there have been many talks and articles written against TDD. The honest truth is TDD rocks, it works, and it offers great benefits when practiced correctly and consistently.

You might probably be wondering, like every developer new to TDD, why write a test first, since you trust your coding instinct to write clean code that always works and usually will test the entire code when you've done coding. Your coding instinct may be right or it may not. There is no way to validate this assumption until the code is validated against a set of written test cases and passes; trust is good, but control is better.

Test cases in TDD are prepared with the aid of user stories or use cases of the software application being developed. The code is then written and refactored iteratively until the tests pass. For example, a method written to validate the length of a credit card might contain test cases to validate the correct length, incorrect length, and even when the null or empty credit card is passed as a parameter to the method.

Many variants of TDD have been proposed ever since it was originally popularized. A variant is **behavior-driven development (BDD)** or **acceptance test–driven development (ATDD)**, which follows all the principles of TDD while the tests are based on expected user-specified behavior.

Origin of TDD

There is literally no written evidence as to when the practice of TDD was introduced into computer programming or by which company it was first used. Nevertheless, there is an excerpt from *Digital Computer Programming*, by D.D. McCracken, in 1957, which indicated that the concept of TDD was not new and had been used by earlier folks, though the nomenclature apparently was different.

The first attack on the checkout problem may be made before coding has begun. In order to fully ascertain the accuracy of the answers, it is necessary to have a hand-calculated check case with which to compare the answers which will later be calculated by the machine. This means that stored program machines are never used for a true one-shot problem. There must always be an element of iteration to make it pay.

Also, in the early 1960s, folks at IBM ran a project (**Project Mecury**) for NASA where they utilized a technique like TDD where half-day iterations were done and the development team performed a review of the changes made. This was a manual process and cannot be compared to the automated tests we have today.

TDD was originally popularized by Kent Beck. He attributed it to an excerpt he read in an ancient book where TDD was described with the simple statements, *you take the input tape, manually type in the output tape you expect, then program until the actual output tape matches the expected output*. The concept of TDD was redefined by Kent Beck when he developed the first xUnit test framework at Smalltalk.

It is safe to say that the Smalltalk community used TDD long before it became widespread because **SUnit** was used in the community. Not until SUnit was ported to **JUnit** by *Kent Beck* and other enthusiasts was it that TDD became widely known. Since then different testing frameworks have been developed. A popular tool is the **xUnit**, with ports available for a large number of programming languages.

TDD misconceptions

Developers have different opinions when it comes to TDD. Most developers do complain about the time and resources required to practice TDD fully and how practicing TDD might not be feasible, based on tight deadlines and schedules. This perception is common among developers just adopting the technique, on the premise that TDD requires writing double code and that time spent doing this could have been used to work on developing other features, and that TDD is best suited for projects with small features or tasks and will be time-wasting with little return on investment for large projects.

Also, some developers complain that mocking can make TDD very difficult and frustrating, as the required dependencies are not to be implemented at the same time the dependent code is being implemented but should be mocked. Using the traditional approach of testing last, the dependencies can be implemented and all the different parts of the code can be tested afterwards.

Another popular misconception is that in the real sense tests cannot be written until the design is determined which relies on code implementation. This is not true, as adopting TDD will ensure there is a clear-cut plan on how the code implementation is to be done, which in turn gives a proper design which can aid the creation of efficient and reliable tests for the intended code to be written.

Some folks at times use TDD and unit testing interchangeably, taking them to be the same. TDD and unit testing are not the same. Unit testing involves practicing TDD at the smallest unit or level of coding, which is a method or function, while TDD is a technique and design approach that encompasses unit testing and integration testing, as well as acceptance testing.

Developers new to TDD often think you must completely write the tests before writing the actual code. The reverse is the case as TDD is an iterative technique. TDD favors exploratory processes where you write the tests and you write enough code. If it fails, you refactor the code until it passes and you can move on to implementing the next feature of your application.

TDD is not a silver bullet that automatically fixes all your bad coding behaviors. You can practice TDD and still write bad code or even bad tests. This is possible if the TDD principles and practices are not correctly used, or even when trying to use TDD where it's not practical to use it.

Benefits of TDD

TDD, when done correctly and appropriately, can give a good return on investment as it facilitates the development of self-testing code, which yields robust software applications with fewer or no bugs. This is because most of the bugs and issues that might appear in production would have been caught and fixed during the development stage.

Documenting the source code is a good coding practice, but in addition to source code documentation, tests are miniature documentations of the source code as they serve as a quick way to understand how a piece of code works. The test will show the expected input together with the expected output or outcomes. The structure of an application can be easily understood from the tests, as there will be tests for all the objects as well as tests for the methods of the objects, showing their usage.

Practicing TDD correctly and continuously helps you to write elegant code with good abstraction, flexible design, and architecture. This is true because, to effectively test all parts of an application, the various dependencies need to be broken down into components that can be tested in isolation and later tested when integrated.

What makes a code clean is when the code has been written using best industry standards, can be easily maintained, is readable, and has tests written to validate its consistent behavior appropriately . This indicates that a code without testing is a bad code as there is no specific way of directly verifying its integrity.

Types of tests

Testing software projects can take different forms and is often carried out by the developers and test analysts or specialists. Testing is carried out to ascertain that the software meets its specified expectation, to identify errors if possible, and to validate that the software is usable. Most programmers often take testing and debugging to be the same. Debugging is carried out to diagnose errors and issues in software and take the possible corrective measures.

Unit tests

This is a level of testing that involves testing each unit that constitutes the components of a software application. This is the lowest level of test and it is done at the method or function level. It is primarily done by programmers, specifically to show code correctness and that the requirement has been correctly implemented. A unit test usually has one or more inputs and outputs.

It is the first level of test usually done in software development and it is designed to isolate units of software systems and test them independently or in isolation. Through unit testing, inherent issues and bugs in systems can be easily detected earlier in the development process.

Integration tests

An integration test is done by combining and testing different units or components that must have been tested in isolation. This test is to ensure that the different units of an application can work together to satisfy the user requirements. Through integration tests, you can uncover bugs in the system when different components interact and exchange data.

This test can be carried out by programmers, software testers, or quality assurance analysts. There are different approaches that can be used for integration testing:

- **Top down**: Top-level components are integrated and tested first before the lower level components
- **Bottom up**: Lower-level components are integrated and tested before top level components
- **Big bang**: All components are integrated together and tested at once

System testing

This level of test is where you validate the entire integrated system to ensure it complies with the specified user requirements. This test is usually performed immediately after the integration test and is carried out by dedicated testers or quality assurance analysts.

The whole software system suite is tested from the user's perspective to identify hidden issues or bugs and usability problems. A rigorous testing of the implemented system is done with the real inputs that the system is meant to process and output is validated against the expected data.

User acceptance testing

User acceptance tests are usually written to specify how software applications work. These tests are intended for business users and programmers and are used to determine if the system meets the expectations and user-specific requirements, and whether the system has been developed completely and correctly based on the specifications. This test is conducted by end users in collaboration with the system developers to determine whether to accept the system formally or make adjustments or modifications.

Principles of TDD

The practice of TDD helps with the design of clean code and serves as a buffer against regression in a large code base. It allows developers to determine easily whether newly implemented features have broken other features that were previously working through the instant feedback obtainable when the tests are run. The working principles of TDD are explained in the following diagram:

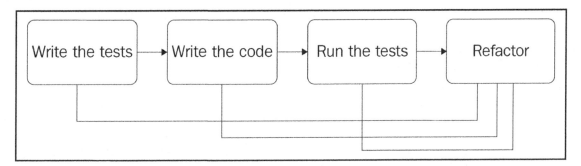

Writing the tests

This is the initial step of the technique, where you have to write the tests that describe a component or feature to be developed. The component can be the user interface, business rule or logic, data persistence routine, or a method implementing a specific user requirement. The tests need to be brief and should contain the required data input and desired outcome expected by the component being tested.

While writing the tests, technically you have solved half of the development task, because the design of the code is usually conceived through the thought pattern and process put into writing the tests. It becomes easier to tackle the difficult code after the easier code, which is the test that has been written. At this point, as a TDD newcomer, the tests are not expected to be 100% perfect or have full code coverage, but with continuous practice and adequate refactoring, this can be achieved.

Writing the code

After the tests have been written, you should write enough code to implement the feature for the tests you wrote earlier. Bear in mind that the goal here is to try to employ good practices and standards in writing the code to make the test pass. All the approaches that lead to writing bad or stinking code should be avoided.

Try to avoid test overfitting, a situation where you write code just to make the tests pass. Instead you should write the code to implement the feature or user requirements fully, so as to ensure that every possible use case of the feature is covered to avoid situations where the code has different behaviors when executed by the test cases and when in production.

Running the tests

When you are sure you have enough code to make the test pass, you should run the test, using the test suite of your choice. At this point, the test might pass or fail. This depends on how you have written the code.

A thumb rule of TDD is to run the tests several times until the tests pass. Initially, when you run the test before the code is fully implemented, the test will fail, which is the expected behavior.

Refactoring

To achieve full code coverage, both the tests and the source code have to be refactored and tested several times to ensure that a robust and clean code is written. Refactoring should be iterative until full coverage is achieved. The refactoring step should remove duplicates from code and attempt to fix any signs of code smell.

The essence of TDD is to write clean code and in turn solid applications, depending on the type of tests being written (unit, acceptance, or integration tests). Refactoring can be localized to just a method or it can affect multiple classes. When refactoring, for example, an interface or multiple methods in a class, it is recommended you make the changes gradually, taking it one test at a time until all the tests and their implementation code are refactored.

Doing TDD the wrong way

As interesting as practicing TDD can be, it can also be wrongly done. Programmers new to TDD can sometimes write monster tests that are way too large and defeat the purpose of test brevity and being able to perform the TDD cycle quickly, leading to a waste of productive development time.

Partial adoption of the technique can also reduce the full benefit of TDD. In situations where only a few developers in a team use the technique and others don't, this will lead to fragmented code where a portion of code is tested and another portion is not, resulting in an unreliable application.

You should avoid writing tests for code that are naturally trivial or not required; for example, writing tests for object accessors. Tests should be run frequently, especially through the use of test runners, build tools, or continuous integration tools. Failing to run the tests often can lead to a situation where the true reflection of the state of the code base is not known even when changes have been made and components are probably failing.

The TDD cycle

The TDD technique follows a tenet known as the red-green-refactor cycle, with the red state being the initial state, indicating the commencement of a **TDD cycle**. At the red state, the test has just been written and will fail when it is run.

The next state is the green state and it shows that the test has passed after the actual application code has been written. Code refactoring is essential to ensure code completeness and robustness. Refactoring will be repeatedly done until the code meets performance and requirement expectations:

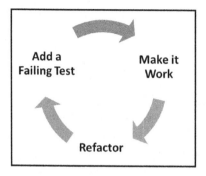

At the beginning of the cycle, the production code to run the test against has not been written, so it is expected that the test will fail. For example, in the following code snippet, the IsServerOnline method has not been implemented yet, and when the Test_IsServerOnline_ShouldReturnTrue unit test method is run, it should fail:

```
public bool IsServerOnline()
{
    return false;
}


[Fact]
public void Test_IsServerOnline_ShouldReturnTrue()
{
    bool isOnline=IsServerOnline();
    Assert.True(isOnline);
}
```

For the test to pass, you have to implement the production code iteratively. When the following IsServerOnline method is implemented, the Test_IsServerOnline_ShouldReturnTrue test method is expected to pass:

```
public bool IsServerOnline()
{
    string address="localhost";
    int port=8034;
    SmppManager smppManager= new SmppManager(address, port);
    bool isOnline=smppManager.TestConnection();
    return isOnline;
}
```

```
[Fact]
public void Test_IsServerOnline_ShouldReturnTrue()
{
    bool isOnline=IsServerOnline();
    Assert.True(isOnline);
}
```

When the test is run and it passes, showing a green color depending on the test runner you are using, this provides an immediate feedback to you on the status of the code. This gives you confidence and inner joy that the code works correctly and behaves as it is intended to.

Refactoring is an iterative endeavor, where you continuously modify the code you have earlier written to pass the test until it has attained the state of production-ready code and that it fully implements the requirements and will work for all possible use cases and scenarios.

Summary

Most potential software project maintenance bottlenecks can be avoided through the use of the principles and coding patterns discussed in this chapter. Attaining professionalism requires consistency to be disciplined and holds true to good coding habits, practices, and having a professional attitude towards TDD.

Writing clean code that is easy to maintain pays off in the long term as less effort will be required to make user-requested changes and users will be kept happy when the application is always available for use with few or no bugs.

In the next chapter, we will explore the .NET Core framework, and its capabilities and limitations. Also, we will take a tour of Microsoft Visual Studio Code before reviewing the new features available in Version 7 of the C# programming language.

Getting Started with .NET Core

2

When Microsoft released the first version of .NET Framework, a platform for creating, running, and deploying services and applications, it was a game changer and a revolution in the Microsoft development community. Several cutting-edge applications were developed with the initial version of the framework and then several versions were released afterwards.

.NET Framework has thrived and matured over the years with support for multiple programming languages and the inclusion of several features to make programming on the platform easy and worthwhile. But as robust and appealing the framework is, there is the limitation of restricting the development and deployment of applications to Microsoft-only operating system variants.

In order to create a cloud-optimized, cross-platform implementation of .NET Framework for developers to solve the limitations of .NET Framework, Microsoft started the development of a .NET Core platform using the .NET Framework. With the introduction of Version 1.0 of .NET Core in 2016, application development on the .NET platform took on a new dimension, as .NET developers could now build applications that worked on Windows, Linux, macOS, and cloud, embedded, and IoT devices with ease. .NET Core is compatible with .NET Framework, Xamarin, and Mono through the .NET Standard.

This chapter will introduce the super cool new cross-platform capabilities of .NET Core and C# 7. We will be learning as we create an ASP.NET MVC application on Ubuntu Linux with TDD. In this chapter, we will cover the following topics:

- .NET Core framework
- The structure of a .NET Core application
- A tour of Microsoft's Visual Studio Code Editor
- A look at the new features of C# 7
- Creating an ASP.NET MVC Core application

.NET Core framework

.NET Core is a cross-platform open source development framework that runs on Windows, Linux, and macOS and cross architecture with support for x86, x64, and ARM. .NET Core was forked from .NET Framework, which technically makes it a subset of the latter, though streamlined line, and modular. .NET Core is a development platform that gives you great flexibility in developing and deploying applications. The new platform frees you from hassles usually experienced during application deployment. Thus, you don't have to worry about managing versions of application runtime on deployment servers.

Currently, in Version 2.0.7, .NET Core includes the .NET runtime with great performance and many features. Microsoft claims it's the fastest version of .NET platform. It has more APIs and more project templates have been added, such as those for developing ReactJS and AngularJS applications that run on .NET Core. Also, Version 2.0.7 has a set of command-line tools that enables you to build and run command-line applications with ease on the different platforms, as well as simplified packaging and support for Visual Studio for Macintosh. A big by-product of .NET Core is the cross-platform modular web framework, ASP.NET Core, which is a total redesign of ASP.NET and runs on .NET Core.

.NET Framework is robust and contains several libraries for use in application development. However, some of the framework's components and libraries can couple with the Windows operating system. For example the `System.Drawing` library depends on Windows GDI, which is why .NET Framework cannot be considered cross-platform even though it has different implementations.

In order to make .NET Core truly cross-platform, components such as Windows Forms and **Windows Presentation Foundation (WPF)** that have strong dependence on the Windows OS have been removed from the platform. ASP.NET Web Forms and **Windows Communication Foundation (WCF)** have also been removed and replaced with ASP.NET Core MVC and ASP.NET Core Web API. Additionally, **Entity Framework (EF)** has been streamlined to make it cross-platform and named Entity Framework Core.

Also, because of the dependency that .NET Framework has on the Windows OS, Microsoft could not open the code base. However, .NET Core is fully open source, hosted on GitHub, and has a thriving developer community, constantly working on new features and extending the scope of the platform.

.NET Standard

.NET Standard is a Microsoft-maintained set of specifications and standards that all .NET platforms must adhere to and implement. It formally specifies the APIs that are meant to be implemented by all variants of the .NET platform. There are currently three development platforms on the .NET platform—.NET Core, .NET Framework, and Xamarin. The .NET platform is needed to provide uniformity, and consistency, and makes it easier to share codes and reuse libraries on the three variants of .NET platform.

.NET platform provides the definition of a set of uniform Base Class Libraries APIs to be implemented by all .NET platforms, to allow developers to easily develop applications and reusable libraries across the .NET platforms. Currently in Version 2.0.7, .NET Standard provides new APIs that were not implemented in Version 1.0 of .NET Core but are now implemented in Version 2.0. More than 20,000 APIs have been added to the runtime components.

Additionally, .NET Standard is a target framework, which means that you can develop your application to target a specific version of .NET Standard, allowing the application to run on any .NET platform that implements the standard, and you can easily share codes, libraries, and binaries among the different .NET platforms. When building your application to target .NET Standard, you should know that higher versions of .NET Standard have more APIs available for use but are not implemented by many platforms. It is always recommended that you target a lower version of the standard, which will guarantee that it's implemented by many platforms:

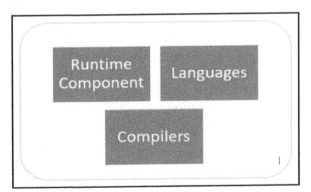

.NET Core components

.NET Core, being a general-purpose application-development platform, is made up of **CoreCLR, CoreFX, SDK and CLI tools**, **application host**, and **dotnet application launcher**:

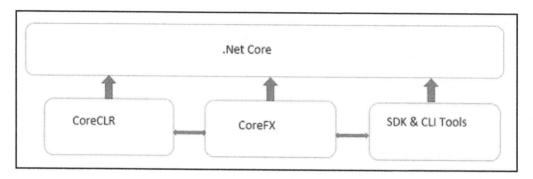

The CoreCLR, also known as .NET Core Runtime, is at the heart of the .NET Core and is a cross-platform implementation of the CLR; the original .NET Framework CLR has been refactored to produce the CoreCLR. The CoreCLR, which is the Common Language Runtime, manages usage and references to objects, communication and interactions of objects written in different programming languages supported in, and performs garbage collection by releasing objects from memory when they are no longer in use. The CoreCLR comprises of the following:

- Garbage collector
- **Just in Time (JIT)** compiler
- Native interop
- Base .NET types

CoreFX is a set of framework or foundational libraries of the .NET Core and it provides primitive datatypes, filesystems, application composition types, consoles, and basic utilities. The CoreFX contains a streamlined library of classes.

.NET Core SDK contains a set of tools including **command-line interface (CLI)** tools and compilers for the different languages supported, used for building applications and libraries to run on .NET Core. The SDK tools and language compilers provide functionalities to make coding easier and faster by giving developers easy access to language components supported by CoreFX libraries.

In order to launch a .NET Core application, the dotnet application host is the component responsible for the selection and hosting of the required runtime for the application. .NET Core has a console application as the main application model and other application models, such as ASP.NET Core, Windows 10 Universal Windows Platform, and Xamarin Forms.

Supported languages

.NET Core 1.0 supported only **C#** and **F#**, but with the release of .NET Core 2.0, **VB.NET** is now supported by the platform. The compilers for the supported languages run on .NET Core and provide access to the underlying features of the platform. This is possible because .NET Core implements .NET Standard specifications and exposes APIs that are available in the .NET Framework. The supported languages and .NET SDK tools can be integrated into different editors and IDEs, giving you different editor options for use in developing applications.

When to choose .NET Core over .NET Framework

Both .NET Core and .NET Framework are well suited for use in *developing robust and scalable enterprise applications*; this is because the two platforms are built on solid code bases and provide a rich set of libraries and routines that simplify most development tasks. The two platforms share many similar components, hence code can be shared across the two development platforms. However, the two platforms are distinct, the selection of .NET Core has the preferred development platform that should be influenced by the development approach as well as the deployment needs and requirements.

Cross-platform requirements

Clearly, when the application you are developing is to be run on multiple platforms, .NET Core should be used. .NET Core being cross-platform makes it suitable for developing services and web applications that can run on **Windows**, **Linux**, and **macOS**. Also, with the introduction of **Visual Studio Code** by Microsoft—an editor with full support for .NET Core that provides intellisense and debugging functionalities, as well as other IDE features that were traditionally available only in **Visual Studio IDE**.

Ease of deployment

With .NET Core, you can install different versions side-by-side, a feature that is not available when using .NET Framework. With the side by side installation of .NET Core, several applications can be installed on a single server, enabling each application to run on its own version of .NET Core. Lately, there has been a lot of attention focused on containers and application containerization. Containers are used for creating standalone packages of software applications, including the runtimes needed to make the applications run in isolation, away from other applications on a shared operating system. Containerizing .NET applications is much better when .NET Core is used as the development platform. This is because of its cross-platform support, thereby allowing deployment of applications to containers of different operating systems. Also, the container images created with .NET Core are smaller and more lightweight.

Scalability and performance

Using .NET Core, developing applications that use microservices architecture is relatively easier. With microservice architecture, you can develop applications that use a mix of different technologies, such as services developed with PHP, Java, or Rails. You can use .NET Core to develop microservices to be deployed on cloud platforms or containers. With .NET Core, you can develop applications that are scalable and can run on high-performance computers or high-end servers, allowing your application to easily serve hundreds of thousands of users.

Limitations of .NET Core

While .NET Core is robust, easy to use, and provides several benefits when used in application development, it is currently not suitable for all development problems and scenarios. Microsoft dropped several technologies that are available on .NET Framework from .NET Core to make it streamlined and cross-platform. Because of this, those technologies are not available for use in .NET Core.

When your application will use a technology not available in .NET Core, for example using WPF or Windows Forms for the presentation layer, WCF Server implementation, or even third-party libraries that do not currently have the .NET Core version, it is preferable and recommended that you develop the application using .NET Framework.

Structure of a .NET Core application

With the release of .NET Core 2.0, new templates were added, providing more options for the different application types that can be run on the platform. In addition to the existing project templates, the following **single-page application (SPA)** templates were added:

- Angular
- ReactJS
- ReactJS and Redux

The console application in .NET Core has a similar structure to that of .NET Framework, whereas ASP.NET Core has several new components, including folders and files, that were not in the previous versions of ASP.NET.

ASP.NET Core MVC project structure

ASP.NET web framework has fully matured over the years, transitioning from web forms to MVC and Web API. ASP.NET core is a new web framework for developing web applications and Web APIs that can run on .NET Core. It is a leaner and more streamlined version of ASP.NET that is easy to deploy with in-built dependency injection. ASP.NET Core can be integrated with frameworks such as AngularJS, Bootstrap, and ReactJS.

ASP.NET Core MVC, similar to ASP.NET MVC, is the framework for building web applications and APIs, using the *Model View Controller pattern*. Like ASP.NET MVC, it supports model binding and validation, tag helpers, and uses *Razor syntax* for the Razor pages and MVC views.

The structure of the ASP.NET Core MVC application differs from that of ASP.NET MVC, with the addition of new folders and files. When you create a new ASP.NET Core project from Visual Studio 2017, Visual Studio for Mac, or through the CLI tools from the solution explorer, you can see the new components added to the project structure.

wwwroot folder

In ASP.NET Core, the newly-added `wwwroot` folder is used to hold libraries and static content, such as images, JavaScript files and libraries, and CSS and HTML for easy access and to serve directly to web clients. The `wwwroot` folder contains `.css`, images, `.js`, and `.lib` folders for organizing the static contents of a site.

Models, Views, and Controllers folders

Similar to the ASP.NET MVC project, an ASP.NET MVC core application's root folder also contains **Models**, **Views**, and **Controllers**, following the convention of the MVC pattern, for proper separation of web application files, codes, and presentation logic.

JSON files – bower.json, appsettings.json, bundleconfig.json

Some other files introduced are `appsettings.json`, which contains all the application settings, `bower.json`, which contains entries for managing client-side packages including CSS and JavaScript frameworks used in the project, and `bundleconfig.json`, which contains entries for configuring bundling and minification for the project.

Program.cs

Like C# console applications, ASP.NET Core has the `Program` class, which is an important class that contains the entry point to the application. The file has the `Main()` method used to run the application and it is used to create an instance of `WebHostBuilder` for creating a host for the application. The `Startup` class to be used by the application is specified in the `Main` method:

```
public class Program
{
    public static void Main(string[] args)
    {
        BuildWebHost(args).Run();
    }

    public static IWebHost BuildWebHost(string[] args) =>
        WebHost.CreateDefaultBuilder(args)
            .UseStartup<Startup>()
            .Build();
}
```

Startup.cs

The `Startup` class is needed by ASP.NET Core applications to manage the application's request pipeline, configure services, and for dependency injection.

Different `Startup` classes can be created for different environments; for example, you can create two `Startup` classes in your application, one for the development environment and the other for production. You can also specify that a `Startup` class be used for all environments.

The `Startup` class has two methods—`Configure()`, which is compulsory and is used to determine how the application should respond to HTTP requests, and `ConfigureServices()`, which is optional and is used to configure services before the `Configure` method is called. Both methods are called when the application starts:

```
public class Startup
    {
        public Startup(IConfiguration configuration)
        {
            Configuration = configuration;
        }

        public IConfiguration Configuration { get; }

        // This method gets called by the runtime. Use this method to add
services to the container.
        public void ConfigureServices(IServiceCollection services)
        {
            services.AddMvc();
        }

        // This method gets called by the runtime. Use this method to
configure the HTTP request pipeline.
        public void Configure(IApplicationBuilder app, IHostingEnvironment
env)
        {
            if (env.IsDevelopment())
            {
                app.UseDeveloperExceptionPage();
            }
            else
            {
                app.UseExceptionHandler("/Home/Error");
            }

            app.UseStaticFiles();

            app.UseMvc(routes =>
            {
                routes.MapRoute(
                    name: "default",
```

```
                                    template: "{controller=Home}/{action=Index}/{id?}");
                });
        }
    }
```

Tour of Microsoft's Visual Studio Code editor

Developing .NET Core applications has been made much easier, not only because of the sleekness and robustness of the platform but also through the introduction of **Visual Studio Code**, a cross-platform editor that runs on Windows, Linux, and macOS. You don't need to have Visual Studio IDE installed on your system before you can create applications on .NET Core.

Visual Studio Code, though not as powerful and features-packed as the Visual Studio IDE, does have in-built productivity tools and features that make creating .NET Core applications with it seamless. You can also install extensions for several programming languages from Visual Studio Marketplace into Visual Studio Code, giving you the flexibility to edit code written in other programming languages.

Installing .NET Core on Linux

To show the cross-platform feature of .NET Core, let's set up a .NET Core development environment on Ubuntu 17.04 desktop version. Before installing Visual Studio Code, let's install .NET Core on the **Ubuntu OS**. First, you need to do a one-time registration of the **Microsoft Product** feed, which is done by registering the Microsoft signature key before adding the Microsoft Product feed to the system:

1. Launch the system terminal and run the following commands to register the Microsoft signature key:

```
curl https://packages.microsoft.com/keys/microsoft.asc | gpg --
dearmor > microsoft.gpg
sudo mv microsoft.gpg /etc/apt/trusted.gpg.d/microsoft.gpg
```

2. Register the Microsoft Product feed with this command:

```
sudo sh -c 'echo "deb [arch=amd64]
https://packages.microsoft.com/repos/microsoft-ubuntu-zesty-pro
d zesty main" > /etc/apt/sources.list.d/dotnetdev.list
```

3. To install .NET Core SDK and the other components required to develop .NET Core applications on the Linux operating system, run the following commands:

```
sudo apt-get update
sudo apt-get install dotnet-sdk-2.0.0
```

4. The commands will update the system and you should see the Microsoft repository from earlier added among the list of repositories where Ubuntu will attempt to get updates from. After the update, the .NET Core tool will be downloaded and installed on the system. The information displayed on your terminal screen should be similar to what is in the following screenshot:

5. When the installation completes, create a new folder inside the `Documents` folder and name it `testapp`. Change the directory to the newly created folder and create a new console application to test the installation. See the following commands, and the screenshot for the outcome of the commands:

```
cd /home/user/Documents/testapp
dotnet new console
```

This gives the following output:

6. You would see on the terminal as .NET Core is creating the project and the required files. After the project has been successfully created, `Restore succeeded` will be displayed on the terminal. Inside the `testapp` folder, an `obj` folder, `Program.cs`, and `testapp.csproj` files would have been added by the framework.

7. You can proceed to run the console application using the `dotnet run` command. This command will compile and run the project before displaying `Hello World!` on the terminal.

Installing and setting up Visual Studio Code on Linux

Visual Studio Code, being a cross-platform editor, can be installed on many variants of Linux OS, with packages for other Linux distributions being added gradually. To install Visual Studio Code on **Ubuntu**, perform the following steps:

1. Download the `.deb` package meant for Ubuntu and Debian variants of Linux from `https://code.visualstudio.com/download`.

2. Install the downloaded file from the terminal, which will install the editor, the `apt` repository, and signing key, to ensure the editor can be automatically updated when the system update command is run:

   ```
   sudo dpkg -i <package_name>.deb
   sudo apt-get install -f
   ```

3. After a successful installation, you should be able to launch the newly installed Visual Studio Code editor. The editor has a slightly similar look and feel to that of Visual Studio IDE.

Exploring Visual Studio Code

With the successful installation of Visual Studio Code on your Ubuntu instance, you need to perform initial environment setup before you can begin writing code using the editor:

1. Launch Visual Studio Code from the Start menu and install the C# extension to the editor from Visual Studio Marketplace. You can launch the extension by pressing *Ctrl + Shift + X*, through the **View** menu and clicking **Extension**, and by clicking directly on the **Extension** tab; this will load a list of available extensions, so click and install the **C#** extension.

2. When the extension has been installed, click on the **Reload** button to activate the C# extension in the editor:

3. Open the folder of the console application you earlier created; to do that, click on the **File** menu and select **Open Folder** or press *Ctrl + K, Ctrl + O*. This will open the file manager; browse to the path of the folder and click open. This will load the content of the project in Visual Studio Code. In the background, Visual Studio Code will attempt to download the required dependencies for the Linux platform, **Omnisharp for Linux** and **.NET Core Debugger**:

4. To create a new project, you can use the **Integrated Terminal** of the editor without having to go through the system terminal. Click on the **View** menu and select **Integrated Terminal**. This will open the **Terminal** tab in the editor, where you can type the commands to create a new project:

5. In the opened project, you will see a notification that requires assets to build and debug the applications that are missing. If you click **Yes**, in the **Explorer** tab, you can see a `.vscode` tree with `launch.json` and `tasks.json` files added. Click the `Program.cs` file to load the file into the editor. From the **Debug** menu select **Start Debugging** or press *F5* to run the application; you should see `Hello World!` displayed on the editor's **Debug Console**:

When you launch Visual Studio Code, it loads with the state it was in when it was closed, opening the files and folders that you last accessed. The editor's layout is easy to navigate and work with, and comes with areas such as:

- Status bar showing you information about the files you currently have opened.
- Activity bar provides access to the **Explorer** view for viewing your project folders and files, and **Source Control** view for managing a project's source versioning. **Debug** view for watching variables, breakpoints and debugging-related activities, **Search** view allows you to search folders and files. **Extension** view allows you to see available extensions that can be installed into the editor.
- Editor area for editing the project files, allowing you to open up to three files for editing simultaneously.

- Panel regions show different panels for **Output**, **Debug Console**, **Terminal**, and **Problems**:

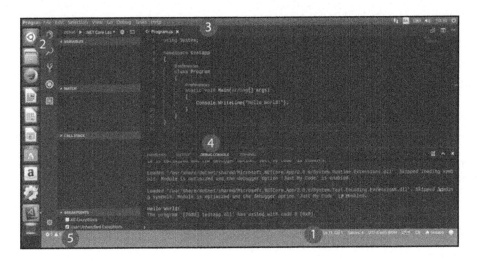

A look at the new features of C# 7

The C# programming language has matured over the years; more language features and constructs are being added with the release of each version. A language that originally was only being developed in house by Microsoft and run only on Windows operating systems is now open source and cross-platform. This is made possible through .NET Core and Version 7 (7.0 and 7.1) of the language, which added flavors and improved the available features of the language. The roadmap of the language, especially Version 7.2 and 8.0, promises to add more features to the language.

Tuples enhancement

Tuples were introduced into C# language in Version 4 and are used in the simplified form to provide structure with two or more data elements, allowing you to create methods that can return two or more data elements. Before C# 7, referencing the elements of a tuple was done by using *Item1, Item2, ...ItemN*, where *N* is the number of elements in the tuple structure. Starting from C# 7, tuples now support semantic naming of the contained fields with the introduction of cleaner and more efficient ways of creating and using tuples.

You can now create tuples by directly assigning each member to a value. This assignment creates a tuple containing elements *Item1, Item2*:

```
var names = ("John", "Doe");
```

You can also create tuples that have semantic names for the elements contained in the tuple:

```
(string firstName, string lastName) names = ("John", "Doe");
```

The names tuple, instead of having fields as *Item1, Item2*, will have fields that can be referenced as `firstName` and `lastName` at compile time.

You can create your method to return a tuple with two or more data elements when using POCO might be overkill:

```
private (string, string) GetNames()
{
    (string firstName, string lastName) names = ("John", "Doe");
    return names;
}
```

Out keyword

In C#, arguments or parameters can be passed by reference or value. When you pass an argument by reference to a method, property, or constructor, the value of the parameter will be changed and the changes made will be retained when the method or constructor goes out of scope. With the use of the `out` keyword, you can pass a method's argument as a reference in C#. Prior to C# 7, to use the `out` keyword, you had to declare a variable before passing it as an `out` argument to a method:

```
class Program
{
    static void Main(string[] args)
    {
        string firstName, lastName;
        GetNames(out firstName, out lastName);
    }
    private static void GetNames(out string firstName, out string lastName)
    {
        firstName="John";
        lastName="Doe";
    }
}
```

In C# 7, you can now pass out variables to a method without having to declare the variables first, with the preceding code snippet now looking like the following, which prevents you from mistakenly using the variables before they are assigned or initialized and gives the code clarity:

```
class Program
{
    static void Main(string[] args)
    {
        GetNames(out string firstName, out string lastName);
    }
    private static void GetNames(out string firstName, out string lastName)
    {
        firstName="John";
        lastName="Doe";
    }
}
```

Support for the implicit type out variable has been added to the language, allowing the compiler to infer the types of variables:

```
class Program
{
    static void Main(string[] args)
    {
        GetNames(out var firstName, out var lastName);
    }
    private static void GetNames(out string firstName, out string lastName)
    {
        firstName="John";
        lastName="Doe";
    }
}
```

Ref locals and returns

C# language has always had the `ref` keyword, which allows you to use and return reference to variables defined elsewhere. C# 7 adds another feature, `ref` locals and `returns`, which improves performance and allows you to declare helper methods that were not possible with the earlier versions of the language. The `ref` locals and `returns` keyword have some restrictions—you cannot use them with the `async` methods and you cannot return a reference to a variable with the same execution scope.

Ref locals

The `ref` local keyword allows you to store references in a local variable by declaring local variables with the `ref` keyword and add the `ref` keyword before a method call or assignment. For example, in the following code, the `day` string variable references `dayOfWeek`; changing the value of `day` also changes the value of `dayOfWeek` and vice versa:

```
string dayOfWeek = "Sunday";
ref string day = ref dayOfWeek;
Console.WriteLine($"day-{day}, dayOfWeek-{dayOfWeek}");
day = "Monday";
Console.WriteLine($"day-{day}, dayOfWeek-{dayOfWeek}");
dayOfWeek = "Tuesday";
Console.WriteLine($"day-{day}, dayOfWeek-{dayOfWeek}");


-----------------
Output:

day: Sunday
dayOfWeek:   Sunday

day: Monday
dayOfWeek:   Monday

day: Tuesday
dayOfWeek:   Tuesday
```

Ref returns

You can also use the `ref` keyword as a return type of methods. To achieve this, add the `ref` keyword to the method signature and inside the method body, add `ref` after the `return` keyword. In the following code snippet, an array of string is declared and initialized. The fifth element of the string array is then returned by the method as a reference:

```
public ref string GetFifthDayOfWeek()
{
    string [] daysOfWeek= new string [7] {"Monday", "Tuesday", "Wednesday",
"Thursday", "Friday", "Saturday", "Sunday"};
    return ref daysOfWeek[4];
}
```

Local function

The **local** or **nested function**, allows you to define a function inside another function. This feature has been available in some programming languages for years, but was just introduced in C# 7. It is desirable to use when you need a function that is small and will not be reusable outside the context of the `container` method:

```
class Program
{
    static void Main(string[] args)
    {
        GetNames(out var firstName, out var lastName);
        void GetNames(out string firstName, out string lastName)
        {
            firstName="John";
            lastName="Doe";
        }
    }
}
```

Patterns matching

C# 7 includes patterns, a language element feature that allows you to perform a method dispatch on properties besides object types. It extends the language constructs already implemented in override and virtual methods for implementing dispatch for types and data elements. The `is` and `switch` expressions have been updated in Version 7.0 of the language to support **pattern matching**, so you can now use the expressions to determine whether an object of interest has a specific pattern.

Using the `is` pattern expression, you can now write code that contains routines with algorithms that manipulate elements with unrelated types. The `is` expressions can now be used with a pattern in addition to being able to test for a type.

The introduced patterns matching can take three forms:

- **Type patterns**: This entails checking whether an object is of a type before extracting the value of the object into a new variable defined within the expression:

```
public void ProcessLoan(Loan loan)
{
    if(loan is CarLoan carLoan)
    {
```

```
            // do something
        }
    }
```

- **Var patterns**: Creates a new variable with the same type as the object and assigns the value:

```
public void ProcessLoan(Loan loan)
{
    if(loan is var carLoan)
    {
        // do something
    }
}
```

- **Constant patterns**: Checks whether the supplied object is equivalent to a constant expression:

```
public void ProcessLoan(Loan loan)
{
    if(loan is null)
    {
        // do something
    }
}
```

With the updated switch expression, you can now use patterns as well as conditions in case causes and switch on any types besides the base or primitive types while allowing you to use the when keyword to additionally specify rules to the pattern:

```
public void ProcessLoan(Loan loan)
{
    switch(loan)
    {
        case CarLoan carLoan:
            // do something
            break;
        case HouseLoan houseLoan when (houseLoan.IsElligible==true):
            //do something
            break;
        case null:
            //throw some custom exception
            break;
        default:
            // do something
    }
}
```

Digit separator and binary literal

A new syntatic sugar has been added to C# 7, which is the **digit separator**. This construct greatly improves code readability, especially when handling large numbers of different numeric types supported in C#. Prior to C# 7, manipulating large numeric values to have separators was a bit messy and unreadable. With the introduction of the digit separator, you can now use an underscore (_) as a separator for digits:

```
var longDigit = 2_300_400_500_78;
```

Also newly introduced in this version is **binary literals**. You can now create binary literals by simply including 0b as a prefix to binary values:

```
var binaryValue = 0b11101011;
```

Creating an ASP.NET MVC Core application

ASP.NET Core provides an elegant way of building web applications and APIs that run on Windows, Linux, and macOS, owing to the .NET Core platform's tool and SDK that simplify developing cutting-edge applications and support side-by-side with application versioning. With ASP.NET Core, your applications have a smaller surface area which improves performance as you only have to include the NuGet packages required to run your applications. ASP.NET Core can also be integrated with client-side libraries and frameworks, allowing you to develop web applications using the CSS and JS libraries you are already familiar with.

ASP.NET Core runs with Kestrel, a web server included in the ASP.NET Core project templates. Kestrel is an in-process cross-platform HTTP server implementation based on **libuv**, a cross-platform asynchronous I/O library that makes building and debugging ASP.NET Core applications much easier. It listens to HTTP requests and then packages the request details and features into an HttpContext object. Kestrel can be used as a standalone web server or with IIS or Apache web servers where the requests received by the other web servers are forwarded to Kestrel, a concept known as reverse proxy.

ASP.NET MVC Core provides you with a testable framework for modern web application development using the *Model View Controller* pattern, which allows you to fully practice test-driven development. Newly added to ASP.NET 2.0 is the support for Razor pages, which is now the recommended approach to develop user interfaces for ASP.NET Core web applications.

To create a new ASP.NET MVC Core project:

1. Open Visual Studio Code and access the integrated terminal panel by selecting **Integrated Terminal** from the **View** menu. On the terminal, run the following commands:

```
cd /home/<user>/Documents/
mkdir LoanApp
cd LoanApp
dotnet new mvc
```

2. After the application has been created, open the project's folder using Visual Studio Code and select the Startup.cs file. You should notice a notification on the top bar of the screen, **Required assets to build and debug are missing from 'LoanApp'. Add them?**; select **Yes**:

3. Press *F5* to build and run the MVC application. This tells the Kestrel web server to run the application and launches the default browser on the computer with the `http://localhost:5000` address:

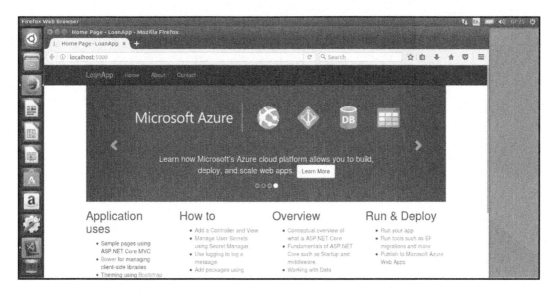

Summary

The .NET Core platform, though new, is rapidly maturing, with Version 2.0.7 introducing many features and enhancements that simplify building different types of cross-platform applications. In this chapter, we have taken a tour of the platform, introduced the new features of C# 7, and set up a development environment on Ubuntu Linux, while creating our first ASP.NET MVC Core application.

In the next chapter, we will explain what to look out for in order to avoid writing codes that are untestable and we will later walk you through SOLID principles that can help you write testable and quality code.

Writing Testable Code

3

In `Chapter 1`, *Exploring Test-Driven Development*, pitfalls that should be avoided when writing code to prevent code smell were explained. While writing good code is in itself an art, the process of writing code that can be efficiently tested requires extra efforts and commitment on the part of the developers to write clean code that can be repeatedly tested without any hassle.

It is true that practicing TDD improves code production and encourages writing good code that is robust and maintainable. Nevertheless, time spent doing TDD can be wasted and the technique's return on investment might not be obtained if developers involved in software projects write code that is untestable. This can usually be traced to the use of bad code design architecture and not adequately or effectively using object-oriented design principles.

Writing tests is as important as writing the main code. It is stressful and really difficult writing tests for code that is untestable, which is the reason why untestable code should be avoided in the first place. Code can be untestable for different reasons, such as when the code does too much (**Monster Code**), it violates the single responsibility principle, there is wrong use of architecture, or faulty object-oriented design.

In this chapter, we will cover the following topics:

- Warning signs when writing untestable code
- Law of Demeter
- The SOLID architecture principles
- Setting up DI Container for ASP.NET Core MVC

Warning signs when writing untestable code

Effective and continuous practice of TDD can improve the code-writing process, making testing easier, which results in improved code quality and robust software application. However, when a project's code base contains portions of codes that are untestable, writing unit or integration tests becomes extremely difficult or nearly impossible.

Software development teams cannot emphatically validate the consistent behavior of the functionalities and features of an application when there is untestable code in a software project's code base. To avoid this preventable situation, writing code that is testable is not an option but a must for every serious development team that values quality software.

Untestable code results from the violation of common standards, practices, and principles that have been proven and tested to improve the quality of code. While professionalism comes with repeated use of good practices and experience, there are some common bad code designs and writing approaches that are common sense even to a beginner, such as the use of global variables when not required, tight coupling of code, hard-coding dependencies, or values that can change in code.

In this section, we will discuss some common anti-patterns and pitfalls that you should watch out for when writing code as they can make writing tests for your production code difficult.

Tight coupling

Coupling is the extent to which objects depend on or are closely related to one another. To explain this further, when a `LoanProcessor` class is tightly coupled to `EligibilityChecker`, changing the latter can affect the behavior or modify the state of the former.

The majority of untestable code is usually a result of inherent dependencies scattered in different portions of the codes, usually through the use of concrete implementations of dependencies causing a mixing of concerns that otherwise should be separated across application boundaries.

Unit testing code with tightly coupled dependencies will lead to testing the different objects that are tightly coupled. Dependencies that should ideally be easy to mock when injected into the constructor, during unit testing will not be possible. This can often slow down the overall testing process as all the dependencies would have to be constructed in the code under test.

In the following snippet, `LoanProcessor` is tightly coupled to `EligibilityChecker`. This is because `EligibilityChecker` has been instantiated with the new keyword in the `LoanProcessor` constructor. Changes made to `EligibilityChecker` will affect `LoanProcessor`, which can cause it to break. Also, unit testing any method contained in `LoanProcessor` will always cause `EligibilityChecker` to be constructed:

```
public class LoanProcessor
{
    private EligibilityChecker eligibilityChecker;

    public LoanProcessor()
    {
        eligibilityChecker= new EligibilityChecker();
    }
    public void ProcessCustomerLoan(Loan loan)
    {
        throw new NotImplementedException();
    }
}
```

An approach to resolve the tight coupling in `LoanProcessor` is through the use of **Dependency Injection (DI)**. Since `LoanProcessor` cannot be tested in isolation, as `EligibilityChecker` object will have to be instantiated in the constructor, `EligibilityChecker` will be injected into `LoanProcessor`, through the constructor:

```
public class LoanProcessor
{
    private EligibilityChecker eligibilityChecker;

    public LoanProcessor(EligibilityChecker eligibilityChecker)
    {
        this.eligibilityChecker= eligibilityChecker;
    }
    public void ProcessCustomerLoan(Loan loan)
    {
        bool isEligible=eligibilityChecker.CheckLoan(loan);
        throw new NotImplementedException();
    }
}
```

With `EligibilityChecker` injected, testing `LoanProcessor` becomes easier as this allows you to write a test where you mock the implementation of `EligibilityChecker`, allowing you to test `LoanProcessor` in isolation.

Alternatively, `EligibilityChecker` can be injected through properties or members of the `LoanProcessor` class instead of passing the dependency through the `LoanProcessor` constructor:

```
public class LoanProcessor
{
    private EligibilityChecker eligibilityChecker;
    public EligibilityChecker EligibilityCheckerObject
    {
        set { eligibilityChecker = value; }
    }
    public void ProcessCustomerLoan(Loan loan)
    {
        bool isEligible=eligibilityChecker.CheckLoan(eligibilityChecker);
        throw new NotImplementedException();
    }
}
```

With the dependency injected either through the constructor or property, `LoanProcessor` and `EligibilityChecker` have now become loosely coupled, thereby making the writing of unit tests and mocking `EligibilityChecker` easy.

To make a class loosely coupled and testable, you have to ensure that the class does not instantiate other classes and objects. Instantiating objects inside constructors or methods of a class can result in preventing the injection of mock or dummy objects while attempting to get the code under a test harness.

Monster Constructor

To test a method, you have to instantiate or construct the class containing the method. The most common mistake developers make is to create what I call **Monster Constructor**, which is simply a constructor that does too much work or real work, such as performing I/O operations, database calls, static initialization, reading some large files, or establishing communication with external services.

When you have a class designed with a constructor that initializes or instantiates objects other than value objects (list, array, and dictionary), the class technically has a nonflexible structure. This is a bad class design because the class automatically becomes strongly tied to the classes it is instantiating, making unit testing difficult. Any class with this design also violates the single responsibility principle, because the creation of an object graph is a responsibility that can be delegated to another class.

Testing methods in a class with a constructor that does a great deal of work comes with great costs. In essence, to test the methods in a class with the preceding design, you are compelled to go through the pain of creating the dependent objects in the constructor. If the dependent object makes a database call when constructed, this call will be repeated each time a method in that class is tested, making testing slow and painful:

```
public class LoanProcessor
{
    private EligibilityChecker eligibilityChecker;
    private CurrencyConverter currencyConverter;

    public LoanProcessor()
    {
        eligibilityChecker= new EligibilityChecker();
        currencyConverter = new CurrencyConverter();
        currencyConverter.DownloadCurrentRates();
        eligibilityChecker.CurrentRates= currencyConverter.Rates;
    }
}
```

In the preceding code snippet, the object graph construction is being done in the LoanProcessor constructor, which will definitely make the class difficult to test. It is a good practice to have a lean constructor, that does little work and has little knowledge of other objects, especially what they can do but not how they do it.

Sometimes developers use a test hack, which involves creating multiple constructors for a class. One of the constructors will be designated as a test-only constructor. While using this approach can allow the class to be tested in isolation, there is a bad side to it. For example, the class created with multiple constructors can have other classes referencing it and instantiating it using the constructor that does a lot of work. This can make testing those dependent classes very difficult.

The following code snippet illustrates the bad design of creating a separate constructor solely for the purpose of testing the class:

```
public class LoanProcessor
{
    private EligibilityChecker eligibilityChecker;
    private CurrencyConverter currencyConverter;

    public LoanProcessor()
    {
        eligibilityChecker= new EligibilityChecker();
        currencyConverter = new CurrencyConverter();
        currencyConverter.DownloadCurrentRates();
```

```
        eligibilityChecker.CurrentRates= currencyConverter.Rates;
    }

    // constructor for testing
    public LoanProcessor(EligibilityChecker
eligibilityChecker,CurrencyConverter currencyConverter)
    {
        this.eligibilityChecker= eligibilityChecker;
        this.currencyConverter = currencyConverter;
    }
}
```

There are important warning signs that can aid you in designing a loosely coupled class with a constructor that does little work. Avoid the use of the `new` operators in the constructor, to allow the injection of dependent objects. You should initialize and assign to the appropriate fields all objects injected through the constructor. Lightweight value objects instantiation should also be done in the constructor.

Also, avoid static method calls, this is because static calls cannot be injected or mocked. Also, the use of iterations or conditional logic inside the constructor should be avoided; each time the class is tested, the logic or loop will be executed, causing excessive overhead.

Design your class with testing in mind, don't create dependent objects or collaborators in the constructor. When your classes need to be dependent on other classes, inject the dependencies. Ensure the creation of value objects only. When you create object graphs in your code, use *factory methods* to achieve this. Factory methods are used for creating objects.

Classes with more than one responsibility

Ideally, a class should have only one responsibility. When you design your class with more than one responsibility, it is possible to have interactions between responsibilities in the class that will make code modifications difficult and testing the interactions in isolation nearly impossible.

There are indicators that can clearly point out that a class is doing too much and has more than one responsibility. For example, when you are struggling with giving a class a name and you probably end up with the word `and` in the class name, it's a clue that the class does too much.

Another sign of a class with multiple responsibilities is when the fields in the class are used only in some methods or when the class has static methods that operate only on parameters and not on the class fields. Additionally, a class does too much when it has a long list of fields or methods and many dependent objects passed into the class constructor.

The `LoanProcessor` class in the following snippet has the dependencies neatly injected into the constructor, making it loosely coupled with the dependencies. However, the class has more than one reason to change; the class has a mix of both methods with code for data retrieval and business rules processing:

```
public class LoanProcessor
{
    private EligibilityChecker eligibilityChecker;
    private DbContext dbContext;
    public LoanProcessor(EligibilityChecker eligibilityChecker, DbContext
dbContext)
    {
       this.eligibilityChecker= eligibilityChecker;
       this.dbContext= dbContext;
    }
    public double CalculateCarLoanRate(Loan loan)
    {
        double rate=12.5F;
        bool isEligible=eligibilityChecker.IsApplicantEligible(loan);
        if(isEligible)
          rate=rate-loan.DiscountFactor;
        return rate;
    }
    public List<CarLoan> GetCarLoans()
    {
        return dbContext.CarLoan;
    }
}
```

The `GetCarLoans` method should not be in `LoanProcessor` in order to make the class maintainable and be easily tested. `LoanProcessor` should be refactored with `GetCarLoans` in a data access layer class.

Classes with the qualities described in this section can be difficult to debug and test. Also, it might be difficult for new team members to understand the inner workings of the class quickly. If you have a class with these attributes in your code base, it is advisable to refactor it by identifying the responsibilities and separating them into different classes and naming the classes as per their responsibilities.

Static objects

Using **static variables**, **methods**, and **objects** in code can be useful as these allow the objects to have the same value throughout all instances of the object, as only one copy of the object is created and put in memory. However, testing code containing statics, especially static methods, can create testing issues because you cannot override static methods in a subclass and using mocking frameworks to mock static methods is a very daunting task:

```
public static class LoanProcessor
{
    private static EligibilityChecker eligibilityChecker= new
EligibilityChecker();
    public static double CalculateCarLoanRate(Loan loan)
    {
        double rate=12.5F;
        bool isEligible=eligibilityChecker.IsApplicantEligible(loan);
        if(isEligible)
          rate=rate-loan.DiscountFactor;
        return rate;
    }
}
```

When you create static methods that maintain states, such as in the `CalculateCarLoanRate` method in `LoanProcessor` in the preceding snippet, the static methods cannot be subclassed or extended using polymorphism. Also, the static method cannot be defined using interfaces, thereby making mocking impossible, since most mocking frameworks work effectively with interfaces.

Law of Demeter

Software applications are complex systems made up of different components that communicate to achieve the overall purposes of solving real-life problems and business process automations. In reality, the components have to coexist, interact, and share information across the component's boundary without the different concerns getting mixed up, to promote component reusability and overall system flexibility.

In software programming, there are technically no hardcore laws defined that must be stringently followed. However, various principles and laws have been formulated that serve as guidelines and can assist software developers and practitioners, and facilitate building software applications that have components with high cohesion and loose coupling to encapsulate data adequately and ensure that quality source codes are produced that can be easily understood and extended, thereby reducing the maintenance costs of software. One of these laws is the **Law of Demeter (LoD)**.

LoD, also known as the **principle of least knowledge**, is an important design approach or rule for developing object-oriented software applications. The rule was formulated at *Northeastern University in 1987 by Ian Holland*. With the proper knowledge of this principle, software developers can write code that is easy to test and build software applications with fewer or no bugs. The formulation of the law is that:

- Each unit should have only limited knowledge about other units: only units "closely" related to the current unit.

- Each unit should only talk to its friends; don't talk to strangers.

LoD emphasizes low coupling, which effectively means an object should have little or very limited information about another object. Relating LoD to a typical class object, the methods in a class should only have limited knowledge about other methods of closely related objects.

LoD serves as heuristics for software developers to facilitate information-hiding in modules and components of software. LoD has two forms—the **object or dynamic form** and **class or static form**.

The class form of LoD is formulated as:

A **method (M)** of a **class (C)** should only send messages to objects of the following classes:

- Argument classes of M including C
- Instance variables of C
- Classes of instances created within M
- Properties or fields of C

And the object form of LoD is formulated as:

Within an M, messages can only be sent to the following objects:

- Parameters of M, which include the enclosing object.
- An immediate part-object, which is the object that M called on the enclosing object returns, including attributes of the enclosing object, or an element of a collection that is an attribute of the enclosing object:

```
public class LoanProcessor
{
    private CurrencyConverter currencyConverter;

    public LoanProcessor(LoanCalculator loanCalculator)
    {
        currencyConverter = loanCalculator.GetCurrencyConverter();
    }
}
```

The preceding code clearly violates LoD, this is because `LoanProcessor` does not really care about `LoanCalculator` as it does not keep any reference to it. In the code, `LoanProcessor` is already talking to `LoanCalculator`, a stranger. This code is not really reusable because both `CurrencyConverter` and `LoanProcessor` will be required by any class or code attempting to reuse them, though technically `LoanCalculator` is not used beyond the constructor.

Writing unit tests for `LoanProcessor` will require that the object graph be created. `LoanCalculator` should be created in order for `CurrencyConverter` to be available. This creates coupling in the system, if `LoanCalculator` is refactored, which is possible anyway, so there is the risk that this might break `LoanProcessor`, causing the unit test to stop running.

While the `LoanCalculator` class can be mocked, to test `LoanProcessor` in isolation, this can sometimes make the test unreadable, it is better that the coupling is avoided so that you can write code that is flexible and can be easily tested.

To refactor the preceding code snippet, and make it comply with LoD and take its dependencies from the class constructor, thereby eliminating an extra dependency on `LoanCalculator` and reduce coupling in the code:

```
public class LoanProcessor
{
    private CurrencyConverter currencyConverter;
```

```
    public LoanProcessor(CurrencyConverter currencyConverter)
    {
        this.currencyConverter = currencyConverter;
    }
}
```

Train Wreck

Another anti-pattern that violates LoD is what is called **Train Wreck** or **Chain Calls**. This is a chain of functions and occurs when you have a series of C# methods that are appended to each other all in a single line of code. You will know you have written a code with Train Wreck when you are spending time trying to figure out what the line of code does:

```
loanCalculator.
    CalculateHouseLoan(loanDTO).
        GetPaymentRate().
            GetMaximumYearsToPay();
```

You might be wondering how this phenomenon violates LoD. First, the code lacks readability and it is not maintainable. Also, the line of code is not reusable as there are three method calls in only a single line of code.

This line of code can be refactored by minimizing the interactions and eliminating the method chaining so as to make it comply with the principle of *don't talk to strangers*. This principle explains that a calling point or method should only interact with one object at a time. With the elimination of the methods chain, the resulting code can be reused elsewhere without having to struggle to understand what the piece of code does:

```
var houseLoan=loanCalculator.CalculateHouseLoan(loanDTO);
var paymentRate=houseLoan.GetPaymentRate();
var maximumYears=paymentRate.GetMaximumYearsToPay();
```

An object should have limited knowledge and information of other objects. Also, methods in an object should have little awareness of the object graph of the application. Through conscious efforts, using LoD, you can build software applications that are loosely coupled and maintainable.

Chapter 3

architecture principles

...velopment procedures and methodologies, from the first step to the
...le and easily understood by both novices and experts. These
...n combination with the right principles, make the process of
...ing software applications easy and seamless.

Developers from time to time adopt and use different development principles and patterns
in order to simplify complexities and make software applications code bases maintainable.
One such principle is the SOLID principle. This principle has proven to be very useful and a
must-know for every serious programmer of object-oriented systems.

SOLID is an acronym of the five basic principles of developing object-oriented systems. The
five principles are for class design and are denoted as:

- **S**: Single Responsibility Principle
- **O**: Open-Closed Principle
- **L**: Liskov Substitution Principle
- **I**: Interface Segregation Principle
- **D**: Dependency Inversion Principle

The principles were first consolidated under the acronym SOLID and popularized by *Robert
C. Martins* (popularly known as **Uncle Bob**) in the early 2000s. The five principles are meant
for class design, and when abided by, can assist with dependency management, which will
avoid the creation of rigid code bases tangled with dependencies here and there.

Proper understanding and use of the SOLID principles can enable software developers to
achieve a very high degree of cohesion and write quality code that can be easily understood
and maintained. With SOLID principles, you can write clean code and build software
applications that are robust and scalable.

Indeed, Uncle Bob clarified that SOLID principles are not laws or rules but are heuristics
that have been observed to work in several cases. To use the principles effectively, you have
to search your code and check for portions where the principles are violated and then
refactor them.

Single Responsibility Principle

The **Single Responsibility Principle (SRP)** is the first of the five SOLID principles. The principle states that a class must at any point in time have only one reason to change. This simply means that a class should only perform one duty at a time or have one responsibility.

The business requirements of software projects are not usually fixed. Before a software project is shipped and, indeed, throughout the life cycle of a software, requirements change from time to time and developers have to adapt the code base to the changes. In order for the software application to meet its business needs and adapt to changes, it is imperative that flexible design patterns are used and classes have a single responsibility at all times.

Additionally, it is important to understand that when a class has more than one responsibility, making even the minutest change can have a great impact on the entire code base. Changes made to the class can cause ripple effects leading to functionalities or other methods that have been working earlier to break. For example, if you have a class that parses a .csv file, while at the same time it makes a call to a web service to retrieve information that is not related to the .csv file parsing, the class has more than one reason to change. Changes in the web service call will affect the class, though the changes are not related to the .csv file parsing.

The design of the LoanCalculator class in the following snippet clearly violates SRP. LoanCalculator has two responsibilities—the first is to calculate house and car loans and the second is to parse loan rates from XML files and XML strings:

```
public class LoanCalculator
{
    public CarLoan CalculateCarLoan(LoanDTO loanDTO)
    {
        throw new NotImplementedException();
    }
    public HouseLoan CalculateHouseLoan(LoanDTO loanDTO)
    {
        throw new NotImplementedException();
    }
    public List<Rate> ParseRatesFromXmlString(string xmlString)
    {
        throw new NotImplementedException();
    }

    public List<Rate> ParseRatesFromXmlFile(string xmlFile)
    {
        throw new NotImplementedException();
```

```
        }
    }
```

The dual responsibility status of the `LoanCalculator` class creates several issues. First, the class becomes very volatile, because changes to one responsibility might affect the other. For instance, a change to the structure of the XML contents to be parsed for the rates might necessitate that the class be rewritten, tested, and redeployed; despite that, changes have not been made to the second concern, which is the loan calculation.

The tangled code in the `LoanCalculator` class can be fixed by redesigning the class and separating the responsibilities. The new design will be to move the responsibility of XML rates parsing into a new `RateParser` class and leaving the loan calculation concern in the existing class:

```
public class RateParser : IRateParser
{
    public List<Rate> ParseRatesFromXml(string xmlString)
    {
        throw new NotImplementedException();
    }
    public List<Rate> ParseRatesFromXmlFile(string xmlFile)
    {
        throw new NotImplementedException();
    }
}
```

With the `RateParser` class extracted from `LoanCalculator`, `RateParser` can now be used as a dependency in `LoanCalculator`. Changes made to any method in `RateParser` will not affect `LoanCalculator` since they now handle different concerns and each class has only one reason to change:

```
public class LoanCalculator
{
    private IRateParser rateParser;
    public LoanCalculator(IRateParser rateParser)
    {
        this.rateParser=rateParser;
    }
    public CarLoan CalculateCarLoan(LoanDTO loanDTO)
    {
        throw new NotImplementedException();
    }
    public HouseLoan CalculateCarLoan(LoanDTO loanDTO)
    {
        throw new NotImplementedException();
    }
```

}

Having the concerns separated creates great flexibility in the code base and allows for easy testing of the two classes. With the new design, changes made to RateParser cannot affect LoanCalculator and the two classes can be unit tested in isolation.

Responsibilities should not be mixed in a class. You should avoid muddling up responsibilities together in a class, which leads to monster classes that do too much. Instead, if you can think of a reason or motivation to change a class, then it already has more than one responsibility; split the class into classes, each containing only a single responsibility.

In a similar manner, a first glance at the LoanRepository class in the following snippet might not outrightly indicate that concerns are muddled up. But if you carefully examine the class, both data access and business logic codes are mixed in the class, making it violate SRP:

```
public class LoanRepository
{
    private DbContext dbContext;
    private IEligibilityChecker eligibilityChecker;
    public LoanRepository(DbContext dbContext,IEligibilityChecker
eligibilityChecker)
    {
        this.dbContext=dbContext;
        this.eligibilityChecker= eligibilityChecker;
    }
    public List<CarLoan> GetCarLoans()
    {
        return dbContext.CarLoan;
    }
    public List<HouseLoan> GetHouseLoans()
    {
        return dbContext.HouseLoan;
    }
    public double CalculateCarLoanRate(CarLoan carLoan)
    {
        double rate=12.5F;
        bool isEligible=eligibilityChecker.IsApplicantEligible(carLoan);
        if(isEligible)
          rate=rate-carLoan.DiscountFactor;
        return rate;
    }
}
```

The class can be refactored by separating the business logic code of calculating a car loan rate into a new class—LoanService, this will allow the LoanRepository class to only contain code related to the data layer, thereby making it adhere to SRP:

```
public class LoanService
{
    private IEligibilityChecker eligibilityChecker;
    public LoanService(IEligibilityChecker eligibilityChecker)
    {
        this.eligibilityChecker= eligibilityChecker;
    }
    public double CalculateCarLoanRate(CarLoan carLoan)
    {
        double rate=12.5F;
        bool isEligible=eligibilityChecker.IsApplicantEligible(carLoan);
        if(isEligible)
          rate=rate-carLoan.DiscountFactor;
        return rate;
    }
}
```

With the business logic code separated into the LoanService class, the LoanRepository class now has has only one dependency, which is the DbContext entity framework. Going forward, LoanRepository can be easily maintained and tested. The new LoanService class also adheres to SRP:

```
public class LoanRepository
{
    private DbContext dbContext;
    public LoanRepository(DbContext dbContext)
    {
        this.dbContext=dbContext;
    }
    public List<CarLoan> GetCarLoans()
    {
        return dbContext.CarLoan;
    }
    public List<HouseLoan> GetHouseLoans()
    {
        return dbContext.HouseLoan;
    }
}
```

When you have concerns in your code well-managed, the code base will have high cohesion and will be flexible and easy to test and maintain in the future. With high cohesion, the classes will be loosely coupled and changes to the classes will have little probability of breaking the entire system.

Open-Closed Principle

The approach for designing and eventually writing production code should be the one that allows new functionalities to be added to a project's code base without having to make many changes, change several portions or classes of the code base, or break existing functionalities that were already working and in good condition.

If, for any reason, you make changes to a method in a class and as a result of the changes, changes have to be made to several parts or modules, it's an indication of a problem with the code design. This is what the **Open-Closed Principle (OCP)** addresses, to allow your code base design to be flexible, so that you can easily make modifications and enhancements.

The OCP states that software entities, such as classes, methods, and modules, should be designed to be open for extension, but closed for modification. This principle can be achieved through inheritance or design patterns, such as factory, observer, and strategy patterns. It is where classes and methods can be designed to allow the addition of new functionalities to be used by the existing code, without actual modification or changes made to the existing code but by extending the behavior of the existing code.

In C#, with the proper use of object abstraction, you can have sealed classes that are closed for modification while the behavior of the classes can be extended through derived classes. Derived classes are children or subclasses of the sealed classes. Using inheritance, you can create classes that add more features by extending their base class without modifying the base class.

Consider the `LoanCalculator` class in the following snippet, which has a `CalculateLoan` method that must be able to calculate the loan details for any type of loan passed into it. Without using the OCP, the requirement can be computed with the use of `if..else if` statements.

The `LoanCalculator` class has a rigid structure, which necessitates much work when a new type is to be supported. For example, if you intend to add more types of customer loans, you have to modify the `CalculateLoan` method and add additional `else if` statements to accommodate the new types of loans. `LoanCalculator` violates the OCP since the class is not closed for modification:

```
public class LoanCalculator
{
    private IRateParser rateParser;
    public LoanCalculator(IRateParser rateParser)
    {
        this.rateParser=rateParser;
    }
    public Loan CalculateLoan(LoanDTO loanDTO)
    {
        Loan loan = new Loan();
        if(loanDTO.LoanType==LoanType.CarLoan)
        {
            loan.LoanType=LoanType.CarLoan;
loan.InterestRate=rateParser.GetRateByLoanType(LoanType.CarLoan);
            // do other processing
        }
        else if(loanDTO.LoanType==LoanType.HouseLoan)
        {
            loan.LoanType=LoanType.HouseLoan;
loan.InterestRate=rateParser.GetRateByLoanType(LoanType.HouseLoan);
            // do other processing
        }
        return loan;
    }
}
```

To make the `LoanCalculator` class open for extension and closed for modification, we can use inheritance to simplify the refactoring. `LoanCalculator` will be refactored to allow subclasses to be created from it. Making `LoanCalculator` a base class will facilitate the creation of two derived classes, `HouseLoanCalculator` and `CarLoanCalulator`. The business logic for calculating the different types of loans has been removed from the `CalculateLoan` method and implemented in the two derived classes, as seen in the following snippet:

```
public class LoanCalculator
{
    protected IRateParser rateParser;
    public LoanCalculator(IRateParser rateParser)
    {
        this.rateParser=rateParser;
```

```
        }
    public Loan CalculateLoan(LoanDTO loanDTO)
    {
        Loan loan = new Loan();
        // do some base processing
        return loan;
    }
}
```

The If conditions have been removed from the CalculateLoan method in the
LoanCalculator class. Instead of having the
if(loanDTO.LoanType==LoanType.CarLoan) line of code, the new CarLoanCaculator
class now contains logic for obtaining car loan calculations:

```
public class CarLoanCalculator : LoanCalculator
{
    public CarLoanCalculator(IRateParser rateParser) :base(rateParser)
    {
        base.rateParser=rateParser;
    }
    public override Loan CalculateLoan(LoanDTO loanDTO)
    {
        Loan loan = new Loan();
        loan.LoanType=loanDTO.LoanType;
        loan.InterestRate=rateParser.GetRateByLoanType(loanDTO.LoanType);
        // do other processing
        return loan
    }
}
```

The HouseLoanCalculator class has been created from LoanCalculator with a
CalculateLoan method that overrides the base CalculateLoan method in
LoanCalculator. Any changes made to HouseLoanCalculator will not affect the
CalculateLoan method of its base class:

```
public class HouseLoanCalculator : LoanCalculator
{
    public HouseLoanCalculator(IRateParser rateParser) :base(rateParser)
    {
        base.rateParser=rateParser;
    }
    public override Loan CalculateLoan(LoanDTO loanDTO)
    {
        Loan loan = new Loan();
        loan.LoanType=LoanType.HouseLoan;
        loan.InterestRate=rateParser.GetRateByLoanType(LoanType.HouseLoan);
```

```
            // do other processing
            return loan;
        }
    }
```

If a new type of loan is introduced, let's say a postgraduate study loan, a new class, `PostGraduateStudyLoan`, can be created to extend `LoanCalculator` and implement the `CalculateLoan` method without having to make any modifications to the `LoanCalculator` class.

Technically, observing the OCP implies that classes and methods in your code should be opened for extension, meaning the classes and methods can be extended to add new behaviors to support new or changing application requirements. And the classes and methods are closed for modification, which means you can't make changes to the source code.

In order to make `LoanCalculator` open for changes, we made it a base class that other types were derived from. Alternatively, we can create an `ILoanCalculator` abstraction, instead of using classical object inheritance:

```
public interface ILoanCalculator
{
    Loan CalculateLoan(LoanDTO loanDTO);
}
```

The `CarLoanCalculator` class can now be created to implement the `ILoanCalculator` interface. Which will necessitate that the methods and properties defined in the interface will be explicitly implemented by the `CarLoanCalculator` class.

```
public class CarLoanCalculator : ILoanCalculator
{
    private IRateParser rateParser;
    public CarLoanCalculator(IRateParser rateParser)
    {
        this.rateParser=rateParser;
    }
    public Loan CalculateLoan(LoanDTO loanDTO)
    {
        Loan loan = new Loan();
        loan.LoanType=loanDTO.LoanType;
        loan.InterestRate=rateParser.GetRateByLoanType(loanDTO.LoanType);
        // do other processing
        return loan
    }
}
```

The `HouseLoanCalculator` class can also be created to implement `ILoanCalculator`, with the `IRateParser` object injected into it through the constructor, similar to `CarLoanCalculator`. The `CalculateLoan` method can be implemented with the specific code required to calculate a house loan. Any other type of loan can be added by simply creating the class and making it implement the `ILoanCalculator` interface:

```
public class HouseLoanCalculator  : ILoanCalculator
{
    private IRateParser rateParser;
    public HouseLoanCalculator (IRateParser rateParser)
    {
        this.rateParser=rateParser;
    }
    public Loan CalculateLoan(LoanDTO loanDTO)
    {
        Loan loan = new Loan();
        loan.LoanType=loanDTO.LoanType;
        loan.InterestRate=rateParser.GetRateByLoanType(loanDTO.LoanType);
        // do other processing
        return loan
    }
}
```

Using OCP, you can create software applications that are flexible with behaviors that can be easily extended, thereby avoiding a code base that is rigid and lacks reusability. Through appropriate use of OCP, by effectively using code abstraction and objects polymorphism, you can make changes to a code base without having to change many parts and with little effort. You really don't have to recompile the code base to achieve this.

Liskov Substitution Principle

The **Liskov Substitution Principle (LSP)**, which can sometimes referred to as **Design by Contract**, is the third of the SOLID principles and was first put forward by *Barbara Liskov*. LSP states that a derived or subclass should be substitutable for the base or superclass without having to make modifications to the base class or generating any runtime errors in the system.

LSP can be further explained using the following mathematical notation—let S be a subset of T, an object of T could be substituted for an object of S without breaking the existing working functionalities of the system or causing any type of errors.

To illustrate the concepts of LSP, let's consider a `Car` super class with a `Drive` method. If `Car` has two derived classes, `SalonCar` and `JeepCar`, both having an overridden implementation of the `Drive` method, wherever `Car` is requested, both `SalonCar` and `JeepCar` should be usable in place of the `Car` class. The derived classes have an *is a* relationship with `Car`, because `SalonCar` is a `Car` and `JeepCar` is a `Car`.

In order to design your classes and implement them to be LSP-compliant, you should ensure that the derived classes elements are designed by contract. The derived classes method definitions should be somewhat similar to that of the base class, though the implementation can be different because of the different business requirements.

Also, it is important that the implementation of the derived classes doesnot violate whatever constraints are implemented in the base classes or interfaces. When you partially implement an interface or base class, by having methods that are not implemented, you are violating LSP.

The following code snippet has a `LoanCalculator` base class, with a `CalculateLoan` method and two derived classes, `HouseLoanCalculator` and `CarLoanCalculator`, which have `CalculateLoan` methods and can have different implementations:

```
public class LoanCalculator
{
    public Loan CalculateLoan(LoanDTO loanDTO)
    {
        throw new NotImplementedException();
    }
}

public class HouseLoanCalculator  : LoanCalculator
{
    public override Loan CalculateLoan(LoanDTO loanDTO)
    {
        throw new NotImplementedException();
    }
}

public class CarLoanCalculator  : LoanCalculator
{
    public override Loan CalculateLoan(LoanDTO loanDTO)
    {
        throw new NotImplementedException();
    }
}
```

If LSP is not violated in the preceding snippet, the `HouseLoanCalculator` and `CarLoanCalculator` derived class can be used in place of `LoanCalculator` wherever a reference to `LoanCalculator` is required. This is demonstrated in the `Main` method, shown in the following snippet:

```
public static void Main(string [] args)
{
    //substituting CarLoanCalulator for LoanCalculator
    RateParser rateParser = new RateParser();
    LoanCalculator loanCalculator= new CarLoanCalculator(rateParser);
    Loan carLoan= loanCalulator.CalculateLoan();
    //substituting HouseLoanCalculator for LoanCalculator
    loanCalculator= new HouseLoanCalculator(rateParser);
    Loan houseLoan= loanCalulator.CalculateLoan();

    Console.WriteLine($"Car Loan Interest Rate - {carLoan.InterestRate}");
    Console.WriteLine($"House Loan Interest Rate -
{houseLoan.InterestRate}");
}
```

Interface Segregation Principle

The **Interface** is an object-oriented programming construct that is used by objects to define the methods and properties they expose, and to facilitate interactions with other objects. An interface contains related methods with empty bodies but no implementation. An interface is a useful construct in object-oriented programming and design; it allows the crafting of software applications that are flexible and loosely coupled.

The **Interface Segregation Principle (ISP)** states that interfaces should be modest, by containing definitions for only properties and methods that are needed, and clients should not be forced to implement interfaces that they don't use, or depend on methods they don't need.

To implement the ISP in your code base effectively, you should favor the creation of simple and thin interfaces that have methods that are logically grouped together to solve a specific business case. With the creation of thin interfaces, the methods contained in the class code can be easily implemented with great flexibility while keeping the code base clean and elegant.

On the other hand, if you have fat or bloated interfaces that have methods with functionalities that are not required in the classes that implement the interface, you are more likely to violate the ISP and create coupling in the code, which will result in a code base that cannot be easily tested.

Instead of having a bloated or fat interface, you can create two or more thin interfaces with the methods logically grouped and have your class implement more than one interface, or let the interfaces inherit from other thin interfaces, a phenomenon known as multiple inheritance, supported in C#.

The IRateCalculator interface in the following snippet violates the ISP. It can be considered a polluted interface because the only class it implements does not require the FindLender method as it is not needed by the RateCalculator class:

```
public interface IRateCalculator
{
    Rate GetYearlyCarLoanRate();
    Rate GetYearlyHouseLoanRate();
    Lender FindLender(LoanType loanType);
}
```

The RateCalculator class has the GetYearlyCarLoanRate and GetYearlyHouseLoanRate methods that are required to fulfill the requirements of the class. By implementing IRateCalculator, RateCalculator is forced to have an implementation for the FindLender method, which is not needed:

```
public class RateCalculator :IRateCalculator
{
    public Rate GetYearlyCarLoanRate()
    {
        throw new NotImplementedException();
    }
    public Rate GetYearlyHouseLoanRate()
    {
        throw new NotImplementedException();
    }
    public Lender FindLender(LoanType loanType)
    {
        throw new NotImplementedException();
    }
}
```

The preceding `IRateCalculator` can be refactored into two cohesive interfaces that have methods that can be logically grouped together. With the small interfaces, the code can be written with great flexibility and unit testing the classes that implement the interface is easy:

```
public interface IRateCalculator
{
    Rate GetYearlyCarLoanRate();
    Rate GetYearlyHouseLonaRate();
}

public interface ILenderManager
{
    Lender FindLender(LoanType loanType);
}
```

With `IRateCalculator` refactored into two interfaces, `RateCalculator` can be refactored to remove the `FindLender` method that is not required:

```
public class RateCalculator :IRateCalculator
{
    public Rate GetYearlyCarLoanRate()
    {
        throw new NotImplementedException();
    }
    public Rate GetYearlyHouseLonaRate()
    {
        throw new NotImplementedException();
    }
}
```

An anti-pattern to watch out for while implementing interfaces that comply with the ISP is the creation of one interface per method, in an attempt to create thin interfaces; these can lead to the creation of several interfaces, resulting in a code base that will be difficult to maintain.

Dependency Inversion Principle

Rigid or bad designs can make changes to components or modules of software applications very difficult and create maintenance issues. These nonflexible designs can often break functionalities that might earlier be working. These can come in the forms of incorrect use of principles and patterns, bad code, and coupling of different components or layers, thereby making the maintenance process a very difficult one.

When you have a rigid design in an application code base, examining the code closely will reveal that the modules are tightly coupled, making changes difficult. Making changes to any of the modules can create the risk of breaking another module that was working before. Observing the last of the SOLID principles—the **Dependency Inversion Principle (DIP)** can eliminate any coupling of modules, making the code base flexible and easy to maintain.

The DIP has two forms, both intended to achieve code flexibility and loose coupling between objects and their dependencies:

- High-level modules should not depend on low-level modules; both should depend on abstractions
- Abstractions should not depend on details; details should depend on abstractions

When high-level modules or entities are directly coupled to low-level modules, making changes to the low-level modules can often have a direct impact on the high-level modules, causing them to change, creating a ripple effect. In practical terms, it is when changes are made to higher level modules that the low-level modules should change.

Also, you can apply DIP wherever you have classes that have to talk to or send messages to other classes. The DIP advocates the well-known principle of layering, or separation of concerns, in application development:

```
public class AuthenticationManager
{
    private DbContext dbContext;
    public AuthenticationManager(DbContext dbContext)
    {
        this.dbContext=dbContext;
    }
}
```

The AuthenticationManager class in the preceding code snippet represents a high-level module, while the DbContext Entity Framework that was passed to the class constructor is a low-level module responsible for CRUD and data layer activities. While a nonprofessional developer might not see anything wrong in the code structure, it violates the DIP. This is because the AuthenticationManager class depends on the DbContext class and an attempt to makes changes to the inner code of DbContext will trickle up to AuthenticationManager, causing it to change which will result in the violation of the OCP.

We can refactor the `AuthenticationManager` class to have a good design and comply with the DIP. This will necessitate the creation of an `IDbContext` interface and make `DbContext` implement the interface:

```
public interface IDbContext
{
    int SaveChanges();
    void Dispose();
}

public class DbContext : IDbContext
{
    public int SaveChanges()
    {
        throw new NotImplementedException();
    }

    public void Dispose()
    {
        throw new NotImplementedException();
    }
}
```

`AuthenticationManager` can be coded against the interface, thereby breaking the coupling or direct dependence on `DbContext` and instead depending on the abstraction. Coding `AuthenticationManager` against `IDbContext` means the interface will be injected in the constructor of `AuthenticationManager` or by using *Property Injection*:

```
public class AuthenticationManager
{
    private IDbContext dbContext;
    public AuthenticationManager(IDbContext dbContext)
    {
        this.dbContext=dbContext;
    }
}
```

With the refactoring done, `AuthenticationManager` now uses dependency inversion and depends on abstraction—`IDbContext`. In future, if changes are made to the `DbContext` class, it can no longer affect the `AuthenticationManager` class and will not violate the OCP.

While `IDbContext` injected to `AutheticationManager` through the constructor is very elegant, the `IDbcontext` can also be injected into `AuthenticationManager` through a public property:

```
public class AuthenticationManager
{
    private IDbContext dbContext;
    private IDbContext DbContext
    {
        set
        {
            dbContext=value;
        }
    }
}
```

Additionally, DI can be done through *Interface Injection*, where object references are passed using interface actions. It simply means interfaces are used to inject dependencies. The following snippet explains the concept of dependency using an interface injection.

`IRateParser` is created with the `ParseRate` method definition. A second interface, `IRepository`, is created containing the `InjectRateParser` method, which accepts `IRateParser` as an argument and will inject the dependency:

```
public interface IRateParser
{
    Rate ParseRate();
}

public interface IRepository
{
    void InjectRateParser(IRateParser rateParser);
}
```

Now, let's create the `LoanRepository` class to implement the `IRepository` interface and have a code implementation for `InjectRateParser`, to inject the `IRateParser` repository into the `LoanRepository` class as dependency for use in the code:

```
public class LoanRepository : IRepository
{
    IRateParser rateParser;

    public void InjectRateParser(IRateParser rateParser)
    {
        this.rateParser = rateParser;
    }
```

```
public float GetCheapestRate(LoanType loanType)
{
    return rateParser.GetRateByLoanType(loanType);
}
}
```

Next, we can create concrete implementations of the `IRateParser` dependency, `XmlRateParser` and `RestServiceRateParser`, which both contain implementations of the `ParseRate` method for parsing loan rates from XML and REST sources:

```
public class XmlRateParser : IRateParser
{
    public Rate ParseRate()
    {
        // Parse rate available from xml file
        throw new NotImplementedException();
    }
}

public class RestServiceRateParser : IRateParser
{
    public Rate ParseRate()
    {
        // Parse rate available from REST service
        throw new NotImplementedException();
    }
}
```

To wrap it up, we can test the *Interface Injection* concept using the interfaces and the classes created in the preceding snippets. A concrete object of `IRateParser` is constructed, which is injected into the `LoanRepository` class, through the `IRepository` interface, and any of the two implementations of the `IRateParser` interface can be used to construct it:

```
IRateParser rateParser = new XmlRateParser();
LoanRepository loanRepository = new LoanRepository();
((IRepository)loanRepository).InjectRateParser(rateParser);
var rate= loanRepository.GetCheapestRate();

rateParser = new RestServiceRateParser();
((IRepository)loanRepository).InjectRateParser(rateParser);
rate= loanRepository.GetCheapestRate();
```

Any of the three techniques described in this section can be effectively used to inject dependencies into your code wherever it is required. Appropriate and effective use of DIP can facilitate the creation of loosely coupled applications that can be easily maintained.

Setting up a DI container for ASP.NET Core MVC

Central to ASP.NET Core is DI. The framework provides built-in DI services to allow developers to create loosely coupled applications and prevent instantiation or construction of dependencies. Using the built-in DI services, your application code can be set up to use DI, and dependencies can be injected into methods in the `Startup` class. While the default DI container has some cool features, you can still use other known, matured DI containers in ASP.NET core applications.

You can configure your code to use DI in two modes:

- **Constructor Injection**: The interfaces required by a class are passed or injected via the class's public constructor. Constructor injection is not possible using a private constructor, an `InvalidOperationException` will be thrown when this is attempted. In a class with an overloaded constructor, only one of the constructors can be used for DI.
- **Property Injection**: Dependencies are injected into a class by using public interface properties in the class. Any of the two modes can be used to request dependencies, which will be injected by the DI container.

A DI container, also known as an **Inversion of Control (IoC)** container, is typically a class or factory that can create classes with their associated dependencies. Before a class with injected dependencies can be successfully constructed, the project must be designed or set up to use DI, and the DI container must have been configured with the dependency types. In essence, the DI will have a configuration containing mappings of the interfaces to their concrete classes and will use this configuration to resolve the requested dependencies for the classes that require them.

The ASP.NET Core built-in IoC container is depicted by the `IServiceProvider` interface and you can configure it using the `ConfigureService` method in the `Startup` class. The container has a default support for constructor injection. In the `ConfigureService` method, services and platform features such as Entity Framework core and ASP.NET MVC core can be defined:

```
public void ConfigureServices(IServiceCollection services)
{
    // Add framework services.
    services.AddDbContext<ApplicationDbContext>(options =>
options.UseSqlServer(Configuration.GetConnectionString("DefaultConnection")
));
    services.AddIdentity<ApplicationUser,
```

```
IdentityRole>().AddEntityFrameworkStores<ApplicationDbContext>().AddDefault
TokenProviders();

    services.AddMvc();
    // Configured DI
    services.AddTransient<ILenderManager, LenderManager >();
    services.AddTransient<IRateCalculator, RateCalculator>();
}
```

The ASP.NET Core inbuilt container has some extension methods, such as `AddDbContext`, `AddIdentity`, and `AddMvc`, that you can use to add additional services. The application dependencies can be configured using the `AddTransient` method, which takes two generic-type arguments, the first is the interface and the second is the concrete class. The `AddTransient` method maps the interface to the concrete class, so the service is created every time it is requested. The container uses this configuration to inject the interfaces for every object that requires it in the ASP.NET MVC project.

Other extension methods for configuring services are the `AddScoped` and `AddSingleton` methods. `AddScoped` only creates a service once per request:

```
    services.AddScoped<ILenderManager, LenderManager >();
```

The `AddSingleton` method creates a service only the first time it is requested and keeps it in memory, making it available for use for subsequent requests of the service. You can instantiate the singleton yourself or simply leave it for the container to do:

```
    // instantiating singleton
    services.AddSingleton<ILenderManager>(new LenderManager());

    // alternative way of configuring singleton service
    services.AddSingleton<IRateCalculator, RateCalculator>();
```

The built-in IoC container for ASP.NET Core is lightweight and has limited features, but basically you can use it for DI configuration in your applications. However, you can replace it with other IoC containers available in .NET, such as **Ninject** or **Autofac**.

Using DI will simplify your application development experience and enable you to craft code that is loosely coupled and can easily be tested. In a typical ASP.NET Core MVC application, you should use DI for dependencies, such as **Repositories**, **Controllers**, **Adapters**, and **Services**, and avoid static access to services or `HttpContext`.

Summary

Using the object-oriented design principles in this chapter will assist you in mastering the skills required to write clean, flexible, easy-to-maintain, and easy-to-test code. The LoD and the SOLID principles explained in the chapter can serve as guidelines for creating loosely coupled, object-oriented software applications.

In order to reap the benefits of a TDD cycle, you must write code that is testable. The SOLID principles covered describes appropriate practices that can facilitate the writing of testable code that can be easily maintained and then enhanced when needed. The last section of the chapter focused on setting up and using a dependency-injection container for an ASP.NET Core MVC application.

In the next chapter, we will discuss the attributes of a good unit test, the .NET ecosystem of unit testing frameworks available for use in creating tests, what to consider when unit testing ASP.NET MVC Core projects, and we will delve into the unit testing property on the .NET Core platform using the xUnit library.

.NET Core Unit Testing

Unit testing has been one of the most discussed concepts in software development in the last few years. Unit testing is not a new concept in software development; it has been around for quite a while, since the early days of the Smalltalk programming language. Based on the increased advocacy for quality and robust software applications, software developers and testers have come to realize the great benefits unit testing can offer in terms of software product quality improvement.

Through unit testing, developers are able to identify errors in code quickly, which increases the development team's confidence in the quality of the software product being shipped. Unit testing is primarily carried out by programmers and tests, and this activity involves the breaking down of the requirements and functionalities of an application into units that can be tested separately.

Unit tests are meant to be small and run frequently, especially when changes are made to the code, to ensure the working functionalities in a code base are not broken. When doing TDD, the unit test must be written before writing the code to be tested. The test usually serves as an aid for designing and writing the code, and is effectively a documentation for the design and specification of the code.

In this chapter, we will explain how to create basic unit tests and prove the results of our unit tests with xUnit assertions. This following topics will be covered in this chapter:

- The attributes of a good unit test
- The current unit testing framework ecosystem for .NET Core and C#
- Unit testing considerations for ASP.NET MVC Core
- Structuring unit tests with xUnit
- Proving unit test results with xUnit assertions
- The test runners available on both .NET Core and Windows

The attributes of a good unit test

A unit test is a piece of code written to test another code. It is sometimes referred to as the lowest-level test because it is used to test code at the lowest level of an application. The unit test calls the method or class under test to validate and assert assumptions about the logic, function, and behavior of the code being tested.

The main purpose of unit testing is to validate a unit of code under test, to ascertain that the piece of code does what it is designed to do and not otherwise. Through unit testing, the correctness of a unit of code can be proven, this can be achieved only if the unit test is written well. While unit testing will prove the correctness and help to discover bugs in code, code quality might not be improved if the code being tested is poorly designed and written.

When you write your unit tests properly, you can to a certain degree, have confidence that your application will behave correctly when shipped. Through the test coverage obtainable from test suites, you can have the metrics of tests written for methods, classes, and other objects in your code base, and you are provided with meaningful information on how frequently they are being run, along with counts of how many times the tests pass or fail.

With the available test metrics, every stakeholder involved in software development can have access to objective information that can be used to improve the software development process. Unit testing, when iteratively done, can add value to the code by improving the reliability and quality of the code. This is possible through testing the code for errors—the test is run repeatedly many times, a concept known as **regression testing**, to locate errors that might occur as the software application matures and components that were working earlier break.

Readable

This characteristic of unit tests can not be overemphasized. Similar to the code under test, unit tests should be easy to read and understand. The coding standards and principles are also applicable to tests. Anti-patterns, such as magic numbers or constants, should be avoided as they can clutter tests and make them difficult to read. Integer 10 in the following test is a magic number, as it was directly used. This affects the test readability and clearity:

```
[Fact]
public void Test_CheckPasswordLength_ShouldReturnTrue() {

    string password = "civic";
```

```
    bool isValid=false;
    if(password.Length >=10)
        isValid=true;
    Assert.True(isValid);
}
```

There is a good test structuring pattern that can be adopted, it's widely known as the **triple A** or **3A pattern**—`Arrange`, `Act`, and `Assert`—which separates the test setup from its verification. You are to ensure that the required data input by the test is arranged, followed by the lines of code to act on the method under test, and assert that the results from the method under test meet the expectation:

```
[Fact]
public void Test_CompareTwoStrings_ShouldReturnTrue() {
    string input = "civic";
    string reversed =  new string(input.Reverse().ToArray());
    Assert.Equal(reversed, input);
}
```

While there is no strict naming convention for tests, you should ensure that the name of a test represents a specific business requirement. The test name should have the expected input as well as state the expected output, `Test_CheckPasswordLength_ShouldReturnTrue`, this is because, besides serving the purpose of testing application-specific functionality, unit tests are also a rich source of documentation of the source code.

Unit independence

A unit test should basically be a unit, it should be designed and written in a form that allows it to run independently. The unit under test, in this case a method, should have been written to depend subtly on other methods. If possible, the data needed by the methods should be taken through the method parameters or should be provided within the unit, it should not have to request or set up data externally for it to function.

The unit test should not depend on or be affected by any other tests. When unit tests are dependent on each other, if one of the tests fails when run, all other dependent tests will also fail. All the needed data by the code under test should be provided by the unit test.

Similar to the *Single Responsibility Principle* discussed in `Chapter 2`, *Getting Started with .NET Core*, a unit should have only one responsibility and only once concern at any time. The unit should have a single task at any point in time to allow it to be testable as a unit. When you have a method that practically does more than a single task, it is simply a wrapper for units and should be decomposed into the basic units for easy testing:

```
[Fact]
 public void Test_DeleteLoan_ShouldReturnNull() {

    loanRepository.ArchiveLoan(12);
    loanRepository.DeleteLoan(12);
    var loan=loanRepository.GetById(12);
    Assert.Null(loan);
 }
```

The issue with the test in this snippet is that there is a lot happening at the same time. And if the test fails, there is no specific way to check which of the method calls caused the failure. This test can be broken down into different tests for clarity and easy maintenance.

Repeatable

A unit test should be easy to run without having to modify it each time it is to run. In essence, a test should be ready to run repeatedly without modification. In the following test, the Test_DeleteLoan_ShouldReturnNull test method is not repeatable, because the test has to be modified each time it is run. To avoid this scenario, it is preferable to mock the loanRepository object:

```
[Fact]
 public void Test_DeleteLoan_ShouldReturnNull() {
    loanRepository.DeleteLoan(12);
    var loan=loanRepository.GetLoanById(12);
    Assert.Null(loan);
 }
```

Maintainable and runs fast

Unit tests should be written in a manner that allows them to run quickly. The test should be easy to implement and any member of a development team should be able to run it. Because software applications are dynamic and continue to evolve, tests for the code base should be easy to maintain as the underlying code under test changes. To have tests that run faster, try to minimize dependencies as much as you can.

Oftentimes, most programmers get this aspect of unit testing wrong, they write unit tests that have inherent dependencies, which in turn makes the tests slower to run. A quick rule of thumb to give you a clue that you are doing something wrong with your unit test, is that they are very slow to run. Also, when you have unit tests that make calls to backend servers or perform some tedious I/O operations, it is an indication of test smells.

Easy to set up, non-trivial, and with good coverage

Unit tests should be easy to set up and decoupled from any direct or external dependencies. The external dependencies should be mocked using a suitable mocking framework. Appropriate object setup should be done in setup methods or test class constructors.

Avoid redundant codes that can clog the tests and ensure the tests contain only codes that are relevant to the methods being tested. Also, tests should be written for units or methods. For example, writing tests for class getters and setters might be considered too trivial.

Lastly, good unit tests should have good code coverage. All execution paths in a method under test should be covered and all the tests should have defined criteria that can be tested.

Unit testing framework ecosystem for .NET Core and C#

The .NET Core development platform has been designed to fully support testing. This can be attributed to the adopted architecture. It makes TDD on the .NET Core platform relatively easy and worthwhile.

There are several unit testing frameworks available for use in .NET and .NET Core. The frameworks essentially provide easy and flexible ways of writing and executing unit tests directly from your preferred IDEs, code editors, through dedicated test runners, or sometimes through the command line.

There exists a thriving ecosystem of test frameworks and suites on the .NET platform. The frameworks contain a variety of adapters that are available for use in creating unit test projects and for continuous integration and deployment.

This ecosystem of frameworks has been inherited by the .NET Core platform. This makes practicing TDDs on .NET Core very easy. Visual Studio IDE is open and extensive, making it faster and easy to install test plugins and adapters from different test frameworks from NuGet for use in test projects.

There are quite a number of testing frameworks that are free and open source, used for various types of tests. The most popular of the frameworks are MSTest, NUnit, and xUnit.net.

.NET Core testing with MSTest

Microsoft MSTest is the default testing framework that ships with Visual Studio and is developed by Microsoft, which originally was part of the .NET framework but is also included in .NET Core. The MSTest framework is used to write load, functional, UI, and unit tests.

MSTest can be used as a uniform application platform support as well as in testing a wide range of applications—Desktop, Store, **Universal Windows Platform** (**UWP**), and ASP.NET Core. MSTest is delivered as a NuGet package.

MSTest-based unit test projects can be added to an existing solution containing projects to be tested following the steps of adding a new project to a solution in Visual Studio 2017:

1. Right-click the existing solution in **Solution Explorer**, select **Add** and select **New Project**. Or, to create a new test project from scratch, click on the **File** menu, select **New**, and select **Project**.
2. In the displayed dialog box, select **Visual C#**, click the **.NET Core** option.
3. Select **MSTest Test Project (.NET Core)** and give a desired name to the project. Then click **OK**:

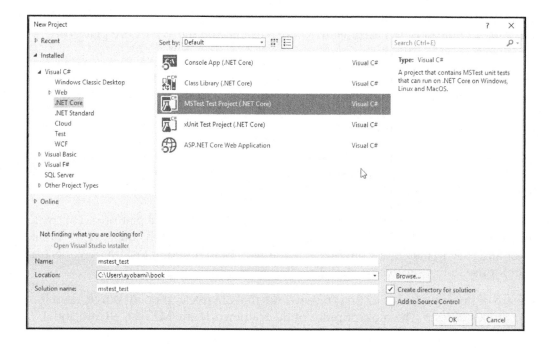

Alternatively, when creating a new project or adding a new project to an existing solution, select the **Class Libary (.NET Core)** option and add references to MSTest from NuGet. Install the following packages to the class library project from NuGet, using the NuGet package manager console or GUI option. You can run the following command from the NuGet package manager console:

```
Install-Package MSTest.TestFramework
Install-Package dotnet-test-mstest
```

Irrespective of which method was used to create the MSTest test project, Visual Studio will automatically create a `UnitTest1` or `Class1.cs` file. You can rename the class or delete it to create a new test class, which will be decorated with an MSTest `TestClass` attribute, which indicates that the class will contain test methods.

The actual test methods will be decorated with the `TestMethod` attribute, marking them as tests, which will make the tests runnable by the MSTest test runner. MSTest has a rich collection of `Assert` helper classes that can be used to verify the expectations of unit tests:

```
using Microsoft.VisualStudio.TestTools.UnitTesting;
using LoanApplication.Core.Repository;
namespace MsTest
{
    [TestClass]
    public class LoanRepositoryTest
    {
        private LoanRepository loanRepository;
        public LoanRepositoryTest()
        {
            loanRepository = new LoanRepository();
        }

        [TestMethod]
        public void Test_GetLoanById_ShouldReturnLoan()
        {
            var loan = loanRepository.GetLoanById(12);
            Assert.IsNotNull(loan);
        }
    }
}
```

You can run the `Test_GetLoanById_ShouldReturnLoan` test method from the **Test Explorer** window in Visual Studio 2017. This window can be opened from the `Test` menu, select **Windows**, and select **Test Explorer**. Right-click on the test and select **Run Selected Tests**:

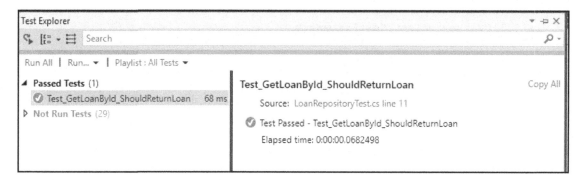

You can also run the tests from the console. Open the command prompt window and change the directory to the folder containing the test project, or the solution folder if you want to run all test projects in the solution. Run the `dotnet test` command. The projects will be built, while the available tests are discovered and executed:

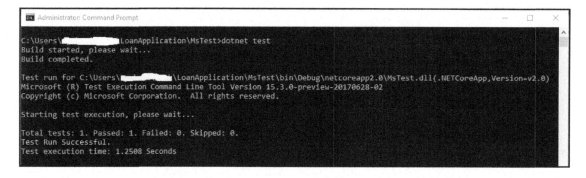

.NET Core testing with NUnit

NUnit is a testing framework originally ported from Java's JUnit and can be used to test projects written in all programming languages available on the .NET platform. Currently on Version 3, its open source testing framework was released under MIT License.

NUnit testing framework includes an engine and console runners. Additionally, it has test runners that are used for testing applications that run on mobile devices—**Xamarin Runners**. The NUnit test adapters and generator can essentially make testing using Visual Studio IDE seamless and relatively easy.

Testing .NET Core or .NET Standards applications using NUnit requires that the NUnit 3 Version of Visual Studio test adapter be used. The NUnit test project template needs to be installed in order to be able to create an NUnit test project, which is usually done once.

NUnit adapters can be installed into Visual Studio 2017 with these steps:

1. Click the **Tools** menu, then select **Extension and Updates**
2. Click on the **Online** option and in the search text box, type `nunit` to filter to available NUnit adapters
3. Select **NUnit 3 Test Adapter** and click **Download**

This will download the adapter and install it as a template into Visual Studio 2017, you have to restart Visual Studio for this to take effect:

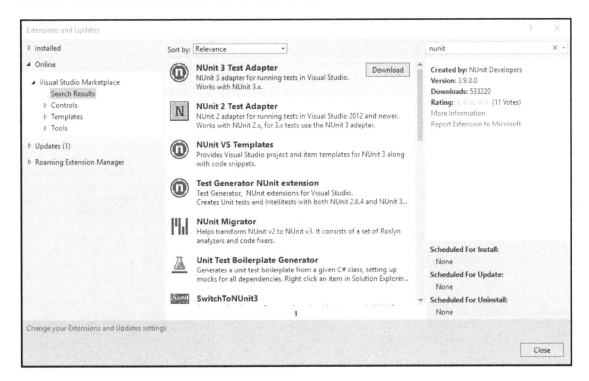

Alternatively, you can install the **NUnit 3 Test Adapter** directly from NuGet each time you want to create a test project.

To add an NUnit test project to your existing solution, follow these steps:

1. Right-click the solution in **Solution Explorer**, select **Add**, **New Project**.
2. In the dialog box, select **Visual C#**, then select the **.NET Core** option.
3. Select **Class Library (.NET Core)** then give the desired name to the project.
4. Add `NUnit3TestAdapter` and `NUnit.ConsoleRunner` packages to the project from NuGet:

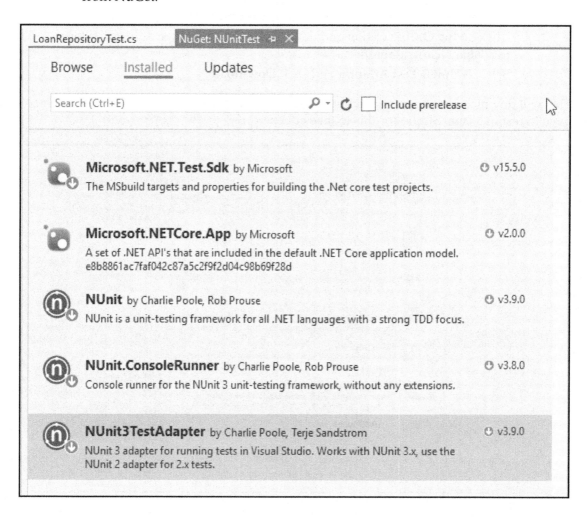

After the project setup is complete, you can write and run unit tests. Similar to MSTest, NUnit has attributes that are used to set up test methods and test classes.

The TestFixture attribute is used to mark a class as a container for test methods. The Test attribute is used to decorate test methods and make the methods callable from the NUnit test runner.

NUnit has other attributes that are used for some setup and testing purposes. The OneTimeSetup attribute is used to decorate a method that is called one time only before all child tests are run. A similar attribute is SetUp, which is used to decorate a method that is called before each test is run:

```csharp
using LoanApplication.Core.Repository;
using NUnit;
using NUnit.Framework;
namespace MsTest
{
    [TestFixture]
    public class LoanRepositoryTest
    {
        private LoanRepository loanRepository;

        [OneTimeSetUp]
        public void SetupTest()
        {
            loanRepository = new LoanRepository();
        }

        [Test]
        public void Test_GetLoanById_ShouldReturnLoan()
        {
            var loan = loanRepository.GetLoanById(12);
            Assert.IsNotNull(loan);
        }
    }
}
```

The test can be run from the **Test Explorer** window, similar to the way it was run with the MSTest test project. Also, the test can be run from the command line, using `dotnet test`. However, you have to add **Microsoft.NET.Test.Sdk Version 15.5.0** as reference to the NUnit test project:

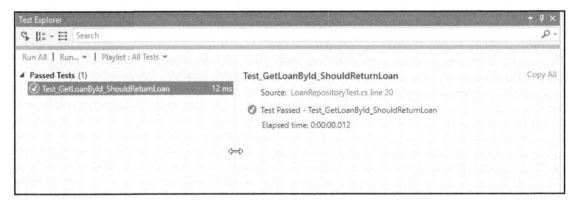

xUnit.net

xUnit.net is an open source unit testing framework for the .NET platform that is used to test projects written in F#, VB.NET, C#, and other .NET-compliant programming languages. xUnit.net was written by the inventor of Version 2 of NUnit and is licensed under Apache 2.

xUnit.net can be used to test traditional .NET platform applications, which includes console and ASP.NET applications, the UWP Application, mobile device applications, and .NET Core applications with ASP.NET Core inclusive.

Unlike in NUnit or MSTest, where the test class is decorated with `TestFixture` and `TestClass` attributes, respectively, the xUnit.net test class does not require attribute decoration. The framework automatically detects all test methods in all public classes in the test project or assembly.

Also, the test setup and tear down attributes are not available in xUnit.net, a parameterless constructor can be used instead to set up test objects or mock dependencies. The test class can implement the `IDisposable` interface and do objects or dependencies cleanup in the `Dispose` method:

```
public class TestClass : IDisposable
{
    public TestClass()
```

```
    {
        // do test class dependencies and object setup
    }
    public void Dispose()
    {
        //do cleanup here
    }
}
```

xUnit.net supports two major types of tests—facts and theories. **Facts** are tests that are always true; they are tests without parameters. **Theories** are tests that will only be true when passed a particular set of data; they are essentially parameterized tests. [Fact] and [Theory] attributes are used to decorate facts and theories tests, respectively:

```
[Fact]
public void TestMethod1()
{
    Assert.Equal(8, (4 * 2));
}

[Theory]
[InlineData("name")]
[InlineData("word")]
public void TestMethod2(string value)
{
    Assert.Equal(4, value.Length);
}
```

The [InlineData] attribute is used in TestMethod2 to decorate a theory test to supply test data to the test methods to be used during test execution.

How to configure xUnit.net

Configuration of xUnit.net comes in two flavors. xUnit.net allows the configuration file to be JSON or XML-based. The xUnit.net configuration must be done for each assembly under test. The configuration file to be used for xUnit.net is dependent on the development platform of the application being tested, though the JSON configuration file can be used on all platforms.

To use a JSON configuration file, after creating your test project in Visual Studio 2017, you should add a new JSON file to the root folder of the test project and name it `xunit.runner.json`:

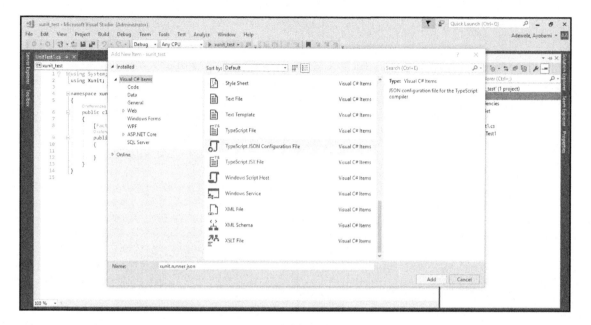

After adding the file to the project, you must instruct Visual Studio to copy the `.json` file to the output folder of your project, where it can be located by xUnit test runners. To do this, you should follow these steps:

1. Right-click the JSON configuration file from **Solution Explorer**. Select **Properties** from the **Menu** option, this will display a dialog with title **xunit.runner.json Property Pages**.
2. On the **Properties Window** page, change the option of **Copy to Output Directory** from **Never** to **Copy if newer** and click the **OK** button:

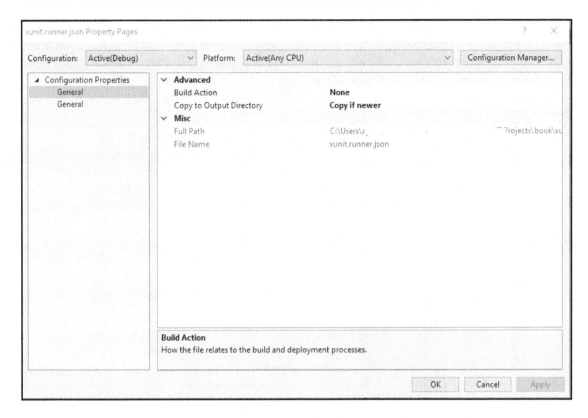

This will ensure that the configuration file is always copied to the output folder when changes are made. The supported configuration elements in xUnit are placed inside a top-level JSON object in the configuration file, as seen in the configuration here:

```
{
    "appDomain": "ifAvailable",
    "methodDisplay": "classAndMethod",
    "diagnosticMessages": false,
    "internalDiagnosticMessages": false,
    "maxParallelThreads": 8
}
```

When a version of Visual Studio that has JSON support is used, it will automatically detect the schema based on the configuration file name. Also, context help will be made available in Visual Studio IntelliSense while editing the `xunit.runner.json` file. The various configuration elements with their acceptable values are explained in this table:

Key	Values
`appDomain`	The `appDomain` configuration element is the `enum` JSON schema type, which can take three values to determine whether application domains are used—`ifAvailable`, `required`, and `denied`. Application domains are used by desktop runners only and will be ignored by non-desktop runners. Default value should always be `ifAvailable`, which indicates that the application domain should be used if available. When set to `required`, it will require the use of application domains, and if set to `denied`, application domains will not be used.
`diagnosticMessages`	The `diagnosticMessages` configuration element is the `boolean` JSON schema type and should be set to `true` if you want to enable diagnostic messages during test discovery and execution.
`internalDiagnosticMessages`	The `internalDiagnosticMessages` configuration element is the `boolean` JSON schema type and should be set to `true` if you want to enable internal diagnostic messages during test discovery and execution.
`longRunningTestSeconds`	The `longRunningTestSeconds` configuration element is the `integer` JSON schema type. You should set this value to a positive integer if you want to enable a long-running test; setting the value to `0` disables the configuration. You should enable `diagnosticMessages` to get notifications for long-running tests.

maxParallelThreads	The maxParallelThreads configuration element is the integer JSON schema type. Set the value to the maximum number of threads to be used when parallelizing. Setting the value to 0 will maintain the default behavior, which is the number of logical processors on your computer. Setting to -1 implies that you do not wish to set a limit to the number of threads used for tests parallelization.
methodDisplay	The methodDisplay configuration element is the enum JSON schema type. When this is set to method, the display name will be the method excluding the class name. Set the value to classAndMethod, which is the default value, indicating that the default display name will be used, which is the class name and method name.
parallelizeAssembly	The parallelizeAssembly configuration element is the boolean JSON schema type. Setting the value to true will make the test assembly parallelize with other assemblies.
parallelizeTestCollections	The parallelizeTestCollections configuration element is the boolean JSON schema type. Setting the value to true will make the tests run in parallel in the assembly, which allows tests in the different test collections to be run in parallel. Tests in the same test collection will still run sequentially. Setting this to false will disable parallelization in the test assembly.
preEnumerateTheories	The preEnumerateTheories configuration element is the boolean JSON schema type and should be set to true to pre-enumerate theories to ensure there is an individual test case for each theory data row. When this is set to false, a single test case for each theory is returned without pre-enumerating the data ahead of time.

shadowCopy	The shadowCopy configuration element is the boolean JSON schema type and should be set to true if you want to enable shadow copying when running tests in different application domains. This configuration element is ignored if the tests are being run without application domains.

The other configuration file option that can be used for desktop and PCL test projects in xUnit.net is the XML configuration. You should add an App.Config file to your test project if it does not already have one.

In the App.Config file, under the appSettings section, you can add the configuration elements with their values. When using the XML configuration file, xUnit has to be appended to the configuration elements explained in the preceding table. For example, the appDomain element in the JSON configuration file will be written as xunit.appDomain:

```xml
<?xml version="1.0" encoding="utf-8"?>
<configuration>
  <appSettings>
    <add key="xunit.appDomain" value="ifAvailable"/>
    <add key="xunit.diagnosticMessages" value="false"/>
  </appSettings>
</configuration>
```

xUnit.net test runners

In xUnit.net, there are two actors responsible for running unit tests written using the framework—xUnit.net runner and the test framework. A **test runner** is the program that can also be a third-party plugin that searches for tests in assemblies and activates the tests discovered. The xUnit.net test runner depends on the xunit.runner.utility library to discover and execute tests.

The test framework is the code with the implementation of test discovery and execution. The test framework links the discovered test against the xunit.core.dll and xunit.execution.dll libraries. The libraries live alongside the unit tests. xunit.abstractions.dll is another useful library of xUnit.net that contains the abstractions that the test runners and tests frameworks use in communicating.

Test parallelism

Test parallelization was introduced in xUnit.net as of Version 2. This feature allows developers to run multiple tests in parallel. Test parallelization is needed because large code bases usually have several thousand tests running, which need to be run multiple times.

These code bases have this huge number of tests because there needs to be assurance that the code for the features works and is not broken. They also take advantage of the super-fast computing resources now available to run parallel tests, thanks to advancements in computer hardware technology.

You can write tests that use parallelization and take advantage of the cores available on the computer, thereby making tests run faster, or let xUnit.net run multiple tests in parallel. The latter is usually preferred, which ensures tests can be run at the speed of the computer running them. In xUnit.net, test parallelism can be at the framework level, where the framework support is running multiple tests in the same assembly in parallel, or parallelism in test runners, where a runner can run multiple test assemblies in parallel.

Tests are run in parallel using test collections. Each test class is a test collection, and tests within a test collection will not be run in parallel against each other. For example, if the tests in `LoanCalculatorTest` are run, the test runner will run the two tests in the class sequentially because they belong to the same test collection:

```
public class LoanCalculatorTest
{
        [Fact]
        public void TestCalculateLoan()
        {
            Assert.Equal(16, (4*4));
        }

        [Fact]
        public void TestCalculateRate()
        {
            Assert.Equal(12, (4*3));
        }
}
```

Tests in separate test classes can run in parallel because they belong to separate test collections. Let's modify `LoanCalculatorTest` and take the `TestCalculateRate` test method into a separate test class, `RateCalculatorTest`:

```
public class LoanCalculatorTest
{
```

```
            [Fact]
            public void TestCalculateLoan()
            {
                Assert.Equal(16, (4*4));
            }
    }

    public class RateCalculatorTest
    {
            [Fact]
            public void TestCalculateRate()
            {
                Assert.Equal(12, (4*3));
            }
    }
```

If we run the tests, the total time spent running both `TestCalculateLoan` and `TestCalculateRate` will be reduced because they are in different test classes, which puts them in different test collections. Also, from the **Test Explorer** window, you can observe the running icon used to mark both tests, to indicate they are both running:

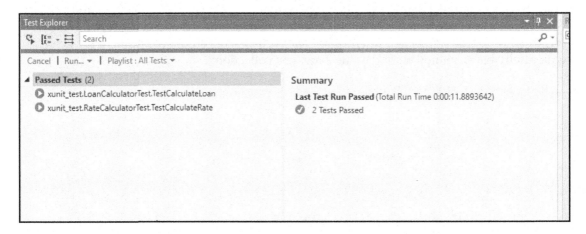

Tests in separate test classes can be configured to not run in parallel. This is done by decorating the classes using the `Collection` attribute with the same name. If the `Collection` attribute is added to `LoanCalculatorTest` and `RateCalculatorTest`:

```
    [Collection("Do not run in parallel")]
    public class LoanCalculatorTest
    {
            [Fact]
            public void TestCalculateLoan()
```

```
        {
            Assert.Equal(16, (4*4));
        }
}

[Collection("Do not run in parallel")]
public class RateCalculatorTest
{
        [Fact]
        public void TestCalculateRate()
        {
            Assert.Equal(12, (4*3));
        }
}
```

Tests in the `LoanCalculatorTest` and `RateCalculatorTest` classes will not be run in parallel because the classes belong to the same test collection based on the attribute decoration.

Unit testing consideration for ASP.NET MVC Core

The ASP.NET Core MVC development paradigm breaks a web application down into three distinct parts—the `Model`, `View`, and `Controller`, as per the tenets of the MVC architectural pattern. The **Model-View-Controller (MVC)** pattern facilitates the creation of web applications that are easy to test and maintain, and have a clear separation of concerns and boundaries.

The MVC pattern provides a clear separation between presentation logic and business logic, with easy scalability and maintainability. It was originally designed for use with desktop applications but has since gained much use and popularity with web applications.

The ASP.NET Core MVC projects can be tested in the same manner that you test other types of .NET Core projects. ASP.NET Core supports the unit testing of controller classes, razor pages, page models, business logic, and the application data access layer. To build robust MVC applications, the various application components have to be tested in isolation and later tested when integrated.

Unit testing controllers

The ASP.NET Core MVC Controller classes handle users interactions, which translates to the request on the browser. The controller gets the appropriate model and selects a view to render that displays the user interface. The controller reads a user's input data, events, and interactions from the view, and passes it to the model. The controller validates the input it receives from the view and then performs the business operation that modifies the state of the data model.

The Controller classes should be lightweight and contain the minimal logic needed to render the view based on a user's interactions to allow easy testing and maintenance. The controller should verify the state of the model and ascertain the validity, call the appropriate code that performs business logic validation and manages data persistence, and later display the appropriate view to the user.

When unit testing the Controller class, the main aim is to test the controller action method's behavior in isolation, this should be done without muddling up the test with other important MVC constructs such as model binding, routing, filters, and other custom controller utility objects. These other constructs, if custom-written, should be unit tested differently and later tested as a whole with the controller using integration testing.

Review the HomeController class of the LoanApplication project, the Controller class contains the four action methods that are added when the project is created in Visual Studio:

```
using System;
using System.Collections.Generic;
using System.Diagnostics;
using System.Linq;
using System.Threading.Tasks;
using Microsoft.AspNetCore.Mvc;
using LoanApplication.Models;

namespace LoanApplication.Controllers
{
    public class HomeController : Controller
    {
        public IActionResult Index()
        {
            return View();
        }

        public IActionResult About()
        {
            ViewData["Message"] = "Your application description page.";
```

```
            return View();
        }
    }
}
```

The `HomeController` class currently contains action methods with the basic logic of returning views. In order to unit test the MVC project, a new xUnit.net test project should be added to the solution, to keep the tests separate from the actual project code. Add the `HomeControllerTest` test class to the newly created test project.

The tests methods to be written in will verify that the `viewResult` objects are returned by both the `Index` and `About` action methods of the `HomeController` class:

```
using System;
using System.Collections.Generic;
using System.Linq;
using System.Threading.Tasks;
using Microsoft.AspNetCore.Mvc;
using LoanApplication.Controllers;
using Xunit;

namespace LoanApplication.Tests.Unit.Controller
{
    public class HomeControllerTest
    {
        [Fact]
        public void TestIndex()
        {
            var homeController = new HomeController();
            var result = homeController.Index();
            var viewResult = Assert.IsType<ViewResult>(result);
        }

        [Fact]
        public void TestAbout()
        {
            var homeController = new HomeController();
            var result = homeController.About();
            var viewResult = Assert.IsType<ViewResult>(result);
        }
    }
}
```

The tests written in the preceding controller test are basic and very simplistic. To demonstrate controller unit testing further, the `Controller` class code can be updated to support dependency injection, which will allow the methods to be tested through object mocking. Also, by using `AddModelError` to add errors, the invalid model state can be tested:

```
public class HomeController : Controller
{
        private ILoanRepository loanRepository;

        public HomeController(ILoanRepository loanRepository)
        {
            this.loanRepository = loanRepository;
        }
        public IActionResult Index()
        {
            var loanTypes=loanRepository.GetLoanTypes();
            ViewData["LoanTypes"]=loanTypes;
            return View();
        }
    }
```

`ILoanRepository` was injected into `HomeController` through the class constructor, and in the test class, `ILoanRepository` will be mocked using the Moq Framework. In the `TestIndex` test method, the mock object is set up with the list of `LoanType` required by the `Index` method in the `HomeController` class:

```
public class HomeControllerTest
{
    private Mock<ILoanRepository> loanRepository;
    private HomeController homeController;
    public HomeControllerTest()
    {
        loanRepository = new Mock<ILoanRepository>();
        loanRepository.Setup(x =>
x.GetLoanTypes()).Returns(GetLoanTypes());
        homeController = new HomeController(loanRepository.Object);
    }
    [Fact]
    public void TestIndex()
    {
        var result = homeController.Index();
        var viewResult = Assert.IsType<ViewResult>(result);
        var loanTypes =
Assert.IsAssignableFrom<IEnumerable<LoanType>>(viewResult.ViewData["LoanTyp
es"]);
```

```
        Assert.Equal(2, loanTypes.Count());
    }
    private List<LoanType> GetLoanTypes()
    {
            var loanTypes = new List<LoanType>();
            loanTypes.Add(new LoanType()
            {
                Id = 1,
                Name = "Car Loan"
            });
            loanTypes.Add(new LoanType()
            {
                Id = 2,
                Name = "House Loan"
            });
            return loanTypes;
    }
}
```

Unit testing razor pages

In ASP.NET MVC, views are the components that are used for rendering a web application's user interface. The view presents information contained in the model in a suitable and easy-to-understand output format, such as HTML, XML, XHTML, or JSON. The view generates output to the user based on the update performed on the model.

Razor pages make coding features on pages relatively easier. A razor page is similar to a razor view, with the addition of the @page directive. The @page directive must be the first directive in the page, it automatically converts the file into an MVC action handling requests without going through the controller.

In ASP.NET Core, razor pages can be tested to ensure they work correctly in isolation and as an integrated application. Razor page testing can involve testing the data access layer codes, page components, and page models.

The following code snippet shows a unit test that verifies that a page model redirects correctly:

```
using Microsoft.AspNetCore.Http;
using Microsoft.AspNetCore.Mvc;
using Microsoft.AspNetCore.Mvc.ModelBinding;
using Microsoft.AspNetCore.Mvc.RazorPages;
using Microsoft.AspNetCore.Mvc.Routing;
using Microsoft.AspNetCore.Mvc.ViewFeatures;
```

```
using Microsoft.AspNetCore.Routing;
using Xunit;

public class ViewTest
{
    [Fact]
    public void TestResultView()
    {
        var httpContext = new DefaultHttpContext();
        var modelState = new ModelStateDictionary();
        var actionContext = new ActionContext(httpContext, new RouteData(),
new PageActionDescriptor(), modelState);
        var modelMetadataProvider = new EmptyModelMetadataProvider();
        var viewData = new ViewDataDictionary(modelMetadataProvider,
modelState);
        var pageContext = new PageContext(actionContext);
        pageContext.ViewData = viewData;
        var pageModel = new ResultModel();
        pageModel.PageContext = pageContext;
        pageModel.Url = new UrlHelper(actionContext);
        var result = pageModel.RedirectToPage();
        Assert.IsType<RedirectToPageResult>(result);
    }
}

public class ResultModel : PageModel
{
    public string Message { get; set; }
}
```

Structuring unit tests with xUnit

Similar to the manner in which an application's code base is structured to allow easy
readability and for effective source code maintenance, unit tests should be structured. This
is to facilitate easy maintenance and quick running of tests using the test runners from
Visual Studio IDE.

A **testcase** is a test class containing test methods. It is usually common to have one test class
per class under test. Another common practice of structuring tests among developers is to
have a nested class for each method being tested or to have one base test class for the class
under test and one subclass for every tested method. Also, there is the test class per feature
approach, where all the test methods that collectively validate a feature of an application
are grouped in a testcase.

These test-structuring approaches promote the DRY principle and essentially faciliate code reusability while writing tests. There is no single approach that is best suited for all purposes, choosing a particular approach should be based on circumstances around the application development and come after effective communication with team members.

Going the one-class-per-test or one-class-per-method route depends on individual preference and sometimes convention or agreement when working in a team, with each approach having it pros and cons. When you use the one-class-per-test approach, you have tests for methods in the class being tested all in the test class, as opposed to the one-class-per-method approach, where you have one test in the class as they pertain to the method being tested, though sometimes it is possible to have more than one test in the class as long as they are relevant to the method:

```
public class HomeControllerTest
    {
        private Mock<ILoanRepository> loanRepository;
        private HomeController homeController;
        public HomeControllerTest()
        {
            loanRepository = new Mock<ILoanRepository>();
            loanRepository.Setup(x =>
x.GetLoanTypes()).Returns(GetLoanTypes());
            homeController = new HomeController(loanRepository.Object);
        }

        private List<LoanType> GetLoanTypes()
        {
            var loanTypes = new List<LoanType>();
            loanTypes.Add(new LoanType()
            {
                Id = 1,
                Name = "Car Loan"
            });
            loanTypes.Add(new LoanType()
            {
                Id = 2,
                Name = "House Loan"
            });
            return loanTypes;
        }
    }
```

Two test classes, `IndexMethod` and `AboutMethod`, will be created. Both classes will extend the `HomeControllerTest` class and will have a method each, following the unit testing approach of one method per test class:

```
public class IndexMethod :HomeControllerTest
     {
         [Fact]
         public void TestIndex()
         {
             var result = homeController.Index();
             var viewResult = Assert.IsType<ViewResult>(result);
             var loanTypes =
Assert.IsAssignableFrom<IEnumerable<LoanType>>(viewResult.ViewData["LoanTyp
es"]);
             Assert.Equal(3, loanTypes.Count());
         }
     }


     public class AboutMethod : HomeControllerTest
     {
         [Fact]
         public void TestAbout()
         {
             var result = homeController.About();
             var viewResult = Assert.IsType<ViewResult>(result);
         }
     }
```

It is important to note that giving test cases and test methods meaningful and descriptive names can go a long way in making them meaningful and easy to understand. It is appropriate that the name of the test methods should contain the names of the method or feature being tested. Optionally, it can be further descriptive to add the expected result in the name of the test method, prefixed by `Should`:

```
[Fact]
public void TestAbout_ShouldReturnViewResult()
{
     var result = homeController.About();
     var viewResult = Assert.IsType<ViewResult>(result);
}
```

xUnit.net shared test context

The test context setup is done in the test class constructor, since the test setup is not applicable in xUnit. For every test, xUnit creates a new instance of the test class, which implies that the codes in the class constructor are run for each test.

Oftentimes, it is desirable for unit test classes to share a test context because it can be expensive to create and clean up test contexts. xUnit offers three approaches to achieve this:

- **Constructor and dispose**: Sharing setup or cleanup code without having to share the object instances
- **Class fixtures**: Sharing object instances across tests in a single class
- **Collection fixtures**: Sharing object instances across multiple test classes

You should use constructor and dispose when you want a fresh test context for every test in a test class. In the following code, the context object will be constructed and disposed for every test method in the `LoanModuleTest` class:

```
public class LoanModuleTest : IDisposable
{
    public LoanAppContext Context { get; private set; }
    public LoanModuleTest()
    {
        Context = new LoanAppContext();
    }

    public void Dispose()
    {
        Context=null;
    }
    [Fact]
    public void TestSaveLoan_ShouldReturnTrue()
    {
        Loan loan= new Loan{Description = "Car Loan"};
        Context.Loan.Add(loan);
        var isSaved=Context.Save();
        Assert.True(isSaved);
    }
}
```

The class fixtures approach is used when you intend to create a test context that will be shared among all the tests in the class and will be cleaned up when the all the tests have finished running. To use the class fixture, you have to create a fixture class with a constructor that will contain the codes for the objects to be shared. The test class should implement `IClassFixture<>` and you should add the fixture class as a constructor argument to the test class:

```
public class EFCoreFixture : IDisposable
{
    public LoanAppContext Context { get; private set; }
    public EFCoreFixture()
    {
        Context = new LoanAppContext();
    }

    public void Dispose()
    {
        Context=null;
    }
}
```

The `LoanModuleTest` class in the following snippet implements `IClassFixture` with `EFCoreFixture` passed as the parameter. `EFCoreFixture` is injected into the test class constructor:

```
public class LoanModuleTest : IClassFixture<EFCoreFixture>
{
    EFCoreFixture efCoreFixture;

    public LoanModuleTest(EFCoreFixture efCoreFixture)
    {
        this.efCoreFixture = efCoreFixture;
    }

    [Fact]
    public void TestSaveLoan_ShouldReturnTrue()
    {
        // test to persist using EF Core context
    }
}
```

Similar to class fixtures, collection fixtures is used to create a test context that is shared among tests, but this time the tests can be in several classes. The test context creation will be done once for all the test classes and the cleanup, if implemented, will be executed after all the tests in the test classes have finished running.

To use the collection fixture:

1. Create a fixture class with a constructor similar to the way you created it with class fixture.

2. You can implement IDisposable on the fixture class if there should be a code cleanup, which will be put in the Dispose method:

```
public class EFCoreFixture : IDisposable
{
    public LoanAppContext Context { get; private set; }
    public EFCoreFixture()
    {
        Context = new LoanAppContext();
    }

    public void Dispose()
    {
        Context=null;
    }
}
```

3. A definition class will be created that will have no code and have ICollectionFixture<> added, since it's purpose is for defining the collection definition. Decorate the class with the [CollectionDefinition] attribute and give a name for the test collection:

```
[CollectionDefinition("Context collection")]
public class ContextCollection : ICollectionFixture<EFCoreFixture>
{
}
```

4. Add the [Collection] attribute to the test classes and use the name earlier used for the collection definition class attribute.

5. Add a constructor with the fixture as argument if the test classes will require instances of the fixture:

```
[Collection("Context collection")]
public class LoanModuleTest
{
    EFCoreFixture efCoreFixture;
```

```
    public LoanModuleTest(EFCoreFixture efCoreFixture)
    {
        this.efCoreFixture = efCoreFixture;
    }

    [Fact]
    public void TestSaveLoan_ShouldReturnTrue()
    {
        // test to persist using EF Core context
    }
}

[Collection("Context collection")]
public class RateModuleTest
{
    EFCoreFixture efCoreFixture;

    public RateModuleTest(EFCoreFixture efCoreFixture)
    {
        this.efCoreFixture = efCoreFixture;
    }

    [Fact]
    public void TestUpdateRate_ShouldReturnTrue()
    {
        // test to persist using EF Core context
    }
}
```

Live unit testing with Visual Studio 2017 Enterprise

Visual Studio 2017, Enterprise edition, has a live unit testing feature that automatically runs tests that are affected by the changes you make to your code base in real time. The tests are run in the background and the results are presented in Visual Studio. This is a cool IDE feature that provides you with instant feedback on the changes you are making to a project's source code.

Live unit testing in Visual Studio currently supports NUnit, MSTest, and xUnit. Live unit testing can be configured from the **Tools** menu—select **Options** from the top-level menu, and select **Live Unit Testing** in the left pane of the **Options** dialog. The **Live Unit Testing** configuration options available can be tweaked from the **Options** dialog:

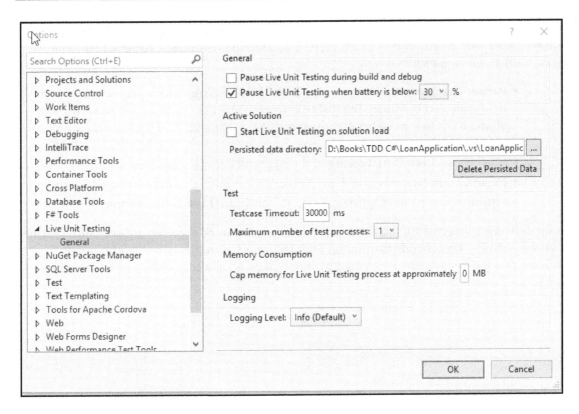

Live Unit Testing can be enabled from the **Test** menu by selecting **Live Unit Testing**, and selecting **Start**:

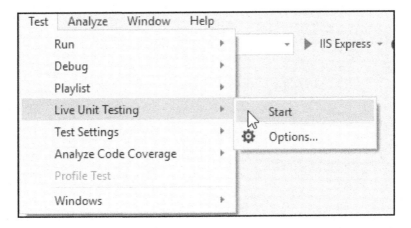

After **Live Unit Testing** is enabled, other available options on the **Live Unit Testing** menu will be displayed. In addition to **Start**, there will be **Pause**, **Stop**, and **Reset Clean**. The menus functions are described here:

- **Pause**: This temporarily suspends **Live Unit Testing**, which preservs unit testing data collected but hides the test coverage `visualization.rk` to catch up with all the edits that have been made while it was paused, and updates the glyphs appropriately
- **Stop**: Stops **Live Unit Testing** and deletes all collected unit test data
- **Reset Clean**: Restarts **Live Unit Testing** by stopping it and starting it again
- **Options**: Opens the **Options** dialog to configure **Live Unit Testing**

In the following screenshot, the coverage visualization can be seen when **Live Unit Testing** is enabled. Every line of code is updated and decorated with green, red, and blue to indicate that the line of code is covered by a passing test, a failing test, or not covered by any test:

Proving unit test results with xUnit.net assertions

xUnit.net assertions verify the behavior of methods under tests. An assertion validates the condition that is expected to be true for the results being expected. When an assertion fails, the current execution of the test is terminated and an exception is thrown. The following table explains the assertions available in xUnit.net:

Assertion	Description
Equal	Validates that an object equals another object
NotEqual	Validates that an object does not equal another object
Same	Verifies that two objects are of the same type
NotSame	Verifies that two objects are not of the same type
Contains	Is an overloaded assertion/method and verifies that a string contains a given substring or a collection contains an object
DoesNotContain	Is an overloaded assertion/method and verifies that a string does not contain a given substring or a collection does not contain an object
DoesNotThrow	Verifies that the code does not throw exceptions
InRange	Verifies that a value is in a given inclusive range
IsAssignableFrom	Verifies that an object is of a given type or derived type
Empty	Verifies that a collection is empty
NotEmpty	Verifies that a collection is not empty
False	Verifies that an expression is false
True	Verifies that an expression is true
IsType<T>	Verifies that an object is of a given type
IsNotType<T>	Verifies that an object is not of a given type
Null	Verifies that an object reference is null
NotNull	Verifies that an object reference is not null
NotInRange	Verifies that a value is not in a given inclusive range
Throws<T>	Verifies that the code throws an exact exception

The following snippet uses some of the xUnit.net assertion methods described in the preceding table. The `Assertions` unit test method shows how assertion methods can be used when doing unit testing in xUnit.net, to verify methods behaviors:

```
[Fact]
public void Assertions()
{
    Assert.Equal(8 , (4*2));
    Assert.NotEqual(6, (4 * 2));

    List<string> list = new List<String> { "Rick", "John" };
    Assert.Contains("John", list);
    Assert.DoesNotContain("Dani", list);

    Assert.Empty(new List<String>());
    Assert.NotEmpty(list);

    Assert.False(false);
    Assert.True(true);

    Assert.NotNull(list);
    Assert.Null(null);
}
```

The test runners available on both .NET Core and Windows

The .NET platform has a large ecosystem of test runners that can be used with the popular test platforms NUnit, MSTest, and xUnit. The test frameworks have test runners shipped with them that facilitate the smooth running of the tests. Additionally, there are also several open source and commercial test runners that can be used with the available test platforms, one of which is ReSharper.

ReSharper

ReSharper is a Visual Studio extension for .NET Developers, developed by JetBrains. Its test runner is by far the most popular among the test runners available on the .NET platform, the ReSharper productivity tool provides other functionalities that enhance programmers' productivity. It has a unit test runner that can assist you in running and debugging unit tests based on xUnit.net, NUnit, MSTest, and couple of other test frameworks.

ReShaper can detect tests written on the .NET and .NET Core platforms for the available test frameworks. ReSharper adds icons to the editor, which can be clicked to **Debug** or **Run** tests:

Unit tests are run by ReSharper using the *Unit Test Sessions* window. **ReSharper's Unit Test Sessions** window allows you to run any number of unit test sessions in parallel, independently of each other. But only one session can be run at a time when running in the debugging mode.

You can filter the tests using the unit test tree, which gives you a structure of your tests. It shows which tests failed, passed, or have not been run. Also, by double-clicking on a test, you can directly navigate to the source:

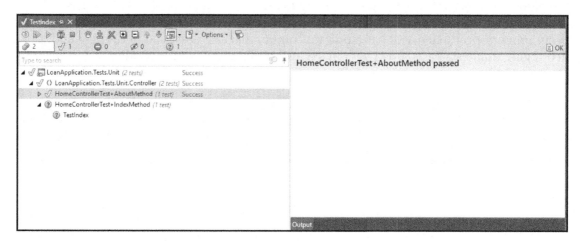

Summary

Unit tests can improve the quality of your code and the overall quality of your application. The tests can also serve as a rich source of commentary and documentation for the source code. Creating high-quality unit tests is a skill that should be consciously learned following the guidelines discussed in this chapter.

In this chapter, attributes of a good unit test were discussed. We also extensively discussed unit testing procedures using the testing features available in the xUnit.net framework. The live unit testing feature in Visual Studio 2017 was explained and, using the xUnit.net Fact attribute, assertions were used to create basic unit tests.

In the next chapter, we will explore data-driven unit tests, another important aspect of unit testing, which facilitates using data from different sources, such as from database or CSV files, to execute unit tests. This is made possible through the xUnit.net Theory attribute.

5
Data-Driven Unit Tests

In the last chapter, we discussed the attributes of good unit tests, as well as the two types of test supported by xUnit.net, **Fact** and **Theory**. Also, we walked through the creation of unit tests using the rich set of test assertions that are available in the xUnit.net unit testing framework.

Unit tests written for a software project should be run repeatedly right from the development stage, during deployment, during maintenance, and, effectively, throughout the life cycle of the project. Often, these tests should be run on different data inputs following the same execution steps, while the tests, and essentially, the code being tested are expected to have consistent behavior, irrespective of the data input.

Running tests on different sets of data can be achieved by creating or replicating existing tests with similar steps operating on the different desired data inputs. The issue with this approach is maintenance, since changes to the test's logic will have to be affected in the various replicated tests. xUnit.net solves this challenge through its data-driven unit tests feature, known as **theories**, which allows tests to be run on different sets of test data.

Data-driven unit tests, which can also be referred to as data-driven testing automation in xUnit.net, are tests decorated with the `Theory` attribute and have data passed in as parameters to these tests. Data passed to data-driven unit tests can come from a variety of sources, which can be inline through the use of the `InlineData` attribute. Data can also come from specific data sources, such as obtaining data from a flat file, web service, or from a database.

The sample data-driven unit tests explained in `Chapter 4`, *.NET Core Unit Testing*, use an inline approach. There are other attributes that can be used for providing data to the tests—`MemberData` and `ClassData`.

In this chapter, we will walk through the creation of data-driven unit tests using the xUnit.net framework and cover the following topics:

- The benefits of data-driven unit testing
- The xUnit.net `Theory` attribute for creating data-driven tests
- Inline data-driven unit tests
- Property data-driven unit tests
- Integrating data from other sources

The benefits of data-driven unit testing

Data-driven unit testing is a concept known to provide great insight into code behavior, due to it being able to execute tests with different sets of data. The insight gained through data-driven unit testing can assist in making informed decisions about application development approaches and can identify potential areas that need improvement. Strategies can be formulated from reports and code coverage available from data unit tests, which can later be used to refactor code with potential performance issues and bugs in the application logic.

Some of the benefits of data-driven unit testing are explained in the following sections.

Tests brevity

Through data-driven tests, it is easier to reduce redundancy while still maintaining comprehensive test coverage. This is because test code duplication can be avoided. Tests that would have been traditionally duplicated to test different datasets can now be reused for different datasets. When there are tests that have similar structures but with dissimilar data, this is an indication that the tests can be refactored as data-driven tests.

Let's review the `CarLoanCalculator` class and the corresponding `LoanCalculatorTest` test class in the following snippets. This will provide a valuable insight into why data-driven testing can simplify testing while providing brevity of code when compared with the traditional approach to writing tests.

CarLoanCalculator extends the LoanCalculator class to override the CalculateLoan method to perform calculations related to a car loan and returns a Loan object that will be validated using xUnit.net assertions:

```
public class CarLoanCalculator : LoanCalculator
{
    public CarLoanCalculator(RateParser rateParser)
    {
        base.rateParser=rateParser;
    }
    public override Loan CalculateLoan(LoanDTO loanDTO)
    {
        Loan loan = new Loan();
        loan.LoanType=loanDTO.LoanType;
        loan.InterestRate=rateParser.GetRateByLoanType(loanDTO.LoanType,
loanDTO.LocationType, loanDTO.JobType);
        // do other processing
        return loan
    }
}
```

To verify the consistent behavior of the CarLoanCalculator class, the Loan object returned by the CalculateLoan method will be validated using the following test scenarios when the method argument LoanDTO has different LoanType, LocationType, and JobType combinations. The Test_CalculateLoan_ShouldReturnLoan test method in the CarLoanCalculatorTest class validates each of the scenarios described:

```
public class CarLoanCalculatorTest
{
    private CarLoanCalculator carLoanCalculator;
    public CarLoanCalculatorTest()
    {
        RateParser rateParser= new RateParser();
        this.carLoanCalculator=new CarLoanCalculator(rateParser);
    }
    [Fact]
    public void Test_CalculateLoan_ShouldReturnLoan()
    {
        // first scenario
        LoanDTO loanDTO1 = new LoanDTO();
        loanDTO1.LoanType=LoanType.CarLoan;
        loanDTO1.LocationType=LocationType.Location1;
        loanDTO1.JobType=JobType.Professional
        Loan loan1=carLoanCalculator.CalculateLoan(loanDTO1);
        Assert.NotNull(loan1);
        Assert.Equal(8,loan1.InterestRate);
```

```
        // second scenario
        LoanDTO loanDTO2 = new LoanDTO();
        loanDTO2.LoanType=LoanType.CarLoan;
        loanDTO2.LocationType=LocationType.Location2;
        loanDTO2.JobType=JobType.Professional;
        Loan loan2=carLoanCalculator.CalculateLoan(loanDTO2);
        Assert.NotNull(loan2);
        Assert.Equal(10,loan2.InterestRate);
    }
}
```

The `Test_CalculateLoan_ShouldReturnLoan` method in the preceding snippet contains lines of code with data to test the `CalculateLoan` method twice. This test clearly contains duplicate code with the test tightly coupled to the test data. Also, the test code is not clean because when more test scenarios are added, the test method will have to be modified by adding more lines of code, thereby making the test large and clumsy. With data-driven testing, this scenario can be avoided and having repeated code in tests can be eliminated.

Inclusive testing

Software application quality can be improved when business people and quality assurance testers are carried along in the automated testing process. They can populate the data source with the data required to execute the tests, with little technical knowledge required, especially when using data files as a data source. The tests can be run multiple times using different datasets to test the code thoroughly in order to ensure robustness.

Using data-driven testing, you have a clear separation of your tests and data. Tests that would have otherwise been muddled up with the data will now be separated using the appropriate logic. This ensures that the data source can be modified without making changes to the tests using them.

The overall quality of the application is improved through data-driven unit tests as you can have good coverage with the various datasets and have metrics to use to fine-tune and optimize the application being developed for improved performance in place.

xUnit.net theory attribute for creating data-driven tests

In xUnit.net, data-driven tests are known as theories. They are tests decorated with the Theory attribute. When a test method is decorated with the Theory attribute, it must additionally be decorated with a data attribute, which will be used by the test runner to determine the source of the data to be used in executing the test:

```
[Theory]
public void Test_CalculateRates_ShouldReturnRate()
{
    // test not implemented yet
}
```

When a test is marked as data theory, the data fed into it from the data source is directly mapped to the parameters of the test method. Unlike the regular test decorated with the Fact attribute, which is executed only once, the number of times a data theory is executed is based on the available data rows fetched from the data source.

At least one data attribute is required to be passed as the test method argument for xUnit.net to treat the test as data-driven and execute it successfully. The data attribute to be passed to the test can be any of InlineData, MemberData, and ClassData. These data attributes are derived from Xunit.sdk.DataAttribute.

Inline data-driven unit tests

Inline data-driven testing is the most basic or simplest way of writing data-driven tests using the *xUnit.net framework*. Inline data-driven tests are written using the InlineData attribute, which is used to decorate the test method in addition to the Theory attribute:

```
[Theory, InlineData("arguments")]
```

Inline data-driven tests can be used when the test method requires parameters that are simple and does not accept class instantiation as an InlineData parameter. The major drawback of using the inline data-driven test is the lack of flexibility. Inline data used with a test cannot be reused with another test.

When you are using the InlineData attribute in a data theory, the data rows are hard-coded and passed inline into the test method. The desired data to be used for the test can be of any data type and is passed as a parameter into the InlineData attribute:

```
public class TheoryTest
{
    [Theory,
    InlineData("name")]
    public void TestCheckWordLength_ShouldReturnBoolean(string word)
    {
        Assert.Equal(4, word.Length);
    }
}
```

An inline data-driven test can have more than one `InlineData` attribute with the parameters to the test method specified. The syntax of multi `InlineData` data theory is specified in the following code:

```
[Theory, InlineData("argument1"), InlineData("argument2"),
InlineData("argumentn")]
```

The `TestCheckWordLength_ShouldReturnBoolean` method can be changed to have three inline data rows, and more data rows can be added to the test as desired. To have clean tests, it is recommended to not have more than the necessary or required inline data per test:

```
public class TheoryTest
{
    [Theory,
    InlineData("name"),
    InlineData("word"),
    InlineData("city")
    ]
    public void TestCheckWordLength_ShouldReturnBoolean(string word)
    {
        Assert.Equal(4, word.Length);
    }
}
```

When writing inline data-driven unit tests, you must ensure that the number of parameters in the test method match the parameters in the data rows passed to the `InlineData` attribute; otherwise, the xUnit test runner will throw a `System.InvalidOperationException`. The `InlineData` attribute in the `TestCheckWordLength_ShouldReturnBoolean` method in the following snippet has been modified to take two parameters:

```
public class TheoryTest
{
    [Theory,
    InlineData("word","name")]
```

```
    public void TestCheckWordLength_ShouldReturnBoolean(string word)
    {
        Assert.Equal(4, word.Length);
    }
}
```

When you run the data theory test in the preceding snippet, the xUnit test runner test fails with `InvalidOperationException`, as shown in the following screenshot, because two parameters "word" and "name" were passed to the `InlineData` attribute instead of the expected one parameter:

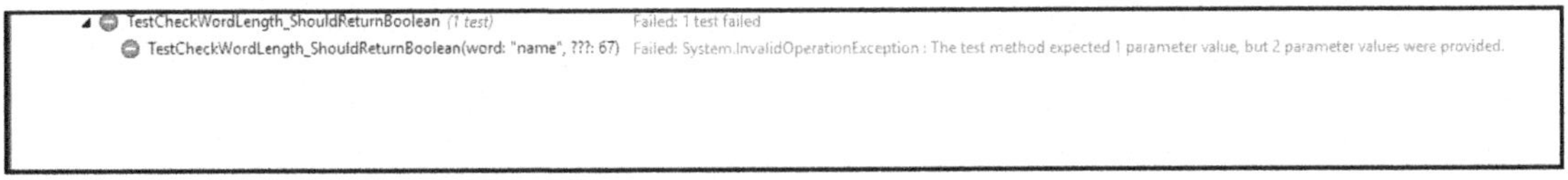

When you run an inline data-driven test, xUnit.net will create the number of tests, based on the number of `InlineData` attributes or data rows added to the test method. In the following snippet, xUnit.net will create two tests, one for the `InlineData` attribute with the argument "name" and the second for the argument "city":

```
[Theory,
    InlineData("name"),
    InlineData("city")]
    public void TestCheckWordLength_ShouldReturnBoolean(string word)
    {
        Assert.Equal(4, word.Length);
    }
```

If you run the `TestCheckWordLength_ShouldReturnBoolean` test method in Visual Studio using the test runner, the test should successfully run and pass. The two tests created based on the attributes can be differentiated by the parameters passed into them from the `InlineData` attribute:

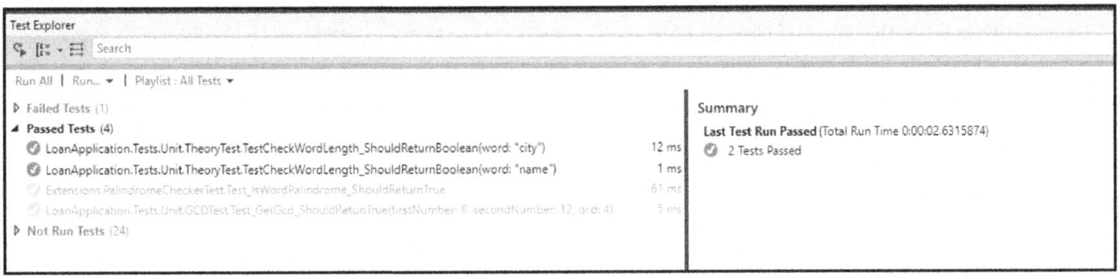

Now, let's modify the `Test_CalculateLoan_ShouldReturnCorrectRate` test method in the section, *The benefits of data-driven unit testing*, to use `InlineData` to load the test data instead of hard-coding the test data directly in the code of the test method:

```
[Theory, InlineData(new LoanDTO{ LoanType =LoanType.CarLoan, JobType
=JobType.Professional, LocationType=LocationType.Location1 })]
 public void Test_CalculateLoan_ShouldReturnCorrectRate(LoanDTO loanDTO)
 {
     Loan loan = carLoanCalculator.CalculateLoan(loanDTO);
     Assert.NotNull(loan);
     Assert.Equal(8, loan.InterestRate);
 }
```

In Visual Studio, the preceding code snippet will give a syntax error, with the IntelliSense context menu showing the error—**An attribute argument must be a constant expression, type of expression or array creation expression of an attribute parameter type**:

```
[Theory,
 InlineData(new LoanDTO { LoanType = LoanType.CarLoan, JobType = JobType.Professional, LocationType = LocationType.Location1 })]
 0 references | 0 exceptions
 public void Test_CalculateLoan_ShouldReturnCorrectRate(Loan   An attribute argument must be a constant expression, typeof expression or array creation expression of an attribute parameter type
 {
     Loan loan = carLoanCalculator.CalculateLoan(loanDTO);    An attribute argument must be a constant expression, typeof expression or array creation expression of an attribute parameter type
     Assert.NotNull(loan);
     Assert.Equal(8, loan.InterestRate);
 }
```

Using properties or custom types as parameter types in the `InlineData` attribute is not allowed, which indicates that the new instance of the `LoanDTO` class cannot be used as an argument to the `InlineData` attribute. This is the limitation of the `InlineData` attribute as it cannot be used to load data from properties, classes, methods, or custom types.

Property data-driven unit tests

The lack of flexibility encountered when writing inline data-driven tests can be overcome through the use of property data-driven tests. Property data-driven unit tests are written in xUnit.net through the use of the `MemberData` and `ClassData` attributes. Using the two attributes, data theories can be created with data loaded from disparate data sources, such as files or databases.

MemberData attribute

The MemberData attribute is used when data theories are to be created and loaded with data rows coming from following data sources:

- Static property
- Static field
- Static method

When using MemberData, the data source must return independent object sets that are compatible with IEnumerable<object[]>. This is because the return property is enumerated by the .ToList() method before the test method is executed.

The Test_CalculateLoan_ShouldReturnCorrectRate test method in the, *The benefits of data-driven unit testing* section, can be refactored to use the MemberData attribute to load the data for the test. A static IEnumerable method, GetLoanDTOs, is created to return a LoanDTO object using the yield statement to return the object to the test method:

```
public static IEnumerable<object[]> GetLoanDTOs()
{
    yield return new object[]
    {
        new LoanDTO
        {
            LoanType = LoanType.CarLoan,
            JobType = JobType.Professional,
            LocationType = LocationType.Location1
        }
    };

    yield return new object[]
    {
        new LoanDTO
        {
            LoanType = LoanType.CarLoan,
            JobType = JobType.Professional,
            LocationType = LocationType.Location2
        }
    };
}
```

The `MemberData` attribute requires that the name of the data source is passed to it as a parameter for subsequent invocation to load the data rows for the test execution. The name of the static method, property, or field can be passed as a string into the `MemberData` attribute in this form—`MemberData("methodName")`:

```
[Theory, MemberData("GetLoanDTOs")]
public void Test_CalculateLoan_ShouldReturnCorrectRate(LoanDTO loanDTO)
{
    Loan loan = carLoanCalculator.CalculateLoan(loanDTO);
    Assert.NotNull(loan);
    Assert.InRange(loan.InterestRate, 8, 12);
}
```

Alternatively, the data source name can be passed to the `MemeberData` attribute through the use of the `nameof` expression, which is a C# keyword that is used to get the string name of a variable, type, or member. The syntax is `MemberData(nameof(methodName))`:

```
[Theory, MemberData(nameof(GetLoanDTOs))]
public void Test_CalculateLoan_ShouldReturnCorrectRate(LoanDTO loanDTO)
{
    Loan loan = carLoanCalculator.CalculateLoan(loanDTO);
    Assert.NotNull(loan);
    Assert.InRange(loan.InterestRate, 8, 12);
}
```

Similar to using static method with the `MemberData` attribute, static fields and properties can be used to provide datasets to data theories.

`Test_CalculateLoan_ShouldReturnCorrectRate` can be refactored to use a static property in place of the method:

```
[Theory, MemberData("LoanDTOs")]
        public void Test_CalculateLoan_ShouldReturnCorrectRate(LoanDTO
loanDTO)
        {
            Loan loan = carLoanCalculator.CalculateLoan(loanDTO);
            Assert.NotNull(loan);
            Assert.InRange(loan.InterestRate, 8, 12);
        }
```

A static property, LoanDTOs, is created to return IEnumerable<object[]>, which is required to make it qualify for use as a parameter to the MemberData attribute. LoanDTOs is subsequently used as a parameter to the attribute:

```
public static IEnumerable<object[]> LoanDTOs
{
        get
        {
            yield return new object[]
            {
                new LoanDTO
                {
                    LoanType = LoanType.CarLoan,
                    JobType = JobType.Professional,
                    LocationType = LocationType.Location1
                }
            };

            yield return new object[]
            {
                new LoanDTO
                {
                    LoanType = LoanType.CarLoan,
                    JobType = JobType.Professional,
                    LocationType = LocationType.Location2
                }
            };
    }
```

Whenever Test_CalculateLoan_ShouldReturnCorrectRate is run, two tests are created that correspond to the two datasets returned by either the static method or property used as the data source.

Following the preceding approach requires that the static method, field, or property used to load the tests data is located in the same class as the data theory. In order to have tests well-organized, it is sometimes required that the tests method is separated in different classes from the static methods or properties used for loading the data:

```
public class DataClass
{
    public static IEnumerable<object[]> LoanDTOs
    {
            get
            {
                    yield return new object[]
                    {
```

```
                                  new LoanDTO
                                  {
                                      LoanType = LoanType.CarLoan,
                                      JobType = JobType.Professional,
                                      LocationType = LocationType.Location1
                                  }
                      };

                  yield return new object[]
                  {
                                  new LoanDTO
                                  {
                                      LoanType = LoanType.CarLoan,
                                      JobType = JobType.Professional,
                                      LocationType = LocationType.Location2
                                  }
                      };
              }
          }
      }
```

When the test method is written in a separate class different from the static method, you have to specify the class containing the method in the MemberData attribute, using MemberType, and assign the containing class, using the class name, as shown in the following snippet:

```
[Theory, MemberData(nameof(LoanDTOs), MemberType = typeof(DataClass))]
public void Test_CalculateLoan_ShouldReturnCorrectRate(LoanDTO loanDTO)
{
      Loan loan = carLoanCalculator.CalculateLoan(loanDTO);
      Assert.NotNull(loan);
      Assert.InRange(loan.InterestRate, 8, 12);
}
```

When using the static method, the method can also have a parameter, which you might want to use when processing the data. For example, you can pass an integer value to the method to specify the number of records to return. This parameter can be passed directly from the MemberData attribute to the static method:

```
[Theory, MemberData(nameof(GetLoanDTOs),  parameters: 1, MemberType =
typeof(DataClass))]
public void Test_CalculateLoan_ShouldReturnCorrectRate3(LoanDTO loanDTO)
{
      Loan loan = carLoanCalculator.CalculateLoan(loanDTO);
      Assert.NotNull(loan);
      Assert.InRange(loan.InterestRate, 8, 12);
}
```

The `GetLoanDTOs` method in `DataClass` can be refactored to take an integer parameter to be used to limit the number of records to be returned for populating the data rows required for the execution of `Test_CalculateLoan_ShouldReturnCorrectRate`:

```
public class DataClass
{
    public static IEnumerable<object[]> GetLoanDTOs(int records)
    {
        var loanDTOs = new List<object[]>
        {
            new object[]
            {
                new LoanDTO
                {
                    LoanType = LoanType.CarLoan,
                    JobType = JobType.Professional,
                    LocationType = LocationType.Location1
                }
            },
            new object[]
            {
                new LoanDTO
                {
                    LoanType = LoanType.CarLoan,
                    JobType = JobType.Professional,
                    LocationType = LocationType.Location2
                }
            }
        };
        return loanDTOs.TakeLast(records);
    }
}
```

ClassData attribute

`ClassData` is another attribute that can be used to create data-driven tests by using data coming from a class. The `ClassData` attribute takes a class that can be instantiated to fetched data that will be used to execute the data theories. The class with the data must implement `IEnumerable<object[]>` with each data item returned as an `object` array. The `GetEnumerator` method must also be implemented.

Let's create a `LoanDTOData` class to be used to provide data to test the `Test_CalculateLoan_ShouldReturnCorrectRate` method. `LoanDTOData` will return `IEnumerable` objects of `LoanDTO`:

```
public class LoanDTOData : IEnumerable<object[]>
{
    private IEnumerable<object[]> data => new[]
    {
            new object[]
            {
                new LoanDTO
                {
                    LoanType = LoanType.CarLoan,
                    JobType = JobType.Professional,
                    LocationType = LocationType.Location1
                }
            },
            new object[]
            {
                new LoanDTO
                {
                    LoanType = LoanType.CarLoan,
                    JobType = JobType.Professional,
                    LocationType = LocationType.Location2
                }
            }
    };

    IEnumerator IEnumerable.GetEnumerator()
    {
        return GetEnumerator();
    }

    public IEnumerator<object[]> GetEnumerator()
    {
        return data.GetEnumerator();
    }
}
```

After the `LoanDTOData` class has been implemented, `Test_CalculateLoan_ShouldReturnCorrectRate` can be decorated with the `ClassData` attribute with `LoanDTOData` passed as the attribute parameter to specify that `LoanDTOData` will be instantiated to return data required for the execution of the test method:

```
[Theory, ClassData(typeof(LoanDTOData))]
```

```
public void Test_CalculateLoan_ShouldReturnCorrectRate(LoanDTO loanDTO)
{
    Loan loan = carLoanCalculator.CalculateLoan(loanDTO);
    Assert.NotNull(loan);
    Assert.InRange(loan.InterestRate, 8, 12);
}
```

Implementing the enumerator can be flexibly done using any suitable approach, either by using a class property or a method. Before the test is run, the xUnit.net framework will call `.ToList()` on the class. While using the `ClassData` attribute for passing data to your tests, you always have to create a dedicated class to contain your data.

Integrating data from other sources

While you can write basic data-driven tests with the xUnit.net theory attributes discussed earlier, there are times where you want to do more, such as connecting to an SQL Server database table to fetch data to be used in executing your tests. Earlier versions of xUnit.net had other attributes from `xUnit.net.extensions` that allow you to easily get data from different sources to be used in your tests. The `xUnit.net.extensions` package is no longer available in **xUnit.net v2**.

However, the classes in `xUnit.net.extensions` are available in sample projects at: `https://github.com/xUnit.net/samples.xUnit.net`. The code from the sample projects can be copied to your project if you wish to use this attribute.

SqlServerData attribute

Inside the `SqlDataExample` folder of the projects, there are files that can be copied to your project to give you the functionality of getting data by connecting directly to an SQL Server database or any data source that can be accessed using *OLEDB*. The four classes located in the folder are `DataAdapterDataAttribute`, `DataAdapterDataAttributeDiscoverer`, `OleDbDataAttribute`, and `SqlServerDataAttribute`.

It is important to note that since .NET Core does not support OLEDB, the preceding extension cannot be used in a .NET Core project. This is because OLEDB technology was based on COM, which is dependent on components that are available only on Windows. But you can use this extension in a regular .NET project.

The code listing provided in the xUnit.net repository on GitHub has the `SqlServerData` attribute that can be used to decorate data theories to fetch data for test execution directly from Microsoft SQL Server database tables.

To test the `SqlServerData` attribute, you should create a database in your instance of SQL Server and name it `TheoryDb`. Create a table with the name `Palindrome`; it should have a column named `varchar`. Populate the table with sample data to be used for the test:

```
CREATE TABLE [dbo].[Palindrome](
    [word] [varchar](50) NOT NULL
) ;

INSERT INTO [dbo].[Palindrome] ([word]) VALUES ('civic')
GO
INSERT INTO [dbo].[Palindrome] ([word]) VALUES ('dad')
GO
INSERT INTO [dbo].[Palindrome] ([word]) VALUES ('omo')
GO
```

The `PalindronmeChecker` class runs with an `IsWordPalindrome` method to verify a word is a palindrome, as shown in the following snippet. A palindrome is a word that can be read in both directions—for example, `dad` or `civic`. A quick way to check this without an algorithm implementation is to reverse the word and use the string `SequenceEqual` method to check if the two words are equal:

```
public class PalindromeChecker
{
    public bool IsWordPalindrome(string word)
    {
        return word.SequenceEqual(word.Reverse());
    }
}
```

To test the `IsWordPalindrome` method, a test method, `Test_IsWordPalindrome_ShouldReturnTrue`, will be implemented which will be decorated with the `SqlServerData` attribute. This attribute requires three parameters—the database server address, the database name, and the select statement for retrieving the data from the table or view containing the data to be loaded for the test:

```
public class PalindromeCheckerTest
    {
        [Theory, SqlServerData(@".\sqlexpress", "TheoryDb", "select word
from Palindrome")]
        public void Test_IsWordPalindrome_ShouldReturnTrue(string word)
        {
```

```
        PalindromeChecker palindromeChecker = new PalindromeChecker();
        Assert.True(palindromeChecker.IsWordPalindrome(word));
    }
}
```

When `Test_IsWordPalindrome_ShouldReturnTrue` is run, the `SqlServerData` attribute is executed to fetch the records from the database table to be used for executing the test method. The number of tests to be created depends on the available records in the table. In this case, three tests will be created and executed:

Extensions.PalindromeCheckerTest.Test_IsWordPalindrome_ShouldReturnTrue   Copy All

Source: PalindromeCheckerTest.cs line 14

✅ Test Passed - Extensions.PalindromeCheckerTest.Test_IsWordPalindrome_ShouldReturnTrue(word: "civic")
Elapsed time: 0:00:00.059

✅ Test Passed - Extensions.PalindromeCheckerTest.Test_IsWordPalindrome_ShouldReturnTrue(word: "dad")
Elapsed time: 0:00:00.001

✅ Test Passed - Extensions.PalindromeCheckerTest.Test_IsWordPalindrome_ShouldReturnTrue(word: "omo")
Elapsed time: 0:00:00.001

Custom attribute

Similar to the `SqlServerData` attribute available in the xUnit.net GitHub repository, you can create a custom attribute to load data from any source. A custom attribute class must implement `DataAttribute`, which is an abstract class that represents a data source to be used by a theory. The custom attribute class must override and implement the `GetData` method. This method returns `IEnumerable<object[]>`, which is used to wrap the content of the dataset to be returned.

Let's create a `CsvData` custom attribute that can be used to load data from a `.csv` file for use in data-driven unit tests. The class will have a constructor that takes two parameters. The first is a string argument containing the full path to the `.csv` file. The second argument is a Boolean value, which when `true`, specifies if the first row of data contained in the `.csv` file should be used as the column header and when `false`, specifies ignoring column headers in the file, meaning the CSV data starts from the first row.

The custom attribute class is `CsvDataAttribute`, which implements the `DataAttribute` class. The class is decorated with the `AttributeUsage` attribute, which has the following parameters—`AttributeTargets` to specify the valid application elements to apply the attribute, `AllowMultiple` to specify if the multiple instances of the attribute can be specified on a single application element, and `Inherited` to specify if the attribute can be inherited by derived classes or overriding members:

```
[AttributeUsage(AttributeTargets.Method, AllowMultiple = false, Inherited =
false)]
    public class CsvDataAttribute : DataAttribute
    {
        private readonly string filePath;
        private readonly bool hasHeaders;
        public CsvDataAttribute(string filePath, bool hasHeaders)
        {
            this.filePath = filePath;
            this.hasHeaders = hasHeaders;
        }
        // To be followed by GetData implementation
    }
```

The next step is to implement the `GetData` method, which will override the implementation available in the `DataAttribute` class. This method uses the `StreamReader` class in the `System.IO` namespace to read the contents of the `.csv` file a line at a time. A second utility method, `ConverCsv`, is implemented to convert the CSV data to an integer for integer values:

```
public override IEnumerable<object[]> GetData(MethodInfo methodInfo)
    {
        var methodParameters = methodInfo.GetParameters();
        var parameterTypes = methodParameters.Select(x =>
x.ParameterType).ToArray();
        using (var streamReader = new StreamReader(filePath))
        {
            if(hasHeaders)
                streamReader.ReadLine();
            string csvLine=string.Empty;
            while ((csvLine = streamReader.ReadLine()) != null)
```

```
        {
            var csvRow = csvLine.Split(',');
            yield return ConvertCsv((object[])csvRow, parameterTypes);
        }
    }
}

 private static object[] ConvertCsv(IReadOnlyList<object> csvRow,
IReadOnlyList<Type> parameterTypes)
 {
    var convertedObject = new object[parameterTypes.Count];
    //convert object if integer
    for (int i = 0; i < parameterTypes.Count; i++)
      convertedObject[i] = (parameterTypes[i] == typeof(int)) ?
Convert.ToInt32(csvRow[i]) : csvRow[i];
    return convertedObject;
 }
```

The created custom attribute can now be used with the xUnit.net `Theory` attribute to provide data to theories from `.csv` files.

The `Test_IsWordPalindrome_ShouldReturnTrue` test method will be modified to use the newly created `CsvData` attribute to get the data for the test execution from a `.csv` file:

```
public class PalindromeCheckerTest
{
        [Theory, CsvData(@"C:\data.csv", false)]
        public void Test_IsWordPalindrome_ShouldReturnTrue(string word)
        {
            PalindromeChecker palindromeChecker = new PalindromeChecker();
            Assert.True(palindromeChecker.IsWordPalindrome(word));
        }
}
```

When you run the `Test_IsWordPalindrome_ShouldReturnTrue` test method in the preceding snippet in Visual Studio, there will be three tests created by the test runner. This should correspond to the number of records or data lines retrieved from the `.csv` file. The test information can be viewed from the **Test Explorer**:

Extensions.PalindromeCheckerTest.Test_IsWordPalindrome_ShouldReturnTrue   Copy All

    Source: PalindromeCheckerTest.cs line 14

✅ Test Passed - Extensions.PalindromeCheckerTest.Test_IsWordPalindrome_ShouldReturnTrue(word: "civic")
    Elapsed time: 0:00:00.059

✅ Test Passed - Extensions.PalindromeCheckerTest.Test_IsWordPalindrome_ShouldReturnTrue(word: "dad")
    Elapsed time: 0:00:00.001

✅ Test Passed - Extensions.PalindromeCheckerTest.Test_IsWordPalindrome_ShouldReturnTrue(word: "omo")
    Elapsed time: 0:00:00.001

The `CsvData` custom attribute can retrieve data from any `.csv` file, irrespective of the numbers of columns present on a single line. The records will be fetched and passed to the `Theory` attribute in the test method.

Let's create a method with two integer parameters, `firstNumber` and `secondNumber`. The method will calculate the greatest common divisor of integer values, `firstNumber` and `secondNumber`. The greatest common divisor of the two integers is the largest value that divides the two integers:

```
public int GetGcd(int firstNumber, int secondNumber)
{
    if (secondNumber == 0)
        return firstNumber;
    else
        return GetGcd(secondNumber, firstNumber % secondNumber);
}
```

Now, let's write a test method to verify the `GetGcd` method. `Test_GetGcd_ShouldRetunTrue` will be a data theory and have three integer parameters—`firstNumber`, `secondNumber`, and `gcdValue`. The method will check if `gdcValue` supplied in the parameter matches what the `GetGcd` method returns when called. The data for the tests will be loaded from a `.csv` file:

```
[Theory, CsvData(@"C:\gcd.csv", false)]
public void Test_GetGcd_ShouldRetunTrue(int firstNumber, int secondNumber,
int gcd)
{
    int gcdValue=GetGcd(firstNumber,secondNumber);
    Assert.Equal(gcd,gcdValue);
}
```

Based on the value provided in the `.csv` file, the tests will be created. The following screenshot shows the outcome of `Test_GetGcdShouldReturnTrue` when run. Three tests were created; one passed and two failed:

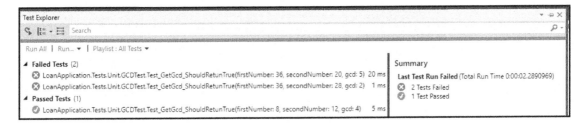

Summary

Data-driven unit testing is an important concept of TDD that brings many benefits, by allowing you to test your code base extensively with real-life data from multiple data sources, giving you the insight needed to tweak and refactor code for better performance and robustness.

In this chapter, we covered the benefits of data-driven testing and how to write effective data-driven tests using the inline and properties attributes of xUnit.net. Furthermore, we explored data-driven unit testing using the `Theory` attribute available in xUnit.net. This allows you to unit test your code for appropriate validation and verification over a wide range of inputs coming from different data sources.

While the default data source attributes provided by xUnit.net are very useful, you can further extend the `DataAttribute` class and create a custom attribute to load data from another source. We walked through the implementation of the `CsvData` custom attribute to load test data from a `.csv` file.

In the next chapter, we will delve into another important and useful TDD concept, dependencies mocking. Mocking allows you to effectively unit test your methods and classes in isolation without having to construct or execute the code of the dependencies directly.

6
Mocking Dependencies

In Chapter 5, *Data-Driven Unit Tests*, we discussed data-driven unit testing using the xUnit framework, which allows us to create tests that run on data from different sources, such as flat files, databases, or inline data. Now, we will explain the concepts of mocking dependencies and explore how to use the Moq framework to isolate your class that is being tested from its dependencies, using mock objects created with Moq.

There are usually objects dependencies in the code base of software projects, whether for a simple or a complex project. This is because the various objects need to interact and share information across boundaries. However, to effectively unit test the objects and isolate their behaviors, each object must be tested in isolation, irrespective of the dependencies it has on other objects.

In order to achieve this, the dependent objects in a class are replaced with mocks to allow the object being tested to be effective when tested in isolation, without having to go through the pain of constructing the dependent objects, which sometimes might not be fully implemented or may be impractical to construct at the time the object being tested is written.

Mock objects are used to simulate or mimic real objects for the purpose of code testing. Mock objects are used to replace real objects; they are created from real interfaces or classes and used to verify interactions. Mock objects are essential instances of classes referenced in another class to be tested and are used to simulate the behavior of these classes. Since the components of a software system need to interact and collaborate, mock objects are used to replace the collaborators. A mock object, when used, verifies that the usage is correct and is as expected. Mocks can be created using a mocking framework or library or, alternatively, by generating code for them through handwritten mock objects.

The Moq framework will be explored in detail in this chapter and will be used to create mock objects. Moq is a fully functional mocking framework that can be set up easily. It can be used to create mock objects for use in unit tests. Moq has several basic and advanced features expected of a mocking framework to create useful mocks and essentially write good unit tests.

In this chapter, we will cover the following topics:

- The benefits of mocking objects
- The shortcomings of mocking frameworks
- Hand-rolling mocks versus using the mocking framework
- Mocking objects using Moq framework

The benefits of mocking objects

In a well-architected software system, there are usually objects that interact and coordinate to accomplish set objectives based on the business or automation requirements. Quite often, these objects are complex and rely on other external components or systems, such as databases, SOAP, or REST services for data and internal state updates.

Most developers are beginning to adopt TDD because of the many benefits that practicing it can offer and due to the awareness that it is the responsibility of programmers to write quality code that is bug free and well tested. However, some developers object to mocking objects due to several assumptions. For example, adding mock objects to unit tests increases the total time required to write unit tests. This assumption is false because using mock objects offers several benefits, as explained in the following sections.

Fast running tests

The main characteristics of a unit test are that it should run very quickly and should give consistent results even when executed multiple times with the same set of data. However, to effectively run a unit test and maintain this attribute of having unit tests that are efficients and run quickly, it is important to have mock objects set up where there are dependencies in the code being tested.

For example, in the following code snippet, the `LoanRepository` class has a dependency on Entity Framework's `DbContext` class which creates a connection to a database server for database operations. To write a unit test for the `GetCarLoans` method in the `LoanRepository` class will necessitate that the `DbContext` object be constructed. The `DbContext` object can be mocked to avoid the expensive operation of opening and closing database connections each time a unit test is run for that class:

```
public class LoanRepository
{
    private DbContext dbContext;
```

```
public LoanRepository(DbContext dbContext)
{
    this.dbContext=dbContext;
}
public List<CarLoan> GetCarLoans()
{
    return dbContext.CarLoan;
}
}
```

In a software system, based on the requirements, there will be the need to access external systems, such as large files, databases, or web connections. Interacting directly with these external systems in a unit test increases the runtime of the test. Therefore, it is desirable to mock these external systems to allow the tests to run quickly. The benefits of unit testing can be lost when you have long running tests that apparently waste productive time. A developer in such a situation can stop running the tests or totally stop unit testing on the assertion that unit testing is time wasting.

Dependencies isolation

Using dependencies mocking, you technically create alternatives to the dependencies in your code that you can experiment with. When you have a mock implementation of dependencies in place, you can make changes and test the effect of the changes in isolation since the tests will be running against mock objects and not the real objects.

When you have the dependencies isolated, you can focus on the test being run, thereby limiting the scope of your test to the code that really matters for the test. In essence, with the reduced scope, you can easily refactor the code being tested as well as the test itself, giving you a clear picture of areas where the code can be improved.

In order to test the `LoanRepository` class in the following snippet in isolation, the `DbContext` object that the class depends on can be mocked out. This will limit the scope of the unit tests to only the `LoanRepository` class:

```
public class LoanRepository
{
    private DbContext dbContext;
    public LoanRepository(DbContext dbContext)
    {
        this.dbContext=dbContext;
    }
}
```

Also, keeping the scope of the test small through isolation of dependencies makes the test easy to understand and facilitates easy maintenance. Increasing the scope of the test by not mocking dependencies eventually makes test maintenance difficult and reduces the high level detailed coverage of the test. Since the dependencies will have to be tested, this can result in less detail being tested due to increased scope.

Refactoring legacy code

Legacy source code is the code that was written by you or someone else usually without tests or using an old framework, architecture, or technology. Such a code base can be difficult to rewrite or maintain. It can sometimes be tangled code that cannot be easily read and understood and as such is very difficult to change.

When faced with the daunting task of maintaining a legacy code base, especially a code base written without adequate or proper testing, writing unit tests for such code can be difficult, and a waste of time, and can result in a lot of hard work. However, using a mocking framework can greatly simplify the refactoring process, as the new code being written can be isolated from the existing code and tested using mock objects.

Wider test coverage

With mocks, you are sure of a wide test coverage, as you can easily use mock objects to simulate possible exceptions, execution scenarios, and conditions that otherwise would be difficult without mocks. For example, if you have a method that purges or drops a database table, it is safer to test this method using mock objects than run it on a live database each time the unit test is run.

The shortcomings of mocking frameworks

While mocking frameworks are very useful during TDD in that they simplify unit testing through the use of mock objects, they, however, have some limitations and downsides that can impact the design of the code or through excessive usage lead to the creation of tangled tests containing irrelevant mock objects.

Interface explosion

The architecture of the majority of the mocking frameworks necessitates that interfaces should be created in order to mock objects. In essence, you cannot mock a class directly; it has to be through the interface implemented by the class. In an attempt to mock dependencies during unit testing, an interface is created for each object or dependency to be mocked, even if the interface is not required to use the dependency in production code. This results in the creation of too many interfaces, a condition known as **interface explosion**.

Extra complexity

Most mocking frameworks use reflection or create proxies to invoke the methods and create the mocks required in unit tests. This process is slow and adds overhead to the unit testing process. This is noticeable especially when it is desired to mock interactions between all classes and dependencies using mocks, which can lead to a situation where a mock returns other mocks.

Mock explosion

With the availability of several mocking frameworks, it is easier to get familiar with mocking concepts and create mocks for unit testing. However, a developer can start to over-mock, a situation where every object seems like a mock candidate. Also, having too many mocks can lead to writing fragile tests, making your tests prone to breaking when the interface changes. When you have too many mocks, this ends up slowing down the test suites and consequently increases development time.

Hand-rolling mocks versus using a mocking framework

Using a mocking framework can facilitate a smooth unit testing experience, especially when unit testing a portion of code with dependencies in which mock objects are created and substituted for the dependencies. While it is easier using mocking frameworks, you might sometimes prefer to hand-roll mock objects for your unit tests and not add extra complexity or additional libraries to your project or code base.

Hand-rolled mocks are classes that are created for the purpose of testing and used to replace production objects. These created classes will have equivalent methods as the production classes with the same definitions and return values to effectively simulate the production classes and to use as substitute for dependencies in unit tests.

Mocking concept

The first step in creating mocks should be dependency identification. The goal of unit testing should be to have clean code and tests that run as quickly as possible with good coverage. You should identify dependencies that can slow down your tests. These are candidates for mocking, for example, a web service or database call.

The approach for creating mock objects can vary based on the type of dependencies being mocked. However, the concepts of mocking can follow the basic concepts that mock objects should return specific predefined values when the methods are invoked. There should be an appropriate validation mechanism in place to ensure the methods of the mock were called and the mock object can throw an exception if configured based on the test requirements.

It is important to understand the types of mock objects to effectively hand-roll mock objects. There are two types of mock objects that can be created—dynamic and static mock objects. **Dynamic objects** can be created through reflection or proxy classes. This is similar to how mocking frameworks work. **Static mock objects** can be created by having classes that implement an interface and sometimes the actual concrete class that is the dependency to be mocked. You are essentially creating static mock objects when you hand-roll mocks objects.

Reflection can be used to create mock objects. Reflection in C# is a useful construct that allows you to create an object that is an instance of a type, as well as getting or binding a type to an existing object and invoking the available fields and method in the type. Additionally, you can use reflection to create objects that describe modules and assemblies.

Benefits of hand-rolling mocks

Hand-rolling your mocks can sometimes be an effective approach to use, when you intend to have full control of your test setup and specify the behavior of the test setup. Also, when the test is relatively simple, using a mocking framework is not an option; it is better to roll the mock and keep everything simple.

When using mocking frameworks, making changes to the real object being mocked will necessitate changes to the mock objects wherever they are used. This is because changes made to the dependency will break the tests. If, for example, the method name on the dependent object changes, you have to change this in the dynamic mocks. Thus, changes have to be made in several parts of the code base. With hand-rolled mocks, you only have to make the changes at one point only since you are in control of what method is presented to the tests.

Mocks and stubs

Mocks and **stubs** are both similar because they are used to replace class dependencies or collaborators and most mocking frameworks provide the features to create both. Stubs can be hand-rolled in the same manner you hand-roll mocks.

So what really differentiates mocks from stubs? Mocks are used to test collaboration. This includes verifying the expectations of the actual collaborator. Mocks are programmed to have the expectation containing the details of method invocations to be received, while stubs are used to simulate collaborators. Let's explain this further with an illustration.

A stub can be used to represent the result from a database. In place of a database call to return a set of data, a C# list can be created with the data that can be used in executing a test. If the stub above the dependency interaction of the test is not validated, the test will only be concerned with the data.

The `LoanService` class in the following snippet has a `GetBadCarLoans` method that accepts a list of `Loan` objects to be retrieved from a database:

```
public class LoanService
{
    public List<Loan> GetBadCarLoans(List<Loan> carLoans)
    {
        List<Loan> badLoans= new List<Loan>();
        //do business logic computations on the loans
        return badLoans;
    }
}
```

The test for the GetBadCarLoans method, Test_GetBadCarLoans_ShouldReturnLoans, in the following snippet uses a stub, which is a list of Loan objects that is passed as a parameter to the GetBadCarLoans method, instead of making a database call to get the list of Loan objects to be used for the Test class:

```
[Fact]
 public void Test_GetBadCarLoans_ShouldReturnLoans()
 {
    List<Loan> loans= new List<Loan>();
    loans.Add(new Loan{Amount=120000, Rate=12.5, ServiceYear=5,
HasDefaulted=false});
    loans.Add(new Loan{Amount=150000, Rate=12.5, ServiceYear=4,
HasDefaulted=true});
    loans.Add(new Loan{Amount=200000, Rate=12.5, ServiceYear=5,
HasDefaulted=false});
    LoanService loanService= new LoanService();
    List<Loan> badLoans = loanService.GetBadCarLoans(loanDTO);
    Assert.NotNull(badLoans);
 }
```

The LoanService class in the following snippet has a LoanRepository DI that connects to the database to fetch records. The class has a constructor, where the ILoanRepository object is injected. The LoanService class has a GetBadCarLoans method that calls the GetCarLoan method on the dependency, which in turn makes a call to get a list of Loan objects from the database:

```
public class LoanService
{
    private ILoanRepository loanRepository;
    public LoanService(ILoanRepository loanRepository)
    {
        this.loanRepository=loanRepository;
    }
    public List<Loan> GetBadCarLoans()
    {
        List<Loan> badLoans= new List<Loan>();
        var carLoans=loanRepository.GetCarLoans();
        //do business logic computations on the loans
        return badLoans;
    }
}
```

Unlike when using a stub, a mock will verify that a method in a dependency is called. This implies that the mock object will have a setup of the method to be called in the dependency. In the `LoanServiceTest` class in the following snippet, a mock object is created from `ILoanRepository`:

```
public class LoanServiceTest
{
        private Mock<ILoanRepository> loanRepository;
        private LoanService loanService;
        public LoanServiceTest()
        {
            loanRepository= new Mock<ILoanRepository>();
            List<Loan> loans = new List<Loan>
            {
                new Loan{Amount = 120000, Rate = 12.5, ServiceYear = 5,
HasDefaulted = false },
                new Loan {Amount = 150000, Rate = 12.5, ServiceYear = 4,
HasDefaulted = true },
                new Loan { Amount = 200000, Rate = 12.5, ServiceYear = 5,
HasDefaulted = false }
            };
            loanRepository.Setup(x => x.GetCarLoans()).Returns(loans);
            loanService= new LoanService(loanRepository.Object);
        }

        [Fact]
        public void Test_GetBadCarLoans_ShouldReturnLoans()
        {
            List<Loan> badLoans = loanService.GetBadCarLoans();
            Assert.NotNull(badLoans);
        }
    }
```

In the constructor of the `LoanServiceTest` class, the data to be returned by the mock object is first created, followed by the method set up in the line `loanRepository.Setup(x => x.GetCarLoans()).Returns(loans);`. The mock object is then passed to the `LoanService` constructor, `loanService= new loanService(loanRepository.Object);`.

Hand-rolled mock

We can hand-roll a mock object to test the `LoanService` class. The mock object to be created will implement the `ILoanRepository` interface and will be used for the purpose of unit testing only since it is not needed in the production code. The mock object will return a list of `Loan` objects, which will simulate the actual call to the database:

```
public class LoanRepositoryMock : ILoanRepository
{
    public List<Loan> GetCarLoans()
    {
        List<Loan> loans = new List<Loan>
        {
            new Loan{Amount = 120000, Rate = 12.5, ServiceYear = 5,
HasDefaulted = false },
            new Loan {Amount = 150000, Rate = 12.5, ServiceYear = 4,
HasDefaulted = true },
            new Loan { Amount = 200000, Rate = 12.5, ServiceYear = 5,
HasDefaulted = false }
        };
        return loans;
    }
}
```

The `LoanRepositoryMock` class created can now be used in the `LoanService` class to mock `ILoanRepository` in place of using a mock object created from a mock framework. In the constructor of the `LoanServiceTest` class, the `LoanRepositoryMock` class will be instantiated and injected into the `LoanService` class, which is used in the `Test` class:

```
public class LoanServiceTest
{
    private ILoanRepository loanRepository;
    private LoanService loanService;
    public LoanServiceTest()
    {
        loanRepository= new LoanRepositoryMock();
        loanService= new LoanService(loanRepository);
    }

    [Fact]
    public void Test_GetBadCarLoans_ShouldReturnLoans()
    {
        List<Loan> badLoans = loanService.GetBadCarLoans();
        Assert.NotNull(badLoans);
    }
}
```

Because `LoanRepositoryMock` is used as a concrete class for the `ILoanRepository` interface, a dependency of the `LoanService` class, whenever the `GetCarLoans` method is called on the `ILoanRepository` interface, the `GetCarLoans` method of `LoanRepositoryMock` will be called to return the data required for the test to run.

Mocking objects using Moq framework

Selecting a mock framework to use for mocking objects is important for a smooth unit testing experience. However, there are no written rules to be followed for this. You can consider some factors and features of the mocking framework when selecting a mocking framework for use in your tests.

Performance and available features should be the first factors to be considered when selecting a mocking framework. You should examine the way the mocking framework creates mocks; frameworks that use inheritance, virtual, and static methods cannot be mocked. Other features to look out for can be methods, properties, events, and even if the framework supports LINQ.

Additionally, nothing beats simplicity and the ease of use of a library. You should go for a framework that is easy to use, with good documentation of the available features. In the subsequent sections of this chapter, the other concepts of mocking will be explained using the Moq framework, an easy-to-use strongly typed library.

When using Moq, the mock object is an actual dummy class that is created for you using reflection, which contains the implementation of methods contained in an interface that is being mocked. In the Moq setup, you will specify the interface you want to mock and the methods that the test class requires to effectively run the tests.

To use Moq, you need to install the library through the NuGet package manager or through the NuGet console:

```
Install-Package Moq
```

To explain mocking with Moq, let's create an `ILoanRepository` interface with two methods, `GetCarLoan`, which retrieves car loans from the database as a list, and a `GetLoanTypes` method that returns a list of `LoanType` objects:

```
public interface ILoanRepository
{
    List<LoanType> GetLoanTypes();
    List<Loan> GetCarLoans();
}
```

The `LoanRepository` class uses the Entity Framework as the ORM for data access and retrieval and implements `ILoanRepository`. The two methods, `GetLoanTypes` and `GetCarLoans`, have been implemented by the `LoanRepository` class:

```
public class LoanRepository :ILoanRepository
{
    public List<LoanType> GetLoanTypes()
    {
        List<LoanType> loanTypes= new List<LoanType>();
        using (LoanContext context = new LoanContext())
        {
            loanTypes=context.LoanType.ToList();
        }
        return loanTypes;
    }

    public List<Loan> GetCarLoans()
    {
        List<Loan> loans = new List<Loan>();
        using (LoanContext context = new LoanContext())
        {
            loans = context.Loan.ToList();
        }
        return loans;
    }
}
```

Let's create a mock object for `ILoanRepository` to test the two methods without having to depend on any concrete class implementation.

Creating a mock object is easy with Moq:

```
Mock<ILoanRepository> loanRepository = new Mock<ILoanRepository>();
```

In the preceding line of code, a mock object has been created which implements the `ILoanRepository` interface. The object can be used as a regular implementation of `ILoanRepository` and injected into any class that has `ILoanRepository` as the dependency.

Mocking methods, properties, and callback

Before the methods of the mock objects can be used in the test, they need to be set up. This setup is preferably done in the constructor of the test class after the mock object is created and before the object is injected into the class that requires the dependency.

First, the data to be returned by the method to be set up will have to be created; this is the dummy data to be used in the test:

```
List<Loan> loans = new List<Loan>
{
    new Loan{Amount = 120000, Rate = 12.5, ServiceYear = 5, HasDefaulted =
false },
    new Loan {Amount = 150000, Rate = 12.5, ServiceYear = 4, HasDefaulted =
true },
    new Loan { Amount = 200000, Rate = 12.5, ServiceYear = 5, HasDefaulted
= false }
};
```

At the point of setting up the method, the return data will be passed to it as well as any method parameter, if applicable. In the following line of code, the GetCarLoans method is set up with the list of the Loan objects passed as the return data. This means that whenever the GetCarLoans method is invoked in the unit test using the mock object, the list created earlier will be returned as the method return value:

```
Mock<ILoanRepository> loanRepository = new Mock<ILoanRepository>();
loanRepository.Setup(x => x.GetCarLoans()).Returns(loans);
```

You can have a lazy evaluation of the method return value. This is a syntax sugar available with the use of LINQ:

```
loanRepository.Setup(x => x.GetCarLoans()).Returns(() => loans);
```

Moq has an It object, which can be used to specify a matching condition for a parameter in the method being set up. It refers to the argument being matched. Assuming the GetCarLoans method has a string parameter, loanType, the syntax of the method setup can be changed to include the parameter with the return value:

```
loanRepository.Setup(x =>
x.GetCarLoans(It.IsAny<string>())).Returns(loans);
```

It is possible to set up a method that returns a different return value each time it is invoked. For example, the setup of the GetCarLoans method can be done to return different sizes of the list each time the method is called:

```
Random random = new Random();
loanRepository.Setup(x => x.GetCarLoans()).Returns(loans).Callback(() =>
loans.GetRange(0,random.Next(1, 3)));
```

In the preceding snippet, a random number is generated between 1 and 3, to set. This will ensure that the size of the list to be returned by the GetCarLoans method varies with each invocation. The first time the GetCarLoans method is called, the Returns method is called, while the code in the Callback is executed with subsequent calls to the GetCarLoans method.

A feature of Moq is the provision of testing for exceptions. You can set up the method to test for exceptions. In the following method setup, the GetCarLoans method throws InvalidOperationException when called:

```
loanRepository.Setup(x =>
x.GetCarLoans()).Throws<InvalidOperationException>();
```

Properties

If you have a dependency that has properties to be set which are used in the method calls, you can set dummy values for such properties using the Moq SetupProperty method. Let's add two properties to the ILoanRepository interface, LoanType and Rate:

```
public interface ILoanRepository
{
    LoanType LoanType{get;set;}
    float Rate {get;set;}
    List<LoanType> GetLoanTypes();
    List<Loan> GetCarLoans();
}
```

With the Moq SetupProperty method, you can specify that the property should have a behavior, which in essence implies that whenever the property is requested, the value set in the SetupProperty method will be returned:

```
Mock<ILoanRepository> loanRepository = new Mock<ILoanRepository>();
loanRepository.Setup(x => x.LoanType, LoanType.CarLoan);
loanRepository.Setup(x => x.Rate, 12.5);
```

The lines of code in the preceding snippet set the LoanType property to an enum value, CarLoan, and Rate to 12.5. Whenever the properties are requested in a test, the set values will be returned to the calling points.

Setting the properties using the SetupProperty method automatically sets the property as a stub and will allow the values of the properties to be tracked and provide a default value for the property.

Also, while setting up the property, you can use the `SetupSet` method, which accepts a lambda expression to specify a type for a call to a property setter and allows you to pass the value into the expression:

```
loanRepository.SetupSet(x => x.Rate = 12.5F);
```

Similar to `SetupSet` is `SetupGet`, which is used to specify a setup on the type for a call to a property getter:

```
loanRepository.SetupGet(x => x.Rate);
```

Recursive mocking allows you to mock complex object types, especially nested complex types. For example, you might want to mock the `Age` property in the `Person` complex type of the `Loan` type. The Moq framework can traverse this graph to mock the property in an elegant way:

```
loanRepository.SetupSet(x => x.CarLoan.Person.Age= 40);
```

You can stub all the properties available on a mock, using the `SetupAllProperties` method. This method will specify that all properties on the mock have a property behavior set. By generating the default value for each property in the mock, the default property is generated using the `Mock.DefaultProperty` property of the Moq framework:

```
loanRepository.SetupAllProperties();
```

Matching parameters

When using Moq to create mock objects, you can match arguments to ensure that the expected parameters are passed during a test. Using this feature, you can ascertain the validity of the arguments passed into a method while the method is called while being tested. This is applicable only to methods that have arguments and the matching will be done during the method setup.

Using Moq's `It` keyword, you can specify different expressions and validations for the method parameter during setup. Let's add a `GetCarLoanDefaulters` method definition to the `ILoanRepository` interface. The implementation in the `LoanRepository` class accepts an integer parameter, which is the service year for a loan and returns a list of car loan defaulters. The `GetCarLoanDefaulters` method code is shown in the following snippet:

```
public List<Person> GetCarLoanDefaulters(int year)
{
    List<Person> defaulters = new List<Person>();
    using (LoanContext context = new LoanContext())
```

```
    {
        defaulters = context.Loan.Where(c => c.HasDefaulted
                        && c.ServiceYear == year).Select(c =>
c.Person).ToList();
    }
    return defaulters;
}
```

Now, let's set up the `GetCarLoanDefaulters` method in the `LoanServiceTest` constructor to accept a different value for the `year` parameter using Moq's `It` keyword:

```
List<Person> people = new List<Person>
{
    new Person { FirstName = "Donald", LastName = "Duke", Age =30},
    new Person { FirstName = "Ayobami", LastName = "Adewole", Age =20}
};

Mock<ILoanRepository> loanRepository = new Mock<ILoanRepository>();
loanRepository.Setup(x => x.GetCarLoanDefaulters(It.IsInRange<int>(1, 5,
Range.Inclusive))).Returns(people);
```

A list of `Person` objects has been created, which will be passed to the `Returns` method of the mock setup. The `GetCarLoanDefaulters` method will now accept the value in the range specified, since the `It.IsInRange` method has been used with both the upper and lower range value supplied.

The `It` class has other useful methods for specifying the matching conditions for a method during setup instead of having to specify a particular value:

- `IsRegex` is used for specifying a regular expression to match a string argument
- `Is` is used to specify a value that matches a given predicate
- `IsAny<>` is used to match any value of the type specified
- `Ref<>` is used to match any value specified in a `ref` parameter

You can create a custom matcher and use it in method setup. For example, let's create a custom matcher, `IsOutOfRange`, for the `GetCarLoanDefaulters` method to ensure a value greater than 12 is not supplied as an argument. Creating a custom matcher is done by using `Match.Create`:

```
public int IsOutOfRange()
{
    return Match.Create<int>(x => x > 12);
}
```

The created `IsOutOfRange` matcher can now be used in a method setup of a mock object:

```
loanRepository.Setup(x =>
x.GetCarLoanDefaulters(IsOutOfRange())).Throws<ArgumentException>();
```

Events

Moq has a feature that allows you to raise an event on the mock object. To raise an event, you use the `Raise` method. The method has two parameters. The first is a Lambda expression with the event subscribed for the event to be raised on the mock. The second argument provides a parameter that will be included in the event. To raise a `LoanDefaulterNotification` event on the `loanRepository` mock object with an empty argument, you can use the following line of code:

```
Mock<ILoanRepository> loanRepository = new Mock<ILoanRepository>();
loanRepository.Raise(x => x.LoanDefaulterNotification+=null,
EventArgs.Empty);
```

Real use cases are used when you want to have a mock object raise an event in response to an action or raise an event in response to a method invocation. When setting up a method on a mock to allow events to be raised, the `Returns` method on the mock is replaced with the `Raises` method, which indicates that when the method is called in the test, an event should be raised:

```
loanRepository.Setup(x => x.GetCarLoans()).Raises(x=>
x.LoanDefaulterNotification+=null, new LoanDefualterEventArgs{OK=true});
```

Callbacks

Using the `Callback` method of Moq, you can specify the callback to be invoked before and after a method is called. There are some test scenarios that might not be easily tested using the simple mock expectations. In such complex scenarios, you can use a callback to execute specific actions when the mock objects are called. The `Callback` method accepts an action parameter, which will be executed based on whether the callback is set up before or after the method invocation. The action can be an expression to be evaluated or another method to be called.

For example, you can have a callback set up to change the data after a specific method has been called. This feature allows you to create tests that offer more flexibility while simplifying test complexities. Let's add a callback to the `loanRepository` mock object.

The callback can be a method that will be invoked or a property that you need to set with values:

```
List<Person> people = new List<Person>
{
    new Person { FirstName = "Donald", LastName = "Duke", Age =30},
    new Person { FirstName = "Ayobami", LastName = "Adewole", Age =20}
};

Mock<ILoanRepository> loanRepository = new Mock<ILoanRepository>();

loanRepository.Setup(x => x.GetCarLoanDefaulters())
.Callback(() => CarLoanDefaultersCallbackAfter ())
.Returns(() => people)
.Callback(() => CarLoanDefaultersCallbackAfter());
```

The preceding snippet has two callbacks set up for the method setup. The `CarLoanDefaultersCallback` method is called before the actual `GetCarLoanDefaulters` method is invoked and `CarLoanDefaultersCallbackAfter` will be called after the `GetCarLoanDefaulters` method has been called on the mock object. `CarLoanDefaultersCallback` adds a new `Person` object to the `List` and `CarLoanDefaultersCallback` removes the first element in the list:

```
public void CarLoanDefaultersCallback()
{
    people.Add(new Person { FirstName = "John", LastName = "Doe", Age =40});
}

public void CarLoanDefaultersCallbackAfter()
{
    people.RemoveAt(0);
}
```

Mock customization

When using the Moq framework, you can further customize mock object, to enhance the effective unit testing experience. The `MockBehavior` enum can be passed into Moq's `Mock` object constructor to specify the behavior of the mock. The enum members are `Default`, `Strict`, and `Loose`:

```
loanRepository= new Mock<ILoanRepository>(MockBehavior.Loose);
```

When a `Loose` member is selected, the mock will not throw any exceptions. The default values will always be returned. This means null will be returned for reference types, and zero or empty arrays and enumerables will be returned for value types:

```
loanRepository= new Mock<ILoanRepository>(MockBehavior.Strict);
```

Selecting a `Strict` member will make the mock throw exceptions for every call on the mock that does not have a proper setup. Lastly, the `Default` member is the default behavior of the mock, which technically equals the `Loose` enum member.

CallBase

`CallBase`, when initialized during a mock construction, is used to specify whether the base class virtual implementation will be invoked for mocked dependencies if no setup is matched. The default value is `false`. This is useful when mocking HTML/web controls of the `System.Web` namespace:

```
loanRepository= new Mock<ILoanRepository>{CallBase=true};
```

Mock repository

Instead of having mock objects creation code scattered across your tests, you can avoid repetitive code by using `MockRepository`, available in Moq for creating and verifying mocks in a single location, thereby ensuring that you can do mock configuration by setting `CallBase`, `DefaultValue`, and `MockBehavior` and verifying the the mocks in one place:

```
var mockRepository = new MockRepository(MockBehavior.Strict) { DefaultValue
= DefaultValue.Mock };
var loanRepository =
repository.Create<ILoanRepository>(MockBehavior.Loose);
var userRepository = repository.Create<IUserRepository>();
mockRepository.Verify();
```

In the preceding code snippet, a mock repository is created with `MockBehaviour.Strict`, and two mock objects are created, each with the `loanRepository` mock, overriding the default `MockBehaviour` specified in the repository. The last statement is an invocation of the `Verify` method to verify all expectations on all the mock objects created in the repository.

Implementing multiple interfaces in a mock

Additionally, you can implement multiple interfaces in a single mock. For example, we can create a mock that implements `ILoanRepository` and later implements the `IDisposable` interface using the `As<>` method, which is used to add an interface implementation to a mock and to specify a setup for it:

```
var loanRepository = new Mock<ILoanRepository>();
loanRepository.Setup(x => x.GetCarLoanDefaulters(It.IsInRange<int>(1, 5,
Range.Inclusive))).Returns(people);

loanRepository.As<IDisposable>().Setup(disposable => disposable.Dispose());
```

Verification method and property invocations with Moq

Mock behaviors are specified during the setup. This is the expected behavior of an object and the collaborator. While unit testing, mocking is not complete until all the mocked dependencie's invocations have been verified. It can be helpful to be aware of the number of times methods were executed or properties accessed.

The Moq framework has useful verification methods that can be used to verify mocked methods and properties. Also, the `Times` structure contains useful members showing the number of calls that can be allowed on a method.

The `Verify` method can be used to verify that a method invocation, together with the supplied parameters performed on a mock, match what was earlier configured during the mock setup and used with the default `MockBehaviour`, which is `Loose`. To explain verification concepts in Moq, let's create a `LoanService` class that depends on `ILoanRepository` for data and add a method, `GetOlderCarLoanDefaulters`, to it to return a list of loan defaulters older than 20 years of age. `ILoanRepository` is injected to `LoanService` through the constructor:

```
public class LoanService
{
    private ILoanRepository loanRepository;
    public LoanService(ILoanRepository loanRepository)
    {
        this.loanRepository = loanRepository;
    }
    public List<Person> GetOlderCarLoanDefaulters(int year)
    {
```

```
        List<Person> defaulters =
loanRepository.GetCarLoanDefaulters(year);
        var filteredDefaulters = defaulters.Where(x => x.Age >
20).ToList();
        return filteredDefaulters;
    }
}
```

To test the `LoanService` class, we will create a `LoanServiceTest` test class that uses dependency mocking to isolate `LoanService` for unit testing. `LoanServiceTest` will contain a constructor for setting up a mock for `ILoanRepository`, required by the `LoanService` class:

```
public class LoanServiceTest
{
    private Mock<ILoanRepository> loanRepository;
    private LoanService loanService;
    public  LoanServiceTest()
    {
        loanRepository= new Mock<ILoanRepository>();
        List<Person> people = new List<Person>
        {
            new Person { FirstName = "Donald", LastName = "Duke", Age =30},
            new Person { FirstName = "Ayobami", LastName = "Adewole", Age
=20}
        };
        loanRepository.Setup(x =>
x.GetCarLoanDefaulters(It.IsInRange<int>(1,12,Range.Inclusive))).Returns(()
=> people);
        loanService = new LoanService(loanRepository.Object);
    }
}
```

The `LoanServiceTest` constructor contains a mock set up for the `GetCarLoanDefaulters` method of the `ILoanRepository` interface, with the arguments expectation and the return value. Let's create a test method, `Test_GetOlderCarLoanDefaulters_ShouldReturnList`, to test `GetCarLoanDefaulters`. After the assert statements, there is the `Verify` method to check if `GetCarLoanDefaulters` was called once:

```
[Fact]
public void Test_GetOlderCarLoanDefaulters_ShouldReturnList()
{
    List<Person> defaulters = loanService.GetOlderCarLoanDefaulters(12);
    Assert.NotNull(defaulters);
    Assert.All(defaulters, x => Assert.Contains("Donald", x.FirstName));
```

```
        loanRepository.Verify(x => x.GetCarLoanDefaulters(It.IsInRange<int>(1,
    12, Range.Inclusive)), Times.Once());
    }
```

The `Verify` method takes two arguments: the method to be verified and the `Time` structure. `Time.Once` was used, which specifies that the mocked method should only be called once.

`Times.AtLeast(int callCount)`, when used, is to specify that a mocked method should be called in the minimum number of times specified in the value of the `callCount` parameter. This can be used to verify that a method was called in the number of times specified:

```
[Fact]
public void Test_GetOlderCarLoanDefaulters_ShouldReturnList()
{
    List<Person> defaulters = loanService.GetOlderCarLoanDefaulters(12);
    Assert.NotNull(defaulters);
    Assert.All(defaulters, x => Assert.Contains("Donald", x.FirstName));
    loanRepository.Verify(x => x.GetCarLoanDefaulters(It.IsInRange<int>(1,
    12, Range.Inclusive)), Times.AtLeast(2));
}
```

In the preceding test snippet, `Times.AtLeast(2)` was passed to the `Verify` method. The test, when run, will fail with `Moq.MoqException` because the `GetCarLoanDefaulters` method was only called once in the code being tested:

Test_GetOlderCarLoanDefaulters_ShouldReturnList failed

```
Moq.MockException :
Expected invocation on the mock at least 2 times, but was 1 times: x => x.GetCarLoanDefaulters
  (It.IsInRange<Int32>(1, 12, Range.Inclusive))

Configured setups:
x => x.GetCarLoanDefaulters(It.IsInRange<Int32>(1, 12, Range.Inclusive))

Performed invocations:
ILoanRepository.GetCarLoanDefaulters(12)
   at Moq.Mock.ThrowVerifyException(MethodCall expected, IEnumerable`1 setups, IEnumerable`1
      actualCalls, Expression expression, Times times, Int32 callCount)
   at Moq.Mock.VerifyCalls(Mock targetMock, MethodCall expected, Expression expression, Times
      times)
   at Moq.Mock.Verify[T,TResult](Mock`1 mock, Expression`1 expression, Times times, String
      failMessage)
   at Moq.Mock`1.Verify[TResult](Expression`1 expression, Times times)
```

`Times.AtLeastOnce` can be used to specify that a mocked method should be called a minimum of one time, which means the method can be called many times in the code being tested. We can modify the `Verify` method in `Test_GetOlderCarLoanDefaulters_ShouldReturnList` to take a second parameter as `Time.AtLeastOnce` to validate after the test is run that the `GetCarLoanDefaulters` was called at least once in the code being tested:

```
[Fact]
public void Test_GetOlderCarLoanDefaulters_ShouldReturnList()
{
    List<Person> defaulters = loanService.GetOlderCarLoanDefaulters(12);
    Assert.NotNull(defaulters);
    Assert.All(defaulters, x => Assert.Contains("Donald", x.FirstName));
    loanRepository.Verify(x => x.GetCarLoanDefaulters(It.IsInRange<int>(1,
12, Range.Inclusive)), Times.AtLeastOnce);
}
```

`Times.AtMost(int callCount)` can be used to specify the maximum number of times that a mocked method should be called in the code being tested. The `callCount` parameter is used to pass the value for the maximum invocation time for a method. This can be used to limit the calls allowed to a mocked method. A Moq exception is thrown if the method is called more than the `callCount` value specified:

```
loanRepository.Verify(x => x.GetCarLoanDefaulters(It.IsInRange<int>(1, 12,
Range.Inclusive)), Times.AtMost(1));
```

`Times.AtMostOnce` is similar to `Time.Once` or `Time.AtLeastOnce`, but with the difference being that the mocked method can only be called at most one time. A Moq exception is thrown if the method is called more than once, but if the method is not called when the code is run, no exception will be thrown:

```
loanRepository.Verify(x => x.GetCarLoanDefaulters(It.IsInRange<int>(1, 12,
Range.Inclusive)), Times.AtMostOnce);
```

`Times.Between(callCountFrom, callCountTo, Range)` can be used in the `Verify` method to specify that the mocked method should be called between `callCountFrom` and `callCountTo` and the `Range` enum used to specify whether to include or exclude the range specified:

```
loanRepository.Verify(x => x.GetCarLoanDefaulters(It.IsInRange<int>(1, 12,
Range.Inclusive)), Times.Between(1,2,Range.Inclusive));
```

`Times.Exactly(callCount)` is very useful when you want to specify that a mocked method should be called at the `callCount` specified. If the mocked method is called fewer times than the `callCount` specified or more times, a Moq exception will be generated with a detailed description of the expectation and what failed:

```
[Fact]
public void Test_GetOlderCarLoanDefaulters_ShouldReturnList()
{
    List<Person> defaulters = loanService.GetOlderCarLoanDefaulters(12);
    Assert.NotNull(defaulters);
    Assert.All(defaulters, x => Assert.Contains("Donald", x.FirstName));
    loanRepository.Verify(x => x.GetCarLoanDefaulters(It.IsInRange<int>(1,
12, Range.Inclusive)), Times.Exactly(2));
}
```

Let's check the code now:

Test_GetOlderCarLoanDefaulters_ShouldReturnList failed

```
Moq.MockException :
Expected invocation on the mock exactly 2 times, but was 1 times: x => x.GetCarLoanDefaulters
  (It.IsInRange<Int32>(1, 12, Range.Inclusive))

Configured setups:
x => x.GetCarLoanDefaulters(It.IsInRange<Int32>(1, 12, Range.Inclusive))

Performed invocations:
ILoanRepository.GetCarLoanDefaulters(12)
    at Moq.Mock.ThrowVerifyException(MethodCall expected, IEnumerable`1 setups, IEnumerable`1
      actualCalls, Expression expression, Times times, Int32 callCount)
    at Moq.Mock.VerifyCalls(Mock targetMock, MethodCall expected, Expression expression, Times
      times)
    at Moq.Mock.Verify[T,TResult](Mock`1 mock, Expression`1 expression, Times times, String
      failMessage)
    at Moq.Mock`1.Verify[TResult](Expression`1 expression, Times times)
```

Also important is `Times.Never`. When used, it can verify that a mocked method is never used. You can use this when you don't want a mocked method to be invoked:

```
loanRepository.Verify(x => x.GetCarLoanDefaulters(It.IsInRange<int>(1, 12,
Range.Inclusive)), Times.Never);
```

A mocked property verification is done in a similar manner to mocked methods using the `VerifySet` and `VerifyGet` methods. The `VerifySet` method is used to verify that a property was set on the mock. Also, the `VerifyGet` method is used to validate that a property was read on a mock, regardless of the value contained in the property:

```
loanRepository.VerifyGet(x => x.Rate);
```

To verify that a property has been set on a mock, irrespective of whatever value was set, you can use the `VerifySet` method with this syntax:

```
loanRepository.VerifySet(x => x.Rate);
```

At times, you might want to validate that a particular value was assigned to a property on the mock. You can do this by assigning the value to verify to the property in the `VerifySet` method:

```
loanRepository.VerifySet(x => x.Rate = 12.5);
```

The `VerifyNoOtherCalls()` method introduced in Moq 4.8 can be used to ascertain that no calls were made other than the ones already verified. The `VerifyAll()` method is used to verify all expectations, irrespective of if they have been flagged as verifiable.

LINQ to mocks

Language-Integrated Query (LINQ) is a language construct introduced in .NET 4.0, which provides query capabilities in the .NET Framework. LINQ has query expressions that are written in a declarative query syntax. There are different implementations of LINQ-LINQ to XML, used for querying XML documents, LINQ to entities, which is used for ADO.NET Entity Framework operations, LINQ to objects used for querying .NET collections, files, strings, and so on.

Throughout this chapter, we have created mock objects using Lambda expressions syntax. Another exciting feature available in the Moq framework is **LINQ to mocks**, which allows you to set up mocks using LINQ like syntax.

LINQ to Mocks is great for simple mocks, and for stubbing out dependencies when you really do not care about the verification. Using the `Of<>` method, you can create a mock object of the specified type.

You can use LINQ to Mocks to have multiple setups done on a single mock and recursive mocks, using LINQ like syntax:

```
var loanRepository = Mock.Of<ILoanRepository>
                    (x => x.Rate==12.5F &&
                        x.LoanType.Name=="CarLoan"&& LoanType.Id==3 );
```

In the preceding mock initialization, the `Rate` and `LoanType` properties were set up as stubs, with the default values for the properties, when accessed during the tests invocation.

Advanced Moq features

Sometimes, the default values provided by Moq might not be suitable for some test scenarios and you need to create a custom default value generation approach to complement what Moq currently provides, which are `DefaultValue.Empty` and `DefaultValue.Mock`. This can be done through extending `DefaultValueProvider` or `LookupOrFallbackDefaultValueProvider`, which are available in Moq 4.8 and higher:

```
public class TestDefaultValueProvider :
LookupOrFallbackDefaultValueProvider
{
    public TestDefaultValueProvider()
    {
        base.Register(typeof(string), (type, mock) => string.empty);
        base.Register(typeof(List<>), (type, mock) =>
Activator.CreateInstance(type));
    }
}
```

The `TestDefaultValueProvider` class created the sub-classes `LookupOrFallbackDefaultValueProvider` and implemented default values for both `string` and `List`. For any type of `string`, `string.empty` is returned and an empty list is created with a `List` of any type. `TestDefaultValueProvider` can now be used in mock creation, in the `Mock` constructor:

```
var loanRepository = new Mock<ILoanRepository> { DefaultValueProvider = new
TestDefaultValueProvider()};
var objectName = loanRepository.Object.Name;
```

The `objectName` variable in the preceding snippet will contain a string of zero characters since the implementation in `TestDefaultValueProvider` indicates that the `string` type should be assigned an empty string.

Mocking internal types

Depending on your project requirements, you might need to create mock objects for internal types. Internal types or members in C# are accessible only within files in the same assembly. Mocking internal types can be done by adding custom attributes to the `AssemblyInfo.cs` file of the concerned projects.

If the assembly containing the internal types does not already have the `AssemblyInfo.cs` file, you can add it. Also, when the assembly is not strongly-named, you can add the `InternalsVisibleTo` attribute, which has the public key excluded. You have to specify the name of the project to share visibility with, which in this case should be the test project.

If you change the `LoanService` access modifier to internal, you will get the error, `LoanService`. It is inaccessible due to its protection level. To be able to test `LoanService`, without changing the access modifier, we then add the `AssemblyInfo.cs` file to the project, and add the required attribute with the test project name specified in order to share the assembly that contains `LoanService` with the test project:

```
 7  using Moq;
 8  using Xunit;
 9
10  namespace LoanApplication.Tests.Unit
11  {
        1 reference
12      public class LoanServiceTest
13      {
14          private Mock<ILoanRepository> loanRepository;
15          private LoanService loanService;
            0 refere
16          public LoanS    'LoanService' is inaccessible due to its protection level
17          {
18                          Cannot access internal class 'LoanService' here
19              loanRepo
20              List<Per   Show potential fixes (Alt+Enter or Ctrl+.)
21              {
22                  new Person { FirstName = "Donald", LastName = "Duke", Age =30},
23                  new Person { FirstName = "Ayobami", LastName = "Adewole", Age =20}
24              };
25              loanRepository.Setup(x => x.GetCarLoanDefaulters(It.IsInRange<int>(1, 12, Range.Inclusive)))
26                  .Returns(() => people);
27              loanService = new LoanService(loanRepository.Object);
```

The attribute added to the `AssemblyInfo.cs` file is shown in the following snippet:

```
[assembly:InternalsVisibleTo("LoanApplication.Tests.Unit")]
```

Summary

The Moq framework, when used together with the xUnit.net framework, can deliver a smooth unit testing experience and make the overall TDD process worthwhile. Moq provides powerful features that, when used effectively, can simplify the creation of dependencies mocking for unit tests.

Mock objects created with Moq can allow you to substitute the concrete dependencies in your unit tests for the created mocks created by you in order to isolate different units in your code for testing and subsequent refactoring, which can facilitate crafting elegant production-ready code. Also, you can use mock objects to experiment and test features available in dependencies that otherwise might not be easily done by using the live dependencies.

In this chapter, we have explored the basics of mocking, and extensively used mocks in unit tests. Also, we configured mocks to set up methods and properties and return exceptions. Some other features provided by the Moq library were explained and mocks verification was covered.

Project hosting and continuous integration will be covered in the next chapter. This will include test and enterprise approaches to automate the running of tests to ensure that quality feedback can be provided on the code coverage.

7
Continuous Integration and Project Hosting

In Chapter 4, *.NET Core Unit Testing*, we explored the various unit testing frameworks available for .NET Core and C# and later explored in detail the xUnit.net framework. We then moved on to the important concepts of data-driven unit tests in Chapter 5, *Data-Driven Unit Tests*, which facilitate the creation of unit tests that can be executed with data loaded from disparate data sources. In Chapter 6, *Mocking Dependencies*, we explained in details dependencies mocking, where we walked through creation of simulated objects using the *Moq framework*.

Effective practice of TDD can assist with providing useful and insightful feedback on the quality of the code base of software projects. With continuous integration, the process of build automation and code automated tests are taken to the next level, allowing development teams to take advantage of the basic and advanced features available in cutting edge modern source code version control systems.

Proper continuous integration setup and practice yield a rewarding continuous delivery where a software project development process is done in such a way that it can be shipped or delivered to production through the life cycle of the project.

In this chapter, we will explore the concepts of continuous integration and continuous delivery. This chapter will cover the following topics:

- Continuous integration
- Continuous delivery
- GitHub online project hosting
- Basic Git commands
- Configuring GitHub WebHooks
- TeamCity continuous integration platform

Continuous integration

Continuous integration (**CI**) is a software development practice where the source code of software projects is integrated by members of a software development team daily into a repository. It is preferably started at an early stage of the development process. The code integration is usually carried out by a CI tool that performs the verification of the code using an automated build script.

In a development team, there are often multiple developers working on different portions of a project, with the source code of the project hosted in a repository. Each developer can have a local version or working copy of the main branch or mainline on their computer.

A developer working on a feature will make a change to the local copy, and test the code using a set of prepared automated tests to ensure that the code works and does not break any existing working functionalities. Once this can be verified, the local copy is updated with the latest from the repository. If there are any conflicts resulting from the update, these conflicts need to be resolved before eventually committing or integrating the work done into the mainline.

The source code repository facilitates adequate versioning of the code base of projects, by keeping snapshots and versions of source files also the changes made overtime. Developers can revert or checkout an earlier version of commits made if necessary. The repository can be hosted locally on the team's infrastructure, such as having an onsite **Microsoft Team Foundation Server** or a cloud-based repository, such as **GitHub**, **Bitbucket**, and a host of others.

CI workflow

CI requires that a proper workflow be put in place. The first major integral part of CI is the setup of a working source code repository. This is needed to keep track of all the changes made by the contributors to the project and for coordinating the different activities.

In order to implement a robust and effective CI setup, the following areas need to be covered and properly set up.

Single source code repository

To effectively use the source code repository, all the required files needed to successfully build a working version of a project should be put in a single source code repository. The files should include the source files, properties files, database scripts, and schema, as well as third-party libraries and assets used.

Other configuration files can also be put in the repository, especially development environment configurations. This will ensure the developers on the project have a consistent environment setup. New members of the development team can easily set up their environment, using the configuration available in the repository.

Build automation

The build automation step of the CI workflow is to ensure that changes in the a project's code base are detected and automatically tested and built. The build automation is usually done with the help of build scripts, which analyze the changes to be made and the compilation needed to be done. The source code should be regularly built, preferably daily or nightly. The success of a commit is measured based on if the code base has been successfully built.

The build automation scripts should be able to build the system with or without the tests. This should be configurable in the build. Irrespective of whether the developer's IDEs have in-built build management in place, there should be a central build script configured on the server to ensure the project can be built and easily run on the development server.

Automated tests

The code base should have automated tests that cover a large percentage of possible test combinations using relevant test data. The automated tests should be developed using a suitable test framework that can cover all tiers or parts of the software project.

With proper automation tests in place, bugs in the source code can be easily detected when the automation build script runs. Integrating automated tests into the build process will ensure that good test coverage and reports of failing or passing tests are provided to facilitate refactoring of the code.

Identical test and production environments

In order to have a smooth CI experience, it is important to ensure that the test and production environments are identical. Both environments should have similar hardware and operating system configurations, as well as environment setup.

Also, for applications that use databases, both the test and production environments should have the same versions. The runtimes and libraries should also be similar. However, sometimes it might not be possible to test in every instance of the production environment, such as desktop applications, but you must ensure that a replica of the production environment is used in testing.

Daily commit

The overall health of the code base is determined by the successful build process run. The project's mainline should be regularly updated with commits from the developers. It is the responsibility of the developer making commits to ensure that the code is tested before pushing to the repository.

In cases where a commit from the developer breaks the build, this should not be procrastinated. A rollback can be done to fix the issue in isolation before committing the changes again. The projects mainline or main branch should always be in good health. Daily commits of changes is usually preferable.

Benefits of CI

Incorporating CI into development process can be greatly valuable to a development team. The CI process provides numerous benefits, some of which are explained next.

Quick bugs detection

With a CI process in place, automated tests are run frequently and bugs can be discovered on time and fixed, yielding a robust system of high quality. CI will not automatically eliminate the bug in the system; developers must strive to write clean code that is well tested. However, CI can facilitate the timely detection of bugs that otherwise would have crept into production.

Improved productivity

A development team's overall productivity can be enhanced through CI as developers are freed from mundane or manual tasks, which would have been automated as part of CI the process. Developers can focus on the important tasks of developing the system's features.

Reduced risks

Sometimes, due to inherent complexities, software projects tend to overshoot budgets and timelines due to underestimation of requirements and other issues. CI can assist in reducing the risks associated with software development. With frequent code commits and integration, a clearer picture of the state of the project can be established and any potential issue can be easily isolated and dealt with.

Facilitating continuous delivery

For a development team that uses CI, continuous or frequent deployment becomes relatively easy. This is because new features or requirements can be quickly delivered and shipped. This will allow the users to provide adequate and useful feedback on the product, which can be used to further refine the software and increase the quality.

CI tools

There are quite a number of CI tools available, each with different features that facilitate easy CI and provide a good structure for the deployment pipeline. The choice of a CI tool depends on several factors, including:

- The development environment, program language, frameworks, and application architecture
- The development team's composition, level of experience, skills, and capabilities
- The deployment environment setup, operating system, and hardware requirements

Some of the popular and most used CI tools are explained next. These CI tools, when effectively used, can assist a development team in achieving quality standards in software projects.

Microsoft Team Foundation Server

Microsoft **Team Foundation Server (TFS)** is an integrated server suit containing a set of collaborative tools to increase the productivity of software development teams. TFS provide tools that can integrate with IDEs, such as **Visual Studio**, **Eclipse**, and many more IDEs and code editors.

TFS provides sets of tools and extensions that facilitate a smooth CI process. Using TFS, the process of building, testing, and deploying applications can be automated. TFS provides great flexibility by supporting wide ranges of programming languages and source code repositories.

TeamCity

TeamCity is an enterprise level CI tool by JetBrains. It has support for a bundled .NET CLI and, similar to TFS, it provides support for automated deployment and composite builds. TeamCity can verify and run automated tests on the server before the code is committed through the plugins available for IDEs.

Jenkins

Jenkins is an open source CI server that can be run as a standalone or in a container, or installed through native system packages. It is self-contained and capable of automating testing, build related tasks, and application deployment. Through a set of chain-tools and plugins, Jenkins can integrate with IDEs and source code repositories.

Continuous delivery

Continuous delivery is a sequel or an extension of CI. It is a set of software development practices that make sure that a project's code can be deployed to a test environment that is identical to the production environment. Continuous delivery ensures that all changes are up-to-date and can be shipped and deployed to production, immediately once the changes have passed the automated tests.

It is widely known that practicing CI will facilitate good communication among team members and can eliminate potential risks. Development teams need to take this a step further by practicing continuous delivery to ensure that their development activities are beneficial to customers. This can be made possible by ascertaining that the application is deployable and production-ready at any stage of the development cycle.

Through effective communication and collaboration of members of a development team, continuous delivery can be achieved. This requires that the major parts of the application delivery process are automated through a developed and refined deployment pipeline. At any point in time, the application being developed should be deployable. The product owner or the customer will determine when the application is deployed.

Benefits of continuous delivery

Through continuous delivery, a software development team's productivity can be improved while also reducing the cost and turnaround time of releasing software applications into production. The following are the reasons why your team should practice continuous delivery.

Lower risks

Similar to CI, continuous delivery assists in lowering risks usually associated with software releases and deployment. This can ensure zero downtime and an application's high availability because the frequent changes made are regularly integrated and production-ready.

Quality software products

Software products are readily made available to the end users due to the automation of the testing, build, and deployment process. Users will be able to give useful and valuable feedback that can be used to further refine and improve the quality of the application.

Reduced costs

Software project development and release costs can be greatly reduced, due to automation of the different parts of the development and deployment processes. This is because costs associated to incremental and continuous changes are eliminated.

GitHub online project hosting

GitHub is a source code hosting platform for version control that allows development team members to collaborate and work on software projects, irrespective of their geographical location. GitHub currently houses several open source and proprietary projects in different programming languages.

GitHub provides basic and advanced features that make collaboration easier. It is essentially a web-based source code repository or hosting service using Git as the version control system, based on Git's distributed versioning behavior.

It is interesting to know that top companies such as **Microsoft**, **Google**, **Facebook**, and **Twitter** host their open source projects on GitHub. Basically, any CI tool can be used with GitHub. This gives development teams the flexibility to choose CI tools based on their budgets, working with GitHub.

In addition to the source code hosting service provided by GitHub, public web pages can also be hosted through GitHub for free. This feature allows GitHub users to create personal websites that are related to the open source projects being hosted.

GitHub supports both public and private project repository hosting. Anyone can see the files and the commit history of a public repository, while private repository access is restricted to only the added members. Private repository hosting on GitHub comes with a cost.

Project hosting

To create a project repository and have access to GitHub's features, you need to first create a GitHub account. This can be done by navigating to `https://github.com`. Upon a successful account creation, you can proceed to create a project repository.

A GitHub repository is used to organize project folders, files, and assets. The files can be images, videos, and source files. It is a common practice in GitHub for a repository to have a `README` file that contains a concise description of the project. Optionally, a software license file can be added to the project.

The following steps describes how to create a new repository in GitHub:

1. Log in to GitHub with the account created.
2. Navigate to `https://github.com/` new or from the upper-right corner of the screen, next to the account's avatar or profile picture, click on the + icon.
3. A drop-down menu is displayed where you can select **New repository**:

4. Name the repository `LoanApplication` and provide a project description.
5. Select **Public**, to make the repository publicly accessible.
6. Select **Initialize this repository with a README**, to include a `README` file in the project.

7. Finally, click on **Create repository**, to create and initialize the repository:

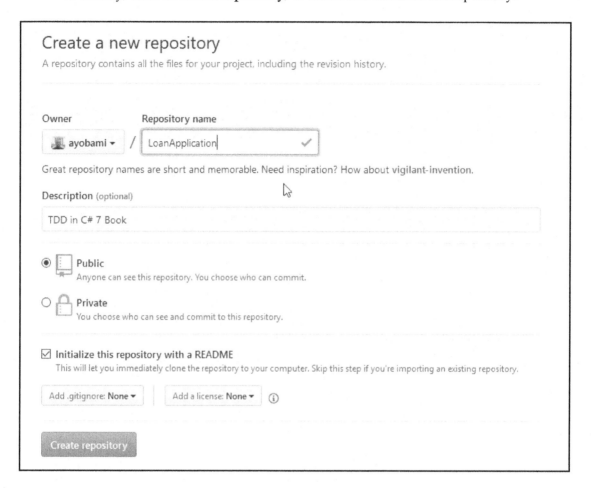

Branching with GitHub Flow

GitHub has a branch-based workflow known as **GitHub Flow**, with great supports and tools for development teams to collaborate and frequently deploy projects.

GitHub Flow facilitates the following:

- Creating branches from a new or existing repository
- Creating, editing, renaming, moving, or deleting files
- Sending a pull request from branches based on agreed changes

- Making changes on a branch as needed
- Merging pull requests when a branch is ready to be merged
- Housekeeping and cleaning up branches by using the delete button in the pull request or on the branches page

Creating branches from a project is core to Git and is an extension to GitHub, which is the central concept of GitHub Flow. **Branches** are created to try out new concepts, and ideas or for working on a feature fix. A branch is a different version of the repository.

When creating a new branch, the usual practice is to create the branch off the master branch. This will create a copy of all the files and configurations contained in the master at that time. The branch is technically independent of the master as changes made on a branch do not affect the master branch. However, new updates can be pulled from the master to the branch and changes made on the branch can be merged back to the master.

The following diagram on GitHub, further explains the GitHub flow of the project branch, where committed changes to a branch are merged to the master through a pull request:

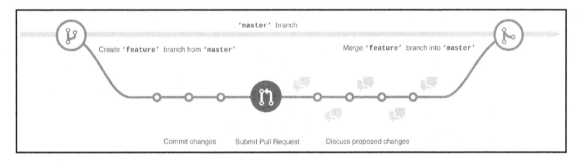

The master branch must always be deployable at any time. Changes on created branches should only be merged to the master branch after a pull request has been opened. The changes will later be carefully reviewed and accepted after passing the necessary validation and automated tests.

To create a new branch from the LoanApplication repository created earlier, perform the following steps:

1. Navigate to the repository.
2. Click the dropdown located at the top of the file list with the caption **Branch: master**.
3. Type a descriptive branch name that provides meaningful information about the branch in the new branch text box.

4. Click on the highlighted link with the branch name supplied to create the branch:

For now, the newly created branch and the master branch are exactly the same. You can begin to make changes to the created branch, by adding and modifying source files. Changes are committed directly to the branch and not the master.

Committing changes facilitates the proper tracking of changes made to the branch over time. A commit message is provided every time changes are to be committed. The commit messages provide a detailed description of what the changes are about. It is important to always provide commit messages because Git tracks changes using commits. This can facilitate easy collaboration on a project, with the commit messages providing a history of the changes made.

In the repository, each commit is a distinct unit of change. If the working code base breaks as a result of a commit, or the commit introduces a bug, the commit can be rolled back.

Pull request

Irrespective of whether the changes you made to the code base are small or large, you can initiate a pull request at any time during the project development process. Pull requests are central to collaboration in GitHub as these facilitate the discussion and review of commits made.

To open a pull request, click the **New pull request** tab. You will be taken to the pull request page, where you can provide a comment or description for the request, and click the **New pull request** button:

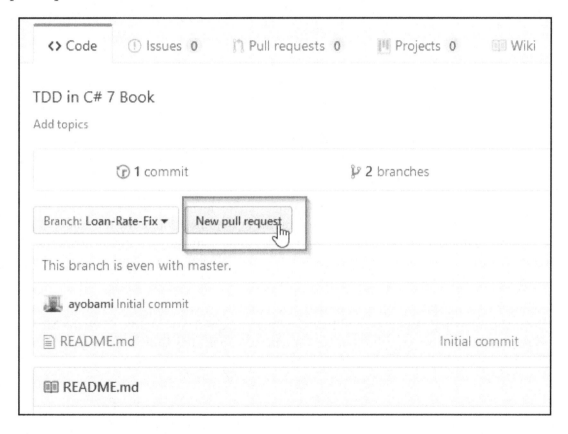

When you open a pull request, the owners or maintainers of the project are notified about the pending changes and your intention to have a merge. Necessary feedback can be provided to further refine the code after an appropriate review has been done on the changes made to the branch. The pull request shows the differences of the files and contents of your branch and the master branch. If the contributions made are deemed to be okay, they will be accepted and merged to the master branch:

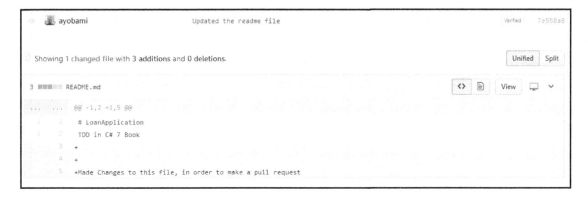

Reviewing changes and merging

After a pull request has been initiated, the changes are reviewed by the participating team members and comments are provided based on the current position of the repository. You can continue to make changes while a pull request is open, and any comments associated with the review will be shown on the unified pull request view. Comments are written in markdown and contain pre-formatted text blocks, images, and emoji.

Once the pull request has been reviewed and accepted, they will be merged into the master branch. The following steps can be followed to merge requests in GitHub. Click the **Merge pull request** button to merge the changes into master. Then click **Confirm merge**, which will merge the commits on the branch to the master:

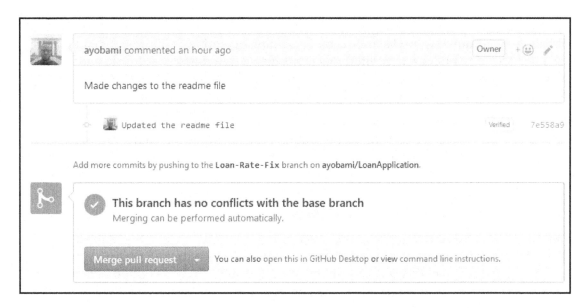

A history of pull requests are kept in GitHub and can be searched later on to determine why the pull requests were initiated while providing access to the review done and the comments added.

Basic Git commands

Git is a **distributed version control system** (**DVCS**). The branching system of Git is very robust and makes it stand out among other version control systems. Using Git, several branches of a project can be created, independent of each other. The process of creation, merging, and deletion of branches are seamless and very fast.

Git greatly supports the concept of frictionless context switching, where you can easily create a branch to explore your ideas, create and apply patches, make commits, merge the branches, and later switch back to the earlier branch you were working on. The branching workflow being used will determine whether to create a branch for each feature or group of features, while easily switching between the branches to test the features.

Your development can get organized and be productive with Git, by having different branches for your production, test, and development, thereby controlling the flow of files and commits that go into each branch. By having a good repository structure, you can easily and quickly experiment with new ideas and delete the branches when done.

Git has a rich set of useful commands that when mastered provide full access to its internals and allow basic and advanced source code versioning operations. Git provides command line interface and graphical user interface clients for the Windows, Macintosh, and Linux operating systems. The commands can be run from the Terminal on Mac and Linux, while in Windows there is Git Bash, an emulator used to run Git from the command line.

The available commands on Git are used to perform the initial setup and configuration of the source code repository, sharing and updating projects, branching and merging, as well as various source code versioning related operations.

Configuration commands

There are a set of commands that can be used to configure user information that cut across all local repositories on the computer where Git is installed. The `git config` command is used to get and set global repository options. It accepts the `--global` option which is followed by the specific configuration to get or set entries from the global `.gitconfig` file.

To set the global username that will be attached to all commit transactions, run the following:

```
git config --global user.name "[name]"
```

The global user email address can also be set. This will attach the set email address to all commit transactions. Run the following command to achieve that:

```
git config --global user.email "[email address]"
```

For good aesthetics, you can enable colorization of the command line output, using the following command:

```
git config --global color.ui auto
```

Initializing repository commands

The `git init` command is used to create an empty Git repository as well as to reinitialize an existing repository. When the `git init` command is run, a `.git` directory is created alongside sub-directories to hold objects, `refs/heads`, `refs/tags`, template files, and an initial HEAD file, which references the HEAD of the master branch. In its simplest form, the `git init` command passes the repository name, and this creates a repository with the specified name:

```
git init [repository-name]
```

To update and pick newly added templates or relocate a repository to another location, `git init` can be rerun in an existing repository. The command will not overwrite the configurations already in the repository. The full `git init` command synopsis is as follows:

```
git init [-q | --quiet] [--bare] [--template=<template_directory>]
     [--separate-git-dir <git dir>]  [--shared[=<permissions>]] [directory]
```

Let's discuss the preceding command in detail:

- The `-q` or `--quiet` option when used will print errors and warning messages while other output messages are suppressed.
- The `--bare` option is used to create a bare repository.
- `--template=<template_directory>` is used to specify the folder where the templates will be used.
- `--separate-git-dir=<git dir>` is used to indicate the directory or path to the repository, or the path to move the repository to, in case of re-initialization.
- `--shared[=(false|true|umask|group|all|world|everybody|0xxx)]` is the option is used to notify Git that the repository is to be shared among many users. Users that are in the same group can push into the repository.

Using the `git clone` command, the existing repository can be cloned into a new directory. The command creates remote-tracking branches for all the branches in the cloned repository. It will download the project and its entire version history. The `git clone` command can simply be used by passing the URL of the repository as an option:

```
git clone [url]
```

The URL passed to the command will contain information of the transport protocol, the address of the remote server, and the repository path. The protocols Git supports are SSH, Git, HTTP, and HTTPS. The command has other options that can be passed to it, to configure the repository to be cloned.

Change commands

Git has a set of useful commands that are used to check the status of files in the repository, review updates made to the files, and commit changes made to the project files.

The git status command is used to show the working status of the repository. The command essentially gives a summary of the files that have changed and are staged for the next commit. It displays the paths of the files that have differences between the current HEAD commit and the index file. It also displays the paths of the files that have differences between the index file and the working tree as well as paths of the files that are not currently being tracked by Git but have not been added in the .gitignore file:

```
git status
```

The git add command uses the content found in the working tree to update the index. It basically adds file content to the index. It is used to add the current content of existing paths. It can be used to remove paths that no longer exist in the tree or add content with the part of the changes made to the working tree.

The practice is usually to run the command several times before performing a commit. It adds the content of the files as it was at the time when the command was run. It takes options that are used for tweaking its behavior:

```
git add [file]
```

The git commit command is used to record or store the content of the index in a commit together with the commit message supplied by the user to describe the changes made to the project files. The changes must have been added, using git add, before the command is run.

The command is flexible and the usage allows different options for recording the changes. An approach is to list the files with changes as parameters to the commit command, which informs Git to ignore changes staged in the index and store the current contents of the listed files.

Also, -a switch can be used with the command to add changes from all files that are listed in the index and are not in the working tree. Switch -m is used to specify the commit message:

```
git commit -m "[commit message]"
```

Sometimes, it is desirable to display the differences or changes between the index and the working tree, changes available between two files or blob objects. The git diff command is used for this purpose. When the --staged option is passed to the command, Git displays the differences between the staging and the last file version:

```
git diff
```

The git rm command removes files from the working tree and the index. The files to be removed are passed as an option to the command. The files passed to the command as arguments are deleted from the working directory and staged for deletion. When the --cached option is passed to the command, Git does not delete the file from the working directory, but removes it from the version control:

```
git rm [files]
```

The git reset command can be used to unstage and preserve the contents of files that have already been staged in a repository. The command is used to reset the current HEAD to a specified state. Also, it can be used to modify the index and working tree, based on the option specified.

The command has three forms. The first and second forms are used to copy the entries from tree to the index, while the last form is used to set the current branch HEAD to a particular commit:

```
git reset [-q] [<tree-ish>] [--] <paths>...
git reset (--patch | -p) [<tree-ish>] [--] [<paths>...]
git reset [--soft | --mixed [-N] | --hard | --merge | --keep] [-q]
[<commit>]
```

Branching and merging commands

The git branch command is core to the Git version control system. It is used to create, move, rename, delete, and list available branches in a repository. The command has several forms and accepts different options used to set up and configure repository branches. When the git branch command is run on Bash, without specifying an option, the available branches in the repository are listed. This is similar to using the --list option.

To create a new branch, the `git branch` command is run with the branch name as the argument:

```
git branch [branch name]
```

The `--delete` option is used to delete the branch specified, and the `--copy` option is used to create a copy of the specified branch alongside its `reflog`.

To update the files in a working tree or branch to match what is available in another working tree, the `git checkout` command is used. The command is used to switch branch or to restore working tree files. Similar to `git branch`, it has several forms and accepts different options.

When the command is run with the branch name passed as an argument, Git switches to the branch specified, updates the working directory, and points the HEAD at the branch:

```
git checkout [branch name]
```

As discussed in the previous section, branching concepts allow development teams to try out new ideas and create new versions of a project from existing ones. The beauty of branching lies in being able to incorporate changes from one branch to another, in essence joining or merging branches or development lines together.

In Git, the `git merge` command is used for the purpose of integrating development branches created from a branch into a single branch. For example, if there is a development branch, created from a master branch to test a certain feature, when the `git merge [branch name]` command is run, Git will retrace the changes that have been made to the branch. This is because it was spurned from the master branch until the latest branch and stores these changes on the master branch in a new commit:

```
git merge [branch name]
git merge --abort
git merge -- continue
```

Quite often, the merge process can result in conflicts between files of the different branches. Running the `git merge --abort` command will abort the merge process and restore the branches back to the pre-merge state. After the conflicts encountered have been resolved, `git merge --continue` can be run to re-run the merge process.

Configuring GitHub WebHooks

A **WebHook** is an event notification delivered through an HTTP POST. A WebHook is often referred to as a web callback or HTTP push API. A WebHook provides a mechanism by which an application delivers data to other applications in real time as they arrive.

A WebHook differs from a regular API in that there is no continuous resource utilization through polling of data to get the latest data. The subscriber or consuming application receives the data when it is available through a URL that must have been registered with the WebHook provider. A WebHook is effective and efficient for both the provider of the data and the consumer.

Consuming WebHooks

To receive notifications or data from a WebHook, the consuming application needs to register a URL with the provider. The provider will deliver the data through POST to the URL. The URL must be publicly accessible from the web and be reachable.

The WebHook provider usually delivers the data through HTTP POST as JSON, XML, or as a form data through multipart or URL encoded. The implementation of the API at the URL of the subscriber will be influenced by the mode of data delivery used by the WebHook provider.

Quite often, there are situations that require that WebHooks be debugged. This might be to troubleshoot an error. This can sometimes be challenging because of the asynchronous nature of WebHooks. First, the data from the WebHook must be understood. This can be achieved using tools that can get and parse WebHook requests. Based on the knowledge of the structure and content of the WebHook data, the requests can be mocked in order to test the URL API code to resolve the issue.

When consuming data from a WebHook, it is important to be security aware and factor this into the design of the consuming application. Because the callback URL that the WebHook provider will POST data to is publicly available, it can be subject to malicious attacks.

A common and easy approach is to append to the URL a mandatory authentication token that will be verified on each request. Also, basic authentication can be built around the URL to verify the party initiating the POST before accepting and processing the data. Alternatively, the provider can sign every WebHook request, if the request signing is already implemented at the provider's end. The signature of every request posted will be verified by the consumer.

Depending on the frequency of events generation from the subscriber, a lot of requests can be raised by WebHooks. If the subscriber is not properly designed to handle such large requests, this can lead to high resource utilization, both in terms of bandwidth and server resources. When resources are fully utilized and used up, the consumer might no longer be able to handle more requests, resulting in a denial of service of the consumer application.

GitHub WebHook

In GitHub, WebHooks serve as a means of delivering notifications to an external web server when events occur. GitHub WebHooks allow you to set up your projects that are hosted on GitHub to subscribe to the desired events available on the `www.github.com` platform. When the event occurs, GitHub sends a payload to the configured endpoint.

WebHooks are configured on any of the repository or at the organizational level. Once successfully configured, the WebHook will be triggered every time a subscribed event or action is triggered. GitHub allows for the creation of up to 20 WebHooks per event for a repository or organization. The WebHooks, after installation, can be triggered on a repository or organization.

Events and payloads

At the point of WebHook configuration in GitHub, you can specify which events you want to receive requests from GitHub. WebHook requests data is termed payloads in GitHub. It is smarter to subscribe to only the events for the data that is needed so as to limit the HTTP requests sent to the application server from GitHub. By default, even a WebHook created on GitHub is subscribed to the `push` event. Event subscriptions can be modified through the GitHub web or API.

Some of the available events that can be subscribed to on GitHub are explained in the following table:

Event	Description
`push`	This is the default event and is raised when there is a Git push to a repository. This also includes editing tags or branches and commits made via API actions that update references
`create`	Raised whenever a branch or tag is created.
`delete`	Raised whenever a branch or tag is deleted.

`issues`	Raised whenever an issue is assigned, unassigned, labeled, unlabeled, opened, edited, milestoned, de-milestoned, closed, or reopened.
`repository`	Raised whenever a repository is created, deleted (organization hooks only), archived, unarchived, made public, or made private.
`*`	This is a wildcard event and indicates that the URL should be notified for any event.

A full list of all available events on GitHub is available at `https://developer.github.com/webhooks/`.

The `push` event has a payload that contains more detailed information. Every event in GitHub has a specific payload format that describes the information required for that event. Besides the specific fields peculiar to an event, each event includes in the payload the user or sender who triggers the event.

Also, included in the payload is the repository or organization that the event occurred on and the application that the event is related to. Payloads cannot exceed 5 MB in size. An event that produces a payload with a size larger than 5 MB will not be fired. A payload delivered to the URL usually contains several headers, some of which are explained in the following table. When a new WebHook is created, GitHub sends a ping to the configured URL, as an indicator that the WebHook configuration was successful:

Header	Description
`User-Agent`	User agent initiating the request. This will always have the prefix `Github-Hookshot`.
`X-GitHub-Event`	Contains the name of the event that triggered the delivery.
`X-GitHub-Delivery`	A GUID to identify the delivery.
`X-Hub-Signature`	This header contains the HMAC hex digest of the response body. This header will be sent if the WebHook is configured with a secret. The content of the header is generated using the `sha1 hash` function and the secret as the HMAC key.

Setting up your first WebHook

To configure a WebHook, we will use the `LoanApplication` repository created earlier. Click on the **Settings** page of the repository, click on **Webhooks**, and click on **Add webhook**:

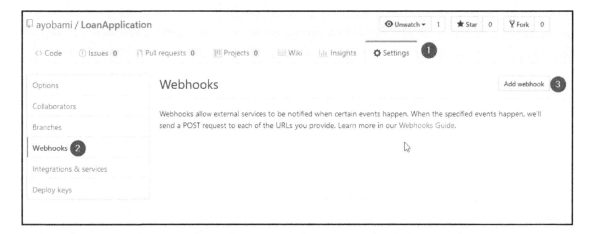

GitHub will ask you to authenticate the action. Supply your GitHub account password to continue. The WebHook configuration page will be loaded, where you can configure the options for the WebHook:

1. In the **Payload URL** field, provide the endpoint of the web application server. Since we will be running the `LoanApplication` from Visual Studio, we will use the following URL: `http://localhost:54113/API/webhook`.
2. Change the **Content type** dropdown to **application/json**, to allow GitHub to send the payload via POST as JSON.
3. Next, choose the option **Let me select individual events**. This will display a full list of available WebHook events.
4. Select the events that you want the WebHook to subscribe to.

5. Finally, click on the **Add webhook** button, to finish the configuration:

Once the WebHook has been created, GitHub will attempt to send a ping to the configured URL in the WebHook. The URL specified, `http://localhost:54113/api/webhook`, is a local development and not publicly available. It is therefore not reachable by GitHub, causing the WebHook request to fail:

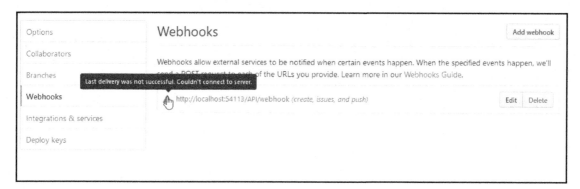

To expose the development environment to the internet to make it accessible to GitHub, we can use **Ngrok**, a tool to create a public URL for exposing a local web server. Navigate to `https://ngrok.com/download` to download Ngrok for your operating system.

Run the following command to tell Ngrok to expose port `54113` to the internet:

```
ngrok http -host-header="localhost:54113" 54113
```

Ngrok will create a public URL that will be accessible and forwarded to the specified port on your development PC. In this case, Ngrok generated `http://d73c1ef5.ngrok.io` as the URL that will be forwarded to port `54113`:

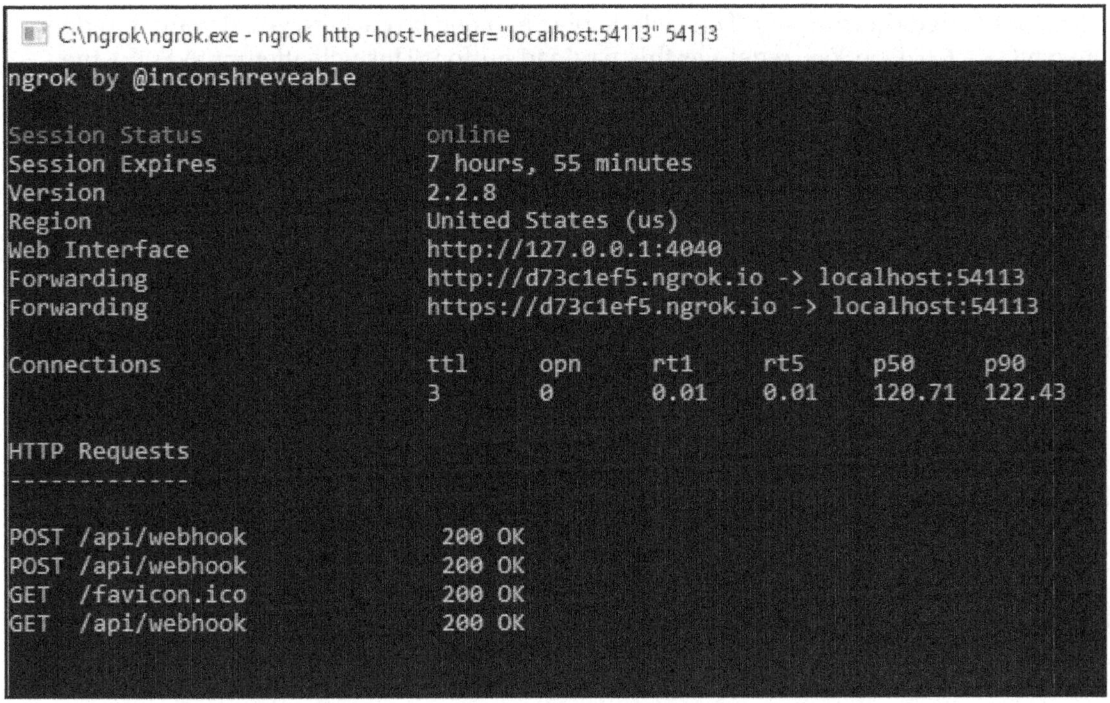

```
■ C:\ngrok\ngrok.exe - ngrok  http -host-header="localhost:54113" 54113

ngrok by @inconshreveable

Session Status                online
Session Expires               7 hours, 55 minutes
Version                       2.2.8
Region                        United States (us)
Web Interface                 http://127.0.0.1:4040
Forwarding                    http://d73c1ef5.ngrok.io -> localhost:54113
Forwarding                    https://d73c1ef5.ngrok.io -> localhost:54113

Connections                   ttl     opn     rt1     rt5     p50     p90
                              3       0       0.01    0.01    120.71  122.43

HTTP Requests
-------------

POST /api/webhook             200 OK
POST /api/webhook             200 OK
GET  /favicon.ico             200 OK
GET  /api/webhook             200 OK
```

Next, update the payload URL for the WebHook created earlier to
`http://d73c1ef5.ngrok.io/api/webhook`. Click on the **Update WebHook** button to
save the changes. Under **Recent Deliveries** tab, click on the GUID for the payload that
failed to deliver. This will open up a screen showing the JSON payload, with a request and
response.

Click on the **Redeliver** button. This will display a dialog box asking you if want to redeliver the payload. Click on **Yes, redeliver this payload** button. This will attempt to POST the JSON payload to the new endpoint specified in the payload URL field. This time, the payload delivery will be successful with HTTP response code 200, indicating that the endpoint was contacted successfully:

You can program the consumer web application to process the payload data the way you want. With the successful configuration, GitHub will POST the payload to the endpoint whenever any event subscribed to in the WebHook is raised.

TeamCity CI platform

TeamCity is a platform-independent CI tool by JetBrains. It is a user-friendly CI tool specifically built with software developers and engineers in mind. TeamCity is a robust and powerful CI tool because of the capability to fully optimize the integration cycle.

TeamCity can also run builds in parallel simultaneously on different platforms and environments. Using TeamCity, you can have customized statistics on code quality, build duration, or even create custom metrics. It has a feature for running code coverage and it has a duplicates finder.

TeamCity concepts

In this section, some basic terms regularly used in TeamCity will be explained. This is necessary in order to understand some of the concepts required to successfully configure the build steps as well as artifacts needed for a quality continuous process. Let's have a look at some basic terms:

- **Project**: This is the software project being developed. It can be a release or specific version. Also, it includes the collection of Build Configurations.
- **Build Agent**: This is the software that executes a build process. It is installed independently from the TeamCity Server. They can both reside on the same machine or on separate machines running similar or different operating systems. For production purposes, it is usually recommended that they both are installed on different machines for optimal performance.
- **TeamCity Server**: The TeamCity Server monitors the Build Agents while using compatibility requirements to distribute builds to connected agents, and it reports the progress and results. The information in the results include the build history, logs, and build data.
- **Build**: This is the process of creating a specific version of a software project. Triggering a build process places it in the Build Queue and will be started when there is an available agent to run it. The Build Agent sends Build Artifacts to the TeamCity Server upon completion of the build.
- **Build Queue**: This is a list containing builds that have been triggered and yet to be started. The TeamCity Server reads the queue for pending builds and distributes the build to compatible Build Agents the moment the agent is idle.
- **Build Artifacts**: These are files generated by a build. These can include dll files, executables, installers, reports, log files, and so on.
- **Build Configuration**: This is a collection of settings describing a build procedure. This includes VCS Roots, Build Steps, and Build Triggers.

- **Build Step**: A Build Step is represented by a build runner with integration with a build tool, such as MSBuild, a code analysis engine, and a testing framework, such as xUnit.net. The build step is essentially a task to be executed, which can contain many steps that are sequentially executed.
- **Build Trigger**: This is a set of rules that triggers a new build on certain events, such as when a VCS triggers a new build when TeamCity detects changes in the configured VCS Roots.
- **VCS Root**: This is a collection of version control settings, including paths to sources, credentials, and other settings that define the way TeamCity communicates with a version control system.
- **Change**: This is a modification to the source code of the project. A Change is termed pending for a certain Build Configuration when the Change has been committed to the version control system, but not yet included in a build.

Installing TeamCity Server

TeamCity can be hosted locally on a development team's server infrastructure or by integrating TeamCity with cloud solutions. This allows virtual machines to be provisioned to run TeamCity. A TeamCity installation will comprise of the server installation and a default Build Agent.

To install the TeamCity Server, navigate to the JetBrains download site to get the free professional edition of the TeamCity Server which comes with free licence key that unlocks 3 Build Agents and 100 Build Configurations. If you are on the Windows operating system, run the download .exe, which is bundled with Tomcat Java JRE 1.8. Follow the dialog prompts to extract and install the TeamCity core files.

During the installation, you can set up the port that TeamCity will be listening to or leave it at default `8080`. If the installation is successful, TeamCity will open in the browser, prompting you to complete the installation process by specifying the Data Directory Location on the server. Specify the path and click **Proceed**:

TeamCity First Start

Please review the settings below before proceeding with the first TeamCity start.

TeamCity server stores server configuration settings, project definitions, build results and caches on disk in a **Data Directory**.

Data Directory location on the TeamCity server machine:

C:\ProgramData\JetBrains\TeamCity

If you already worked with TeamCity on this machine you can specify existing Data Directory.

Proceed

TeamCity 2017.2.2 (build 50909)

After the Data Directory Location path has been initialized, you will be taken to the database selection page, where you will be given the option of selecting any of the supported databases. Select **Internal (HSQLDB)** and click the **Proceed** button:

Database connection setup

TeamCity server stores builds history and users-related data in an SQL database. ⓘ

Select the database type*: | Internal (HSQLDB) ⌄ |

The internal database suits evaluation purposes only and is not intended for production. We strongly recommend using an external database in a production environment. ⓘ

You can start with the internal database and then migrate the data to an external one after successful evaluation.

| Proceed |

TeamCity 2017.2.2 (build 50909)

The database configuration will take a few seconds, before you are presented with the license agreement page. Accept the license agreement and click on the **Continue** button. The next page is the admin account creation page. Create the account with the desired credentials to finish the installation. After the installation is completed, you will be directed to the overview page:

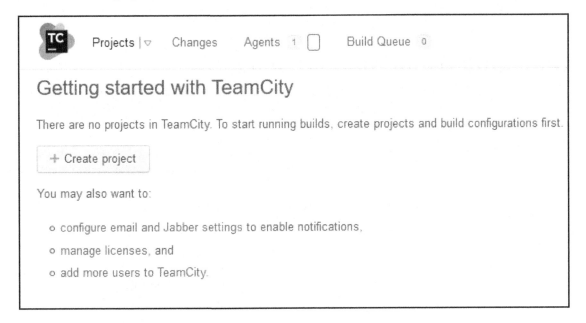

TeamCity CI workflow

The TeamCity build life cycle describes the data flow between the server and the agents. This is basically the information passed to the agents and the process of retrieving the results by TeamCity. The workflow describes the manner in which configured build steps for projects are executed end to end:

1. The TeamCity Server detects a change in the VCS Root and persists this in the database.
2. The Build Trigger notices the change in the database and adds a build to the queue.
3. The TeamCity Server assigns the build on the queue to a compatible idle Build Agent.

4. The Build Agent executes the build steps. During the execution of the build steps, the agents sends reports of the build progress to the server. The Build Agent reports the build progress to the TeamCity Server to allow for real time monitoring of the build process.

5. The Build Agent sends Build Artifacts to the TeamCity Server upon completion of the build.

Configuring and running build

Essentially, a project should contain configuration and project properties required to run a successful build. Using the TeamCity CI server, the steps required to run tests, perform environmental checks, compile, build, and make available a deploy-ready version of a project can be automated end to end.

The installed TeamCity Server can be accessed locally at the port specified during installation. In this case, we will use `http://localhost:8060`. To create a TeamCity project, navigate to the server URL and log in using the earlier created credentials. Click on the **Projects** menu and click on the **Create Project** button.

You will be presented with several project options for creating the project from a repository, manually, or connecting to any of GitHub, Bitbucket, or Visual Studio Team Services. Click on the **From GitHub.com** button to connect TeamCity to the `LoanApplication` repository we created earlier on GitHub:

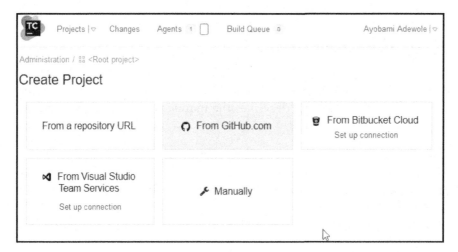

The **Add Connection** dialog is displayed where TeamCity will be connected to GitHub. A new GitHub OAuth application needs to be created to successfully connect TeamCity to GitHub. To create a new OAuth application in GitHub, perform the following steps:

1. Navigate to `https://github.com/settings/applications/new`.
2. In the homepage URL field, supply the URL of the TeamCity Server: `http://localhost:8060`.
3. Supply `http://localhost:8060/oauth/github/accessToken.html` in the **Authorization callback URL**.
4. Click on the **Register application** button to complete the registration. A new client secret and client ID will be created for you:

5. The new client ID and client secret created will be used to fill the fields in the add connection dialog on TeamCity to create a connection from TeamCity to GitHub. Click on the **Save** button to save the settings:

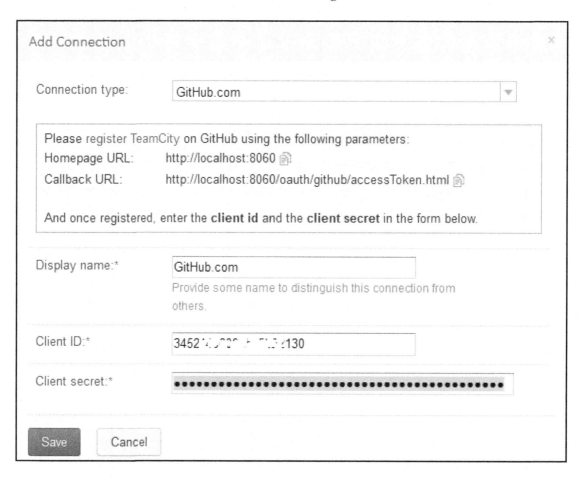

6. The next step is to authorize TeamCity to have access to the VCS. This can be done by clicking the **Sign in to GitHub** button. A page will be displayed where you have to authorize TeamCity to access both public and private repositories in the GitHub account. Click **Authorize** to complete the process.

7. TeamCity will initiate a connection to GitHub to retrieve the list of available repositories that you can select from. You can filter the list to select the desired repository:

8. Connection to the selected repository will be verified by TeamCity. If this is successful, **Create Project** will be displayed. On this page, the project and **Build configuration name** will be displayed. You can modify this if required. Click the **Proceed** button to continue with the project setup:

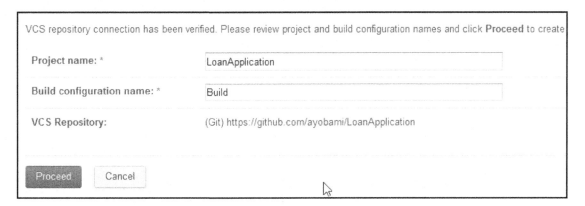

9. In the next screen, TeamCity will scan the connected repository for available configured build steps. You can click on the **Create Build Step** button to add a build step:

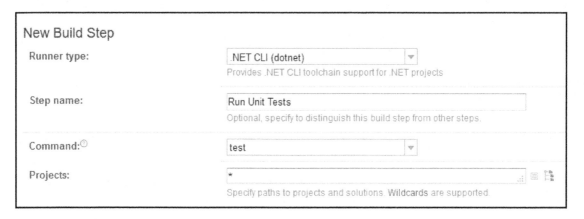

10. In the **New Build Step** screen, you have to select the build runner from the dropdown.
11. Specify a descriptive name for the build step.
12. Next select the command that you want the build runner to execute. Fill in all the other required fields
13. Click the **Save** button to save the build step:

14. Once the build step is saved, the list of the available build steps will be displayed where you can add more build steps as desired following the same procedure. Also, you can reorder the build steps and can detect build steps, by clicking the **Auto-detect build steps** button.

15. After configuring the build steps, you can run the build by clicking on the run link on the top menu of the TeamCity web page. This will redirect to you to the build result page where you can view the progress of the build and subsequently review it or edit the Build Configuration:

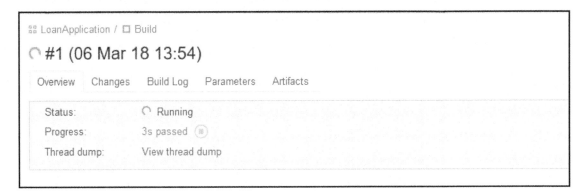

Summary

In this chapter, we have extensively explored the concept of CI, a software development practice that assists development teams in integrating their code frequently. Developers are expected to check the code several times a day, which is then verified by an automated build process, using a CI tool.

Also, common terminologies of CI be for continuous delivery were discussed. We explained the steps on how to host software projects on GitHub and online hosting platforms and later discussed basic Git commands.

The process of creating GitHub WebHooks to configure integrations with build management systems was explored. Finally, a step-by-step description of installing and configuring the TeamCity CI platform was given.

In the next chapter, we will explore Cake Bootstrapper and configure TeamCity to use a cross-platform build automation system called Cake to clean, build, and restore package dependencies and test our `LoanApplication` project.

Creating Continuous Integration Build Processes

8

Continuous feedback, frequent integration, and timely deployment, which all result from the practice of continuous integration, can greatly reduce the risks associated with the software development process. A development team can improve productivity, reduce the amount of time required to deploy, and benefit tremendously from CI.

In Chapter 7, *Continuous Integration and Project Hosting*, we set up TeamCity, a robust continuous integration tool, that simplifies and automates the process of managing source code check-ins and changes, testing, building, and deploying the software project. We walked through the creation of build steps in TeamCity and connected it to our LoanApplication project in GitHub. TeamCity has in-built features that allow it to connect to software projects hosted on GitHub or Bitbucket.

The CI process brings many different steps together into an easily repeatable process. These steps vary based on the software project type, but there are steps that are common and applicable to most projects. These steps can be automated using a build automation system.

In this chapter, we will configure TeamCity to use a cross-platform build-automation system, called **Cake**, to clean, build, and restore package dependencies, and test the LoanApplication solution. Later in the chapter, we will explore the build-step creation with a Cake task in **Visual Studio Team Services**. We will cover the following topics:

- Installing the Cake Bootstrapper
- Writing build scripts in C#
- Cake extension for Visual Studio
- Using Cake tasks to build steps
- CI with Visual Studio Team Services

Installing the Cake Bootstrapper

Cake is a cross-platform build-automation framework. It is a build-automation framework for compiling codes, running tests, copying files and folders, as well as running build-related tasks. Cake is open source with the source code hosted on GitHub.

Cake has the feature to make working with file system paths easy and has functionality for manipulating XML, starting processes, I/O operations, and parsing Visual Studio Solutions. Using Cake build-related activities can be automated using C# domain-specific language.

It employs a dependency-based programming model for build automation, through which tasks are declared alongside dependencies between the tasks. The dependency-based model is ideal and suitable for build automation because the majority of automation build steps are idempotent.

Cake is truly cross-platform; its NuGet package, Cake.CoreCLR, allows it to run on Windows, Linux, and Mac using .NET Core. It has a NuGet package that can be used to run on Windows relying on .NET Framework 4.6.1. Also, it can use the Mono framework to run on Linux and Max, with Mono Version 4.4.2 recommended.

Irrespective of the CI tool being used, Cake has consistent behavior across all supported tools. It has wide support for most tools used during builds, which include **MSBuild**, **ILMerge**, **Wix**, and **Signtool**.

Installation

In order to use the Cake Bootstrapper, Cake needs to be installed. The easy approach to install Cake and test run the installation is to clone or download a `.zip` file, which is the Cake build example repository located at: `https://github.com/cake-build/example`. The example repository contains a simple project and all the files necessary to run the Cake script.

In the example repository, there are certain files of interest—`build.ps1` and `build.sh`. They are the bootstrapper scripts that ensure that the needed dependencies by Cake together with Cake and the necessary files are installed. These scripts make invoking Cake easier. The `build.cake` file is the build script; the build script can be renamed, but the bootstrapper will locate the `build.cake` file by default. The `tools.config/packages.config` file is the package configuration that instructs the bootstrapper script which NuGet packages to install in the `tools` folder.

Extract the downloaded example repository archive file. On Windows, open a PowerShell prompt and execute the bootstrapper script by running `.\build.ps1`. On Linux and Mac, open the terminal and run `.\build.sh`. The bootstrapper script will detect that Cake is not installed on the computer and automatically download it from NuGet.

Based on the bootstrapper script execution, upon completion of Cake download, the downloaded sample `build.cake` script will run, which will clean up the output directory, and restore referenced NuGet packages before building the project. When the `build.cake` file runs, it should clean the test project, restore the NuGet packages, and run the unit tests in the project. The `Run Settings` and `Test Run Summary` will be presented as shown in the following screenshot:

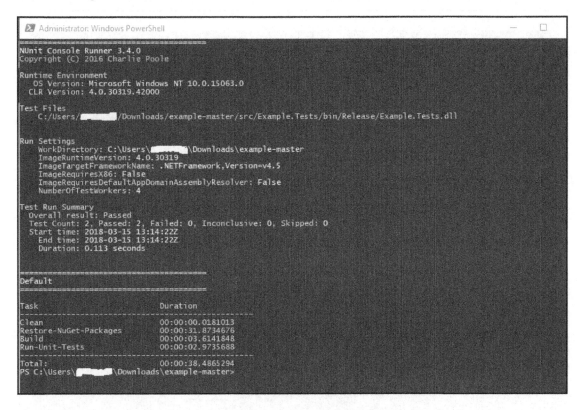

The Cake Bootstrapper can be installed by downloading it from the *Cake Resources* repository hosted on GitHub (`https://github.com/cake-build/resources`), which contains configuration files and bootstrappers. The bootstrapper will download Cake and the necessary tools required by the build script, thereby avoiding storing binaries in the source code repository.

PowerShell security

Often, PowerShell can prevent the running of the `build.ps1` file. You can get an error on the PowerShell screen that `build.ps1` cannot be loaded because running scripts is disabled on the system. This restriction in running the file is due to the default security settings available in PowerShell.

Open the PowerShell window and change the directory to the folder of the Cake build example repository that was downloaded earlier, and run the `.\build.ps1` command. If the execution policy on the system has not been changed from the default, this should give you the following error:

To view the current execution policy configurations on the system, run the `Get-ExecutionPolicy -List` command on the PowerShell screen; this command will present a table with the available scopes and execution policies, like in the following screen. Based on the way you run PowerShell, you might have different settings on your instance:

To change the execution policy to allow the scripts to run subsequently, run the `Set-ExecutionPolicy RemoteSigned -Scope Process` command, which is intended to change the process scope from undefined to `RemoteSigned`. Running the command will display a warning with a prompt on the PowerShell screen stating your PC might be exposed to security risks. Type *Y* for Yes and press *Enter*. The following screenshot shows what is displayed on the PowerShell screen when the command is run:

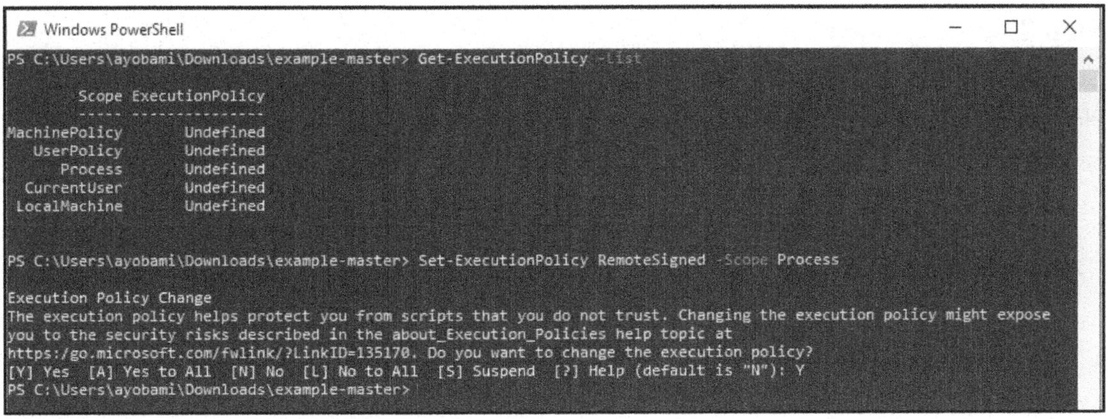

This will change the execution policy of the PC and allow PowerShell scripts to be run.

Cake Bootstrapper installation steps

The steps to install Cake Bootstrapper are similar for the platforms with little differences. Perform the following steps to set up the boostrapper.

Step 1

Navigate to the Cake resource repository to download the boostrapper. For Windows, download the PowerShell `build.ps1` file and for Mac and Linux, download the `build.sh` bash file.

On Windows, open a new PowerShell window and run the following command:

```
Invoke-WebRequest https://cakebuild.net/download/bootstrapper/windows -OutFile build.ps1
```

On Mac, run the following command from a new shell window:

```
curl -Lsfo build.sh https://cakebuild.net/download/bootstrapper/osx
```

On Linux, open a new shell to run the following command:

```
curl -Lsfo build.sh https://cakebuild.net/download/bootstrapper/linux
```

Step 2

Create a Cake script to test the installation. Create a build.cake file; which should be placed in the same location as the build.sh file:

```
var target = Argument("target", "Default");

Task("Default")
  .Does(() =>
{
  Information("Installation Successful");
});

RunTarget(target);
```

Step 3

The Cake script created in *Step 2* can now be run by invoking the Cake Bootstrapper.

On Windows, you need to instruct PowerShell to allow running scripts, this is done by changing the Windows PowerShell script execution policy. The PowerShell script execution can fail due to the execution policy.

To execute the Cake script, run the following command:

```
./build.ps1
```

On Linux or Mac, you should run the following command to give the current owner permission to execute the script:

```
chmod +x build.sh
```

Once the command has been run, the bootstrapper can be invoked to run the Cake script created in *Step 2*:

```
./build.sh
```

Writing build scripts in C#

Automating the build and deployment tasks using Cake allows you to avoid issues and headaches associated with project deployments. A build script usually contains the steps and logic required to build and deploy the source code alongside configuration files and other artifacts of a project.

Using the sample `build.cake` file available on the Cake resource repository can be a starting point for writing a build script for a project. However, to achieve more, we will walk through some basic Cake concepts that can facilitate writing robust scripts for automating build and deployment tasks.

Task

At the core of the build automation with Cake is the task. A **task** in Cake is a simple unit of work that is used to carry out a specific action or activity in a desired defined order. Tasks in Cake can have specified criteria, associated dependencies, and error handling.

A task can be defined by using the `Task` method, with the task name or caption passed into it as an argument:

```
Task("Action")
    .Does(() =>
{
    // Task code goes here
});
```

For example, the `build` task in the following snippet cleans the `debugFolder` folder to delete the contents. When the task is run, the `CleanDirectory` method will be invoked:

```
var debugFolder = Directory("./bin/Debug");

Task("CleanFolder")
    .Does(() =>
{
    CleanDirectory(debugFolder);
});
```

Cake allows you to use C# to use the async and await features in a task to create asynchronous tasks. Essentially, a task itself will run synchronously with a single thread, but the code contained in a task can benefit from the asynchronous programming features and utilize asynchronous APIs.

Cake has the `DoesForEach` method that can be used to add a collection of items or a delegate that yields a collection of items as actions to a task. When a delegate is added to a task, the delegate will be executed after the task is executed:

```
Task ("LongRunningTask")
    .Does(async () =>
    {
        // use await keyword to multi thread code
    });
```

Define `DoesForEach` by chaining it to the `Task` method, as in the following snippet:

```
Task ("ProcessCsv")
    .Does (() =>
{
})
.DoesForEach(GetFiles("**/*.csv"), (file) =>
{
    // Process each csv file.
});
```

TaskSetup and TaskTeardown

`TaskSetup` and `TaskTeardown` are used to wrap code to execute actions that you want the build to perform before and after the execution of each task. These methods are especially useful when performing actions such as configuration initializations and custom logging:

```
TaskSetup(setupContext =>
{
    var taskName =setupContext.Task.Name;
    // perform action
});

TaskTeardown (teardownContext =>
{
    var taskName =teardownContext.Task.Name;
    // perform action
});
```

Similar to `TaskSetup` and `TaskTeardown` for task, Cake has the `Setup` and `Teardown` methods that can be used to execute actions that are intended to run before the first task and after the last task, respectively. These methods are useful in a build automation, with a good use case being, for example, when you intend to start up some server and services before running tasks and for the cleanup activities afterwards. The `Setup` or `Teardown` methods are to be called before `RunTarget` to ensure they work correctly:

```
Setup(context =>
{
    // This will be executed BEFORE the first task.
});

Teardown(context =>
{
    // This will be executed AFTER the last task.
});
```

Configuration and preprocessor directives

Cake operations can be controlled through the use of environment variables, configuration files, and by passing arguments into the Cake executable file. This is based on a specified priority in which the configuration file overrides the environment variables and arguments passed into Cake, and then overrides entries defined in both environment variables and the configuration file.

For example, if you intend to specify the tool path, which is the directory that cake checks when restoring tools, you can create the `CAKE_PATHS_TOOLS` environment variable name and set the value to the Cake tools folder path.

When using configuration file, the file should be placed in the same directory as the `build.cake` file. The Cake tools path can be specified in the configuration file, like in the following snippet, which overrides whatever is set in the environment variable:

```
[Paths]
Tools=./tools
```

The Cake tools path can be passed directly into Cake, which will override what is set in both the environment variable and configuration file:

```
cake.exe --paths_tools=./tools
```

Cake has values that are used by default for the configuration entries, if they are not overridden using any of the methods for configuring Cake. The available configuration entries are shown here with their default values and how to configure them using the configuration methods:

Configuration option	Description	Default value	Environment variable name	Config file content	Direct argument
Tools path	This option is used to tell Cake which folder contains the tools to be used by Cake when restoring.	./tools	CAKE_PATHS_TOOLS	[Paths]Tools=./tools	cake.exe --paths_tools=./tools
Addins path	This config option is used to specify the Addins folder to be used by cake while restoring Add-ins.	./tools/Addins	CAKE_PATHS_ADDINS	[Paths]Addins=./tools/Addins	cake.exe --paths_addins=./tools/Addins
NuGet download URL	Using this option, you can specify where Cake should download Nuget packages from when you are using the addin and tool preprocessor.	https://packages.nuget.org/api/v2	CAKE_NUGET_SOURCE	[Nuget]Source=http://someurl/nuget/	cake.exe --nuget_source=http://someurl/nuget/
Modules path	This is used for configuring the Modules folder for use by Cake when loading custom modules.	./tools/Modules	CAKE_PATHS_MODULES	[Paths]Modules=./tools/Modules	cake.exe --paths_modules=./tools/Modules
Skip verification	This option is used to avoid runtime errors that can occur during script execution. When exceptions occur during script execution, Cake will abort the execution of the script.	false	CAKE_SETTINGS_SKIPVERIFICATION	[Settings]SkipVerification=true	cake.exe --settings_skipverification=true
Add-in NuGet dependencies	A configuration option that became available since Cake Version 0.220 to install and reference NuGet package dependencies.	false	CAKE_NUGET_LOADDEPENDENCIES	[NuGet]LoadDependencies=true	cake.exe --nuget_loaddependencies=true

Preprocessor directives are used in Cake to reference assemblies, namespaces, and scripts. The preprocessor line directives run before the script is executed.

Dependencies

Often, you will create tasks whose execution will depend on the completion of other tasks; to achieve this, you use the `IsDependentOn` and `IsDependeeOf` methods. To create a task that is dependent on another task, use the `IsDependentOn` method. In the following build script, Cake will execute `Task1` before `Task2` is executed:

```
Task("Task1")
    .Does(() =>
{
});

Task("Task2")
    .IsDependentOn("Task1")
    .Does(() =>
{
});
```

```
RunTarget("Task2");
```

Using the `IsDependeeOf` method, you can define task dependencies with reversed relationships. This implies that where the tasks that depend on a task are defined in that task. The preceding build script can be refactored to use the reversed relationship:

```
Task("Task1")
    .IsDependeeOf("Task2")
    .Does(() =>
{
});

Task("Task2")
    .Does(() =>
{
});

RunTarget("Task2");
```

Criteria

When criteria is used in the Cake script, it allows you to control the flow of the execution of the build script. A **criteria** is a predicate that must be fulfilled for the task to execute. The criteria does not affect the execution of the succeeding task. Criteria is used to control task execution based on specified configurations, environmental states, repository branches, and any other desired options.

In the simplest form, you can use the `WithCriteria` method to specify the criteria of the execution of a particular task. For example, if you want to clean the `debugFolder` folder only in the afternoon, you can specify the criteria as in the following script:

```
var debugFolder = Directory("./bin/Debug");

Task("CleanFolder")
    .WithCriteria(DateTime.Now.Hour >= 12)
    .Does(() =>
{
    CleanDirectory(debugFolder);
});

RunTarget("CleanFolder");
```

You can have a task whose execution is dependent on another task; in the following script, the criteria for the `CleanFolder` task will be set when the task is created, while the criteria for the `ProcessCsv` task evaluation will be done during task execution:

```
var debugFolder = Directory("./bin/Debug");

Task("CleanFolder")
    .WithCriteria(DateTime.Now.Hour >= 12)
    .Does(() =>
{
    CleanDirectory(debugFolder);
});
Task("ProcessCsv")
    .WithCriteria(DateTime.Now.Hour >= 12)
    .IsDependentOn("CleanFolder")
    .Does(() =>
{
})
.DoesForEach(GetFiles("**/*.csv"), (file) =>
{
    // Process each csv file.
});
RunTarget("ProcessCsv");
```

A more useful use case will be to write a Cake script with criteria that checks a local build and executes some actions that will clean, build, and deploy a project. Four tasks will be defined, one for each of the actions to be performed and the fourth to chain the actions together:

```
var isLocalBuild = BuildSystem.IsLocalBuild
Task("Clean")
    .WithCriteria(isLocalBuild)
    .Does(() =>
    {
        // clean all projects in the soution
    });

Task("Build")
    .WithCriteria(isLocalBuild)
    .Does(() =>
    {
        // build all projects in the soution
    });

Task("Deploy")
    .WithCriteria(isLocalBuild)
    .Does(() =>
```

```
    {
        // Deploy to test server
    });

Task("Main")
    .IsDependentOn("Clean")
    .IsDependentOn("Build")
    .IsDependentOn("Deploy")
    .Does(() =>
    {
    });
RunTarget("Main");
```

Cake's error handling and finally block

Cake has error handling techniques that you can use to recover from errors or graciously handle exceptions whenever they occur during the build process. Sometimes build steps call external services or processes; invocation of these external dependencies might cause errors that can cause the overall build to fail. A robust build should handle such exceptions without stopping the entire build process.

The OnError method is a task extension that is used when you need to act on an exception generated in the build. Instead of forcefully terminating the script, you can write code to handle the error in the OnError method:

```
Task("Task1")
.Does(() =>
{
})
.OnError(exception =>
{
    // Code to handle exception.
});
```

Sometimes you might want to ignore the error thrown and just continue the execution of a task that generates the exception; you can use the ContinueOnError task extension to achieve this. When using the ContinueOnError method, you cannot use the OnError method with it:

```
Task("Task1")
    .ContinueOnError()
    .Does(() =>
{
});
```

If you wish to report the exception generated in a task, and still allow the exception to propagate and take its course, use the `ReportError` method. If, for any reason, an exception is thrown inside the `ReportError` method, it is swallowed:

```
Task("Task1")
    .Does(() =>
{
})
.ReportError(exception =>
{
    // Report generated exception.
});
```

Also, you can use the `DeferOnError` method to defer any thrown exception till the task being executed is completed. This will ensure that the task executes all actions specified in it before the exception is thrown and the script fails:

```
Task("Task1")
    .Does(() =>
{
})
.DeferOnError();
```

Lastly, you can use the `Finally` method to execute any action, irrespective of the outcome of the task's execution:

```
Task("Task1")
    .Does(() =>
{
})
.Finally(() =>
{
    // Perform action.
});
```

LoanApplication build script

To demonstrate the power of Cake, let's write a Cake script to build the `LoanApplication` project. The Cake script will clean the project folder, restore all package references, build the entire solution, and run unit test projects in the solution.

The following script sets arguments to be used throughout the script, defines the directories and the tasks to clean the bin folder of the LoanApplication.Core project, and restores packages using the DotNetCoreRestore method. NuGet packages can be restored by using the DotNetCoreRestore method, which in turn uses the dotnet restore command:

```
//Arguments
var target = Argument("target", "Default");
var configuration = Argument("configuration", "Release");
var solution = "./LoanApplication.sln";

// Define directories.
var buildDir = Directory("./LoanApplication.Core/bin") +
Directory(configuration);

//Tasks
Task("Clean")
    .Does(() =>
{
    CleanDirectory(buildDir);
});

Task("Restore-NuGet-Packages")
    .IsDependentOn("Clean")
    .Does(() =>
{
    Information("Restoring NuGet Packages");
    DotNetCoreRestore();
});
```

The later portion of the script contains tasks to build the entire solution using the DotNetCoreBuild method, which builds the solution using the dotnet build command, using settings provided in the DotNetCoreBuildSettings object. The test projects are executed using the DotNetCoreTest method, which runs the tests in all the test projects in the solution using dotnet test and the settings provided in the DotNetCoreTestSettings object:

```
Task("Build")
    .IsDependentOn("Restore-NuGet-Packages")
    .Does(() =>
{
    Information("Build Solution");
    DotNetCoreBuild(solution,
            new DotNetCoreBuildSettings()
                {
                    Configuration = configuration
```

```
                        });
    });

    Task("Run-Tests")
        .IsDependentOn("Build")
        .Does(() =>
    {
        var testProjects = GetFiles("./LoanApplication.Tests.Units/*.csproj");
            foreach(var project in testProjects)
            {
                DotNetCoreTool(
                    projectPath: project.FullPath,
                    command: "xunit",
                    arguments: $"-configuration {configuration} -diagnostics -
stoponfail"
                );
            }
    });

    Task("Default")
        .IsDependentOn("Run-Tests");

    RunTarget(target);
```

The Cake Bootstrapper can be used to run the Cake `build` file by invoking the bootstrapper from the PowerShell window. When the bootstrapper is invoked, Cake will use the task definition available in the `build` file to commence execution of the defined build tasks. When the execution begins, the progress and status of the execution is presented in the PowerShell window:

```
Preparing to run build script...
Running build script...

========================================
Clean
========================================


========================================
Restore-NuGet-Packages
========================================
Restoring NuGet Packages

Welcome to .NET Core!
---------------------
Learn more about .NET Core @ https://aka.ms/dotnet-docs. Use dotnet --help to see available commands or go to https://ak
a.ms/dotnet-cli-docs.

Telemetry
---------
The .NET Core tools collect usage data in order to improve your experience. The data is anonymous and does not include c
ommand-line arguments. The data is collected by Microsoft and shared with the community.
You can opt out of telemetry by setting a DOTNET_CLI_TELEMETRY_OPTOUT environment variable to 1 using your favorite shel
l.
```

The progress of the execution of each task will be displayed on the PowerShell window with all the activities that Cake is currently undergoing. When the build execution completes, the duration of the execution of each task in the script will be displayed along with the total execution time of all the tasks:

```
      0 Error(s)

Time Elapsed 00:01:07.79


========================================
Run-Tests
========================================


========================================
Default
========================================

Task                              Duration
----------------------------------------------------
Clean                             00:00:00.0248073
Restore-NuGet-Packages            00:00:29.1532166
Build                             00:01:17.0493209
Run-Tests                         00:00:00.0128710
----------------------------------------------------
Total:                            00:01:46.2433470
```

Cake Extension for Visual Studio

The **Cake Extension for Visual Studio Add-in** brings language support for Cake build scripts to Visual Studio. The extension supports new templates, a task runner explorer, and the ability to bootstrap Cake files. **Cake Extension** for Visual Studio can be downloaded at **Visual Studio Market Place** (https://marketplace.visualstudio.com/items?itemName=vs-publisher-1392591.CakeforVisualStudio).

The `.vsix` file downloaded from the marketplace is essentially a `.zip` file. This file contains the contents of the Cake extensions to be installed in Visual Studio. When the downloaded `.vsix` file is run, it will install Cake support for Visual Studio 2015 and 2017:

Cake templates

After installing the extension, a **Cake template** will be added to the available options in Visual Studio when creating new projects. The extension will add four different Cake project templates types:

- **Cake Addin**: This is a project template for creating Cake Addin
- **Cake Addin Unit Test Project**: This is the project template for creating unit tests for Cake Addin and it includes samples that serve as guidelines
- **Cake Addin Unit Test Project (empty)**: This is the project template for creating unit tests for Cake Addin but without the sample included
- **Cake Module**: This template is used to create the Cake module and it comes with samples

The following image shows the different Cake project templates:

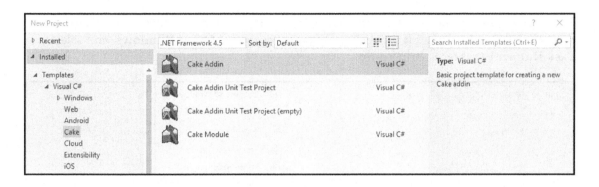

Task Runner Explorer

In a Visual Studio solution that uses a Cake script for build automation, the Cake task runner will be triggered when the `build.cake` file is discovered. Cake Extension activates the **Task Runner Explorer** integration, which allows you to run Cake tasks with the bindings included directly in Visual Studio.

To open the Task Runner Explorer, right-click the **Cake Script** (`build.cake` file) and select **Task Runner Explorer** from the displayed context menu; it should open the **Task Runner Explorer** with all the tasks available in the Cake script listed in the window:

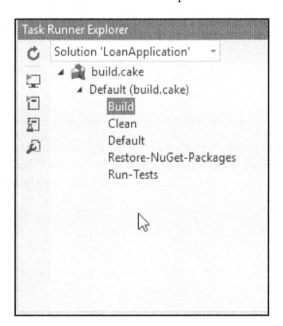

Sometimes, Task Runner Explorer might not be displayed in the context menu when you right-click the **Cake Script**. If so, click on **View** menu, select **Other Windows**, and select **Task Runner Explorer** to bring it up:

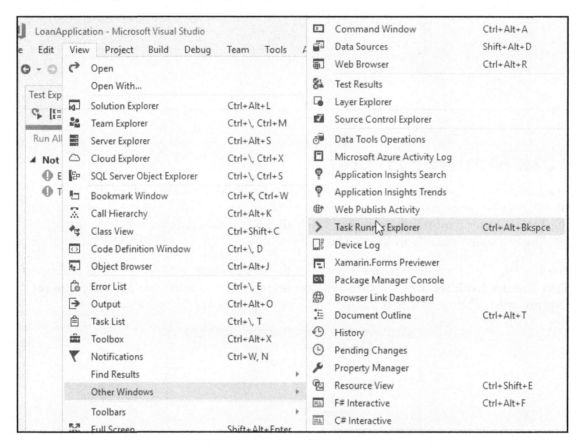

As a result of the Cake Extension installation, the **Build** menu of Visual Studio will now have an entry for **Cake Build**, which can be used to install the Cake config file, PowerShell bootstrapper, and Bash bootstrapper if they are not already configured in the solution:

You can now execute each task directly from **Task Runner Explorer** by double-clicking it or through right-clicking it and selecting **Run**. The progress of the task execution will be displayed on **Task Runner Explorer**:

Syntax highlighting

Cake extension adds a syntax highlighting feature to Visual Studio. This is a common feature of IDEs, where source code are presented in different formats, colors, and fonts. The source code highlighting is done based on defined groups, categories, and sections.

After the installation of the extension, any file with the `.cake` extension can be opened in Visual Studio with complete task and syntax highlighting. There is currently no IntelliSense support for the `.cake` script files in Visual Studio; this feature is expected to come later.

The following screenshot shows the syntax highlighting of a `build.cake` file in Visual Studio:

```
build.cake    LoanRepositoryTest.cs
    1     //Arguments
    2     var target = Argument("target", "Default");
    3     var configuration = Argument("configuration", "Release");
    4     var solution = "./LoanApplication.sln";
    5
    6     // Define directories.
    7     var buildDir = Directory("./LoanApplication.Core/bin") + Directory(configuration);
    8
    9     //Tasks
   10     Task("Clean")
   11         .Does(() =>
   12     {
   13         CleanDirectory(buildDir);
   14     });
   15
   16     Task("Restore-NuGet-Packages")
   17         .IsDependentOn("Clean")
   18         .Does(() =>
   19     {
   20         Information("Restoring NuGet Packages");
   21         DotNetCoreRestore();
   22     });
   23
   24     Task("Build")
   25         .IsDependentOn("Restore-NuGet-Packages")
   26         .Does(() =>
   27     {
   28         Information("Build Solution");
   29         DotNetCoreBuild(solution,
   30             new DotNetCoreBuildSettings()
```

Using Cake tasks to build steps

Using Task Runner Explorer to run build tasks written in Cake scripts is easier and more convenient. This is usually done through Cake Extension for Visual Studio or by directly invoking the Cake bootstrapper file. However, there is an alternative that is more efficient, which is to run the Cake build script using the TeamCity CI tool.

The TeamCity build steps can be used to execute Cake scripts as part of the build steps execution processes. Let's create a build step that executes the Cake script for the `LoanApplication` project by following these steps:

- Click on **Add Build Step** to open a **New Build Step** window.
- In the **Runner type**, select **PowerShell**, since the Cake bootstrapper file will be invoked by PowerShell.
- Give the build step a descriptive name in the text field.

- In the **Script** option, select **File**. This is because it is a `.ps1` file that will be invoked and not a direct PowerShell script.
- To select the **Script file**, click on the tree icon; this will load the available files and folders available in the project hosted on GitHub. Select the `build.ps1` file in the list of displayed files.
- Click on the **Save** button to save the changes and create the build step:

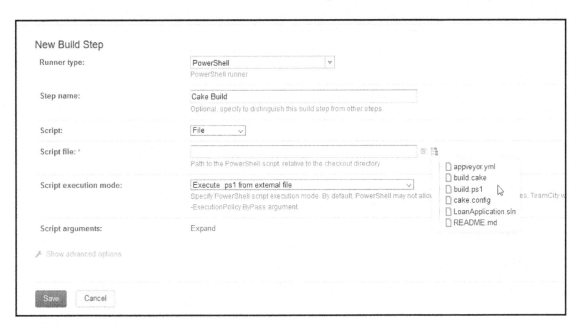

The new build step should appear in the list of available build steps configured for the project in TeamCity. In the **Parameters Description** tab, information about the build step will be displayed showing the runner type and PowerShell file to be executed, as seen in the following screenshot:

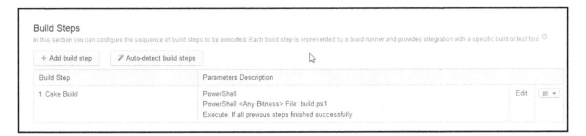

CI with Visual Studio Team Services

Microsoft Visual Studio Team Services (**VSTS**) is the cloud version of the **Team Foundation Server** (**TFS**). It provides great features that allow developers to collaborate on software project development. Similar to TFS, it provides an easy and simplified server management experience with enhanced connectivity with remote sites.

VSTS provides great experience for development teams practicing CI and **Continuous Delivery** (**CD**). It has support for Git repositories for source control, easy-to-understand reports, and customizable dashboards for monitoring the overall progress of software projects.

Also, it has in-built features and tools for build and release management, planning and tracking projects, managing code defects, and issues using the *Kanban* and *Scrum* methods. It equally has an in-built wiki for information dissemination with a development team.

You connect to VSTS through the internet, using Microsoft accounts that need to have been created by the developers. However, development teams in an organization can configure VSTS authentication to work with **Azure Active Directory** (**Azure AD**), or set up Azure AD with security features, such as IP address restrictions and multi-factor authentication.

Setting up a project in VSTS

To get started with VSTS, navigate to `https://www.visualstudio.com/team-services/` to create a free account. You can sign in with a Microsoft account, if you have created one, or using your organization's Active Directory authentication. You should be redirected to the following screen:

Host my projects at:

ayobami   .visualstudio.com

Manage code using:

◉ ◈ Git

○ ⚮ Team Foundation Version Control

We will host your projects in **Central US** location.

You can share work with other   users.

✎ **Change details**

Continue

To keep our lawyers happy:
By continuing, you agree to the Terms of Service, Privacy
Statement, and Code of Conduct.

In VSTS, each account has it own customized URL, which contains a team project collection, for example, `https://packt.visualstudio.com`. You should specify the URL; in the field and select the **Version control** to use with the projects. VSTS currently supports Git and Team Foundation Version Control. Click continue to proceed with the account creation.

After the account creation, click on the **Projects** menu to navigate to the **Projects** page, and then click on **New Project** to create a new project. This will load the project creation screen where you will specify the project name, description, the **Version control** to use, and the work item process. Click on the **Create** button to complete the project creation:

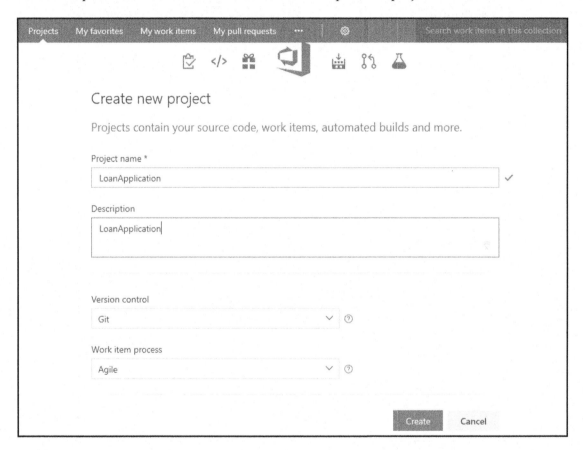

After the project creation is completed, you will be presented with the getting started screen. The screen provides options of cloning existing projects or pushing an existing project to it. Let's import the `LoanApplication` project we created earlier on GitHub. Click on the **Import** button to begin the import process:

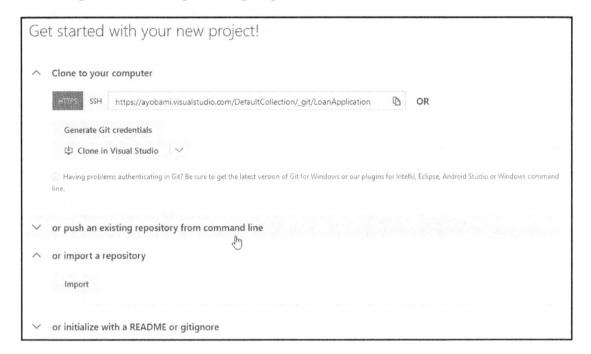

At the **Import** screen, specify the source type, and URL to the GitHub repository, and provide the GitHub login credentials. Click on the **Import** button to begin the import process:

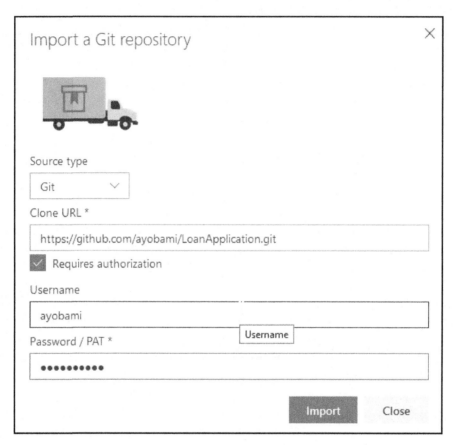

You will be presented with a screen showing the import progress. The import process might take some time based on the size of the project to be imported. When the process completes, an **Import successful** message will be displayed on the screen:

Import successful!

Congratulations! Your https://github.com/ayobami/LoanApplication.git repository has been successfully imported.

If you are not automatically redirected to your repository page Click here to navigate to code view.

Click on **Click here to navigate to code view** to view the files and folders imported by VSTS. The **Files** screen will present the available files and folders in the project with the commits and date details:

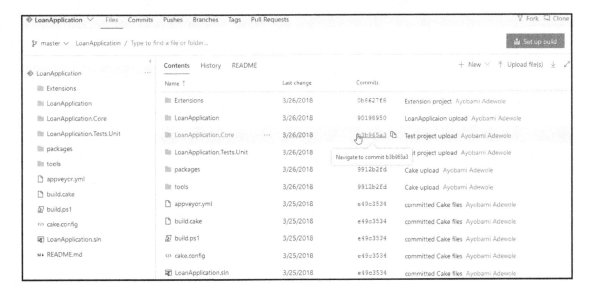

Installing Cake into VSTS

Cake has a VSTS extension that allows you to run the Cake script directly from the VSTS build task relatively easily. With the extension installed into VSTS, the Cake script would not have to be run using PowerShell, like when running Cake scripts in TeamCity.

Navigate to the Cake Build URL on Visual Studio Marketplace: `https://marketplace.visualstudio.com/items/cake-build.cake`. Click on the **Get it free** button to begin the installation of the Cake extension into VSTS:

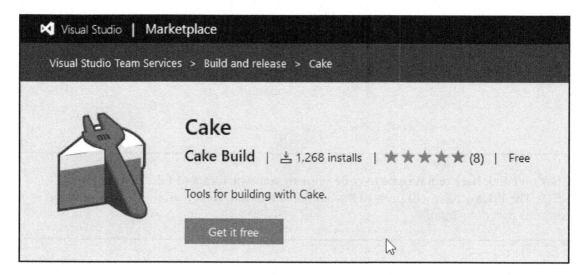

Clicking the **Get it free** button will redirect to the VSTS **Visual Studio** | **Marketplace** integration page. On this page, select the account where you intend to install Cake and click the **Install** button:

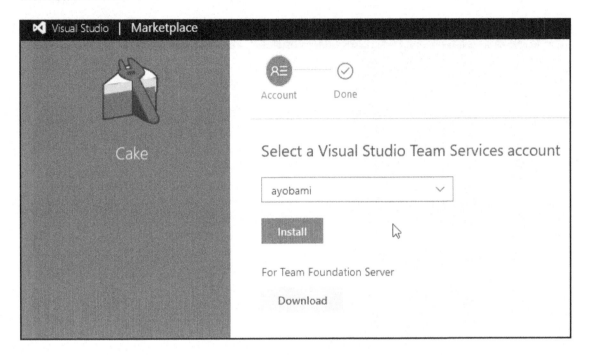

When the installation is successful, you will be presented with a message stating that all is set, similar to what is in the following screenshot. Click on **Proceed to account** button to redirect you to your VSTS account page:

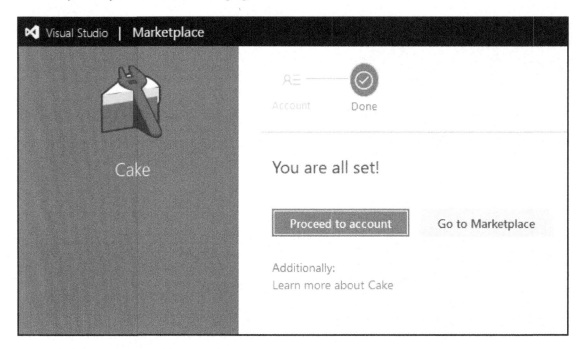

Adding a build task

After the successful installation of Cake into VSTS, you can proceed to configure how your code will be built and how the software will be deployed. VSTS provides easy approaches for building your source code and shipping your software.

To create a VSTS build that is powered by Cake, click on **Build and Release** and select the **Builds** submenu. This will load the build definition page; click the **+New** button on this page to begin the build-creation process.

A screen will be displayed, where the repository is selected, see the following screenshot. The screen provides options of selecting the repository from different sources:

After selecting the repository source, click on the **Continue** button to load the template screen. On this screen, you can choose the build template to use for configuring the build. VSTS has featured templates for the various supported project types. Each template is configured with build steps related to the template project:

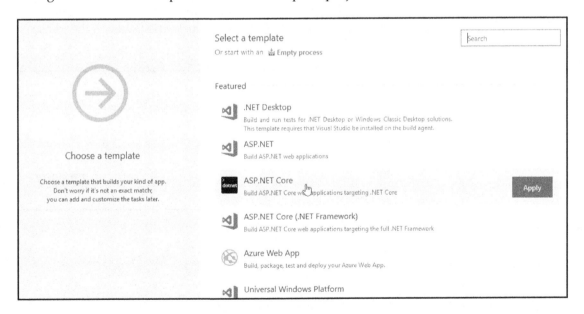

Scroll down to the bottom of the template list or simply type `Empty` in the search box to select the **Empty** template. Hover the mouse over the template to activate the **Apply** button, and click on the button to proceed to the task creation page:

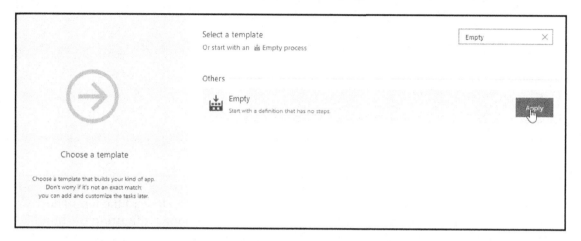

When the **Tasks** screen loads, click on the **+** button to add a task to the build. Scroll through the list of displayed task templates to select **Cake** or use the search box to filter the list to **Cake**. Click the **Add** button to add the **Cake** task to the list of tasks available on the phase of the build:

After adding the **Cake** task, click on the task to load the property screen. Click on the **Browse** button to select the `build.cake` file containing the build scripts for the `LoanApplication` project to be associated with the build task. You can modify the **Display name** and change the **Target** and **Verbosity** properties. Also, if there are arguments to be passed to the Cake script, you can supply them in the provided field:

Click on the **Save & queue** menu and select **Save & queue** to ensure the build created will be queued on the hosted agent. This will load up the build definition and queue screen where you can specify the comment and the **Agent queue**:

A hosted agent is the software that runs the build job. Using a hosted agent is the simplest and easiest way for build execution. The hosted agent is managed by the VSTS team.

If the build is queued successfully, you should get a notification on the screen showing the build number stating that the build has been queued:

Click on the build number to navigate to the build execution page. The hosted agent will process the queue and execute the configured tasks for the build in the queue. The build agent will show the progress of build execution. After the completion of the execution, the success or failure of the build will be reported:

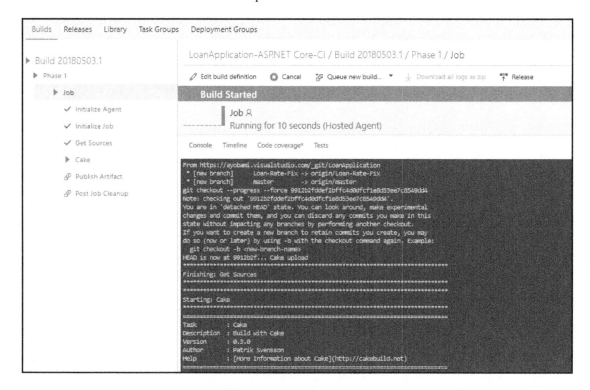

VSTS offers great benefits and simplifies the CI and CD processes. It provides tools and features that allow different IDE to easily integrate with it and makes end-to-end development and project testing relatively easy.

Summary

In this chapter, we explored the Cake build automation in detail. We walked through the steps of installing Cake and the Cake Bootstrapper. Later, we explored the process of writing Cake build scripts and task creation with sample tasks that can be used for various build activities.

Also, we created a build script for the `LoanApplication` project, with the build script containing tasks to clean, restore, and build all projects in the solution and build the unit test projects contained in the solution.

We later created a build step in TeamCity that executes the Cake script by using PowerShell as the runner type. Later in the chapter, we walked through setting up Microsoft Visual Studio Team Services, installing Cake into VSTS, and configuring a build step with the Cake task.

In the final chapter, we will explore how to execute xUnit.net tests with Cake scripts. Later in the chapter, we will explore .NET Core versioning, .NET Core packaging, and metapackages. We will package the `LoanApplication` project for NuGet distribution.

Testing and Packaging the Application

9

In `Chapter 8`, *Creating Continuous Integration Build Processes*, we walked through the installation and setup of the Cake automation building tool. Also, we extensively demonstrated the process of writing build scripts using Cake with its rich, C# domain-specific languages. We also covered installing Cake Extension for Visual Studio and running Cake scripts using the *Task Explorer* window.

The benefits of CI process brings to software development cannot be overemphasized; it facilitates the easy fixing of bugs in project's code base through early and quick detection. Using CI, running and reporting test coverage of unit tests projects can be automated alongside the project build and deployment.

In order to utilize the features of the CI process effectively, the unit test projects in a code base should run and test coverage reports that should be generated by the CI tool. In this chapter, we will modify the Cake build script to run our suite of xUnit.net tests.

Later in this chapter, we will explore .NET Core versioning and how it can affect application development. We will finish up the chapter by packaging the `LoanApplication` project for distribution on the various platforms .NET Core supports. Later, we will explore how to package the .NET Core application for sharing on NuGet.

The following topics will be covered in this chapter:

- Executing xUnit.net tests with Cake
- .NET Core versioning
- .NET Core packages and metapackages
- Packaging for NuGet distribution

Executing xUnit.net tests with Cake

In Chapter 8, *Creating Continuous Integration Build Processes*, in the *LoanApplication build script* section, we walked through the process of creating and running build steps using the Cake automation build script. Running unit tests and getting the test results and coverage from Visual Studio IDE, Visual Studio Code, or any other suitable IDE for building .NET and .NET Core applications is easier with the assistance of the xUnit console runner and xUnit adapter. However, for the CI process and the build process to be complete and effective, unit test projects should be compiled and executed as part of the build steps.

Executing xUnit.net tests in .NET projects

Cake has a rich support for running xUnit.net tests. Cake has two aliases for running the different versions of xUnit.net tests—xUnit for running earlier versions of xUnit.net and xUnit2 for Version 2 of xUnit.net. To use commands for the alias, the **ToolPath** to xUnit.net must be specified within the XUnit2Settings class or include the tool directive in the build.cake file, to instruct Cake to get the binaries required to run xUnit.net tests from NuGet.

Here is the syntax for including the tool directive for xUnit.net:

```
#tool "nuget:?package=xunit.runner.console"
```

Cake's XUnit2Alias is overloaded with different forms for running the xUnit.net version tests in the specified assemblies. The alias resides in Cake's Cake.Common.Tools.XUnit namespace. The first form is XUnit2(ICakeContext, IEnumerable<FilePath>), which is used to run all xUnit.net tests in the specified assemblies in the IEnumerable parameter. The following script shows how to get the test assemblies to be executed into the IEnumerable object using the GetFiles method and passing it to the XUnit2 method:

```
#tool "nuget:?package=xunit.runner.console"

Task("Execute-Test")
    .Does(() =>
    {
        var assemblies =
GetFiles("./LoanApplication.Tests.Unit/bin/Release/LoanApplication.Tests.Un
it.dll");
        XUnit2(assemblies);
    });
```

The XUnit2(ICakeContext, IEnumerable<FilePath>, XUnit2Settings) alias is similar to the first form, with the addition of the XUnit2Settings class for specifying options of how Cake should execute the xUnit.net tests. The following snippet describes the usage:

```
#tool "nuget:?package=xunit.runner.console"

Task("Execute-Test")
    .Does(() =>
    {
        var assemblies =
GetFiles("./LoanApplication.Tests.Unit/bin/Release/LoanApplication.Tests.Un
it.dll");
        XUnit2(assemblies,
          new XUnit2Settings {
              Parallelism = ParallelismOption.All,
              HtmlReport = true,
              NoAppDomain = true,
              OutputDirectory = "./build"
          });
    });
```

Alternatively, the XUnit2 alias allows the passing of the IEnumerable of string, which is expected to contain the paths to the assemblies of the xUnit.net Version 2 test projects to be executed. The form is XUnit2(ICakeContext, IEnumerable<string>) and the following snippet describes the usage:

```
#tool "nuget:?package=xunit.runner.console"

Task("Execute-Test")
    .Does(() =>
    {
        XUnit2(new []{
"./LoanApplication.Tests.Unit/bin/Release/LoanApplication.Tests.Unit.dll",
          "./LoanApplication.Tests/bin/Release/LoanApplication.Tests.dll"
    });
    });
```

Executing xUnit.net tests in .NET Core projects

In order to complete a build process successfully, it is important to run test projects in a solution to verify that the code works correctly. Running xUnit.net tests in a .NET Core project is relatively easy, by using the dotnet test command through the `DotNetCoreTest` alias. To have access to some other features of the **dotnet-xunit** tool, it is preferred to run the test using `DotNetCoreTool`.

Unit tests in .NET Core projects are executed by running the `dotnet test` command. This command supports all the major unit test frameworks available for writing .NET Core tests, provided that the framework has a test adapter that the `dotnet test` command can integrate to expose available unit test features.

Using the dotnet-xunit framework tool to run .NET Core tests provides access to features and settings in xUnit.net and is the preferred way of executing .NET Core tests. To get started, the dotnet-xunit tool should be installed into a .NET Core test project by editing the `.csproj` file and including the `DotNetCliToolReference` entry in the `ItemGroup` section. The `xunit.runner.visualstudio` and `Microsoft.NET.Test.Sdk` packages should be added so as to be able to execute the tests using the `dotnet test` or `dotnet xunit` commands:

```
<ItemGroup>
  <DotNetCliToolReference Include="dotnet-xunit" Version="2.3.1" />
  <PackageReference Include="xunit" Version="2.3.1" />
  PackageReference Include="xunit.runner.visualstudio" Version="2.3.1" />
</ItemGroup>
```

Additionally, there are other arguments which can be used to customize the behavior of xUnit.net framework during .NET Core unit tests execution when the `dotnet xunit` command is used. These arguments and their usages can be displayed by running `dotnet xunit --help` command on the terminal.

Cake has aliases that can be used to invoke the dotnet SDK commands to execute xUnit.net tests. The `DotNetCoreRestore` alias restores NuGet packages used in a solution using the `dotnet restore` command. Also, `DotNetCoreBuild` alias is responsible for building a .NET Core solution by using the `dotnet build` command. Unit tests in test project are executed using the `DotNetCoreTest` alias which uses the `dotnet test` command. See the following Cake snippet for the usage of the aliases.

```
var configuration = Argument("Configuration", "Release");

Task("Execute-Restore")
    .Does(() =>
```

```
    {
        DotNetCoreRestore();
    });

Task("Execute-Build")
    .IsDependentOn("Execute-Restore")
    .Does(() =>
    {
        DotNetCoreBuild("./LoanApplication.sln"
            new DotNetCoreBuildSettings()
                {
                    Configuration = configuration
                }
        );
    });

Task("Execute-Test")
    .IsDependentOn("Execute-Build")
    .Does(() =>
    {
        var testProjects =
GetFiles("./LoanApplication.Tests.Unit/*.csproj");
        foreach(var project in testProjects)
        {
            DotNetCoreTest(
                project.FullPath,
                new DotNetCoreTestSettings()
                {
                    Configuration = configuration,
                    NoBuild = true
                }
            );
        }
    });
```

Alternatively, the `DotNetCoreTool` alias can be used to execute xUnit.net tests for .NET Core projects. `DotNetCoreTool` is a general purpose alias in Cake that can be used to execute any dotnet tool. This is done by supplying the tool name and the required arguments, if any. `DotNetCoreTool` exposes the additional features available in the `dotnet xunit` command, which gives the flexibility of effectively tweaking the way the unit tests are executed. When the `DotNetCoreTool` alias is used, command-line arguments are to be passed manually into the alias. See the usage of the alias in the following snippet:

```
var configuration = Argument("Configuration", "Release");

Task("Execute-Test")
```

```
        .Does(() =>
        {
            var testProjects =
GetFiles("./LoanApplication.Tests.Unit/*.csproj");
            foreach(var testProject in testProjects)
            {
                DotNetCoreTool(
                    projectPath: testProject.FullPath,
                    command: "xunit",
                    arguments: $"-configuration {configuration} -diagnostics -
stoponfail"
                );
            }
        });
```

.NET Core versioning

Versioning the .NET Core SDK and runtime makes the platform easy to understand and allows better agility. The .NET Core platform essentially is distributed as a unit that consists of the different distributions of the frameworks, tools, installer, and NuGet packages. Also, versioning the .NET Core platform gives great flexibility as regards side-by-side application development on different platforms of .NET Core.

Beginning from .NET Core 2.0, a top-level version number that is easy to comprehend was used to version .NET Core. Some components of .NET Core version together while some do not. However, starting from Version 2.0, there is a consistent versioning strategy adopted for .NET Core distributions and components, these include the web pages, installers, and NuGet packages.

The versioning model used in .NET Core is based on the framework's runtime component [major].[minor] version numbers. Similar to the runtime versioning, the SDK version uses [major].[minor] version numbers with an additional independent [patch] that combines features and patch semantics for the SDK.

Versioning principle

As of Version 2.0 of .NET Core, the following principles were adopted:

- Version all .NET Core distributions as *x.0.0*, for example 2.0.0 for the first release and then move forward together

- File and package names should clearly represent the component or collection and its version, leaving version divergence reconciliation to minor and major version boundaries
- Clear communication should exist between the high-order versions and installers that chain multiple components

Also, beginning from .NET Core 2.0, the version numbers were unified for the shared framework and associated runtime, the .NET Core SDK and the associated .NET Core CLI and `Microsoft.NETCore.App` metapackage. Using single version numbers makes it easier to identify the version of the SDK to install on the development machine and what version the shared framework should be when moving application production environments.

Installer

Downloads for the daily builds and releases conforms to the new naming scheme. The installer UI available in the downloads was also modified to display both the names and versions of the components being installed as from .NET Core 2.0. The naming scheme format is here:

```
[product]-[component]-[major].[minor].[patch]-[previewN]-[optional build
#]-[rid].[file ext]
```

Also, the format shows in detail what is being downloaded, the version it is, on what OS it can be used, and whether it is readable. See the examples of the format as shown below:

```
dotnet-runtime-2.0.7-osx-x64.pkg                    # macOS runtime
installer
dotnet-runtime-2.0.7-win-x64.exe                    # Windows SDK installer
```

Descriptions of the website and UI strings contained in the installers are maintained and kept simple, accurate, and consistent. Sometimes an SDK release can contain more than one version of the runtime. In that case, the installer UX shows only the SDK version and installed runtime on the summary page when the installation process completes. This is applicable to the installers for both Windows and macOS.

Also, .NET Core Tools might be required to be updated, without necessarily updating the runtime. In which case, the SDK version is incremented, for example, to 2.1.2. The Runtime version will be incremented when next there is an update, while for example, both the Runtime and SDK, when updated the next time, will be shipped as 2.1.3.

Package manager

The flexibility of the .NET Core platform allows the distribution not to be done solely by Microsoft; the platform can be distributed by other entities. The platform's flexibility makes it easy to distribute installers and packages for Linux distribution owners. As well making it seamless for package maintainers to add .NET Core packages to their package managers.

The minimum package set details include `dotnet-runtime-[major].[minor]` which is the .NET runtime with the specific major+minor version combination indicated and available in the package manager for this package. The `dotnet-sdk` includes forward major, minor, patch versions as well as update rolls. Also included in the package set is the `dotnet-sdk-[major].[minor]` which is the SDK with the highest specified version of the shared frameworks and the latest host which is `dotnet-host`.

Docker

Similar to the installer and package manager, the docker tag takes the naming convention in which the version number is placed before the component name. The available docker tags include the runtime versions listed here:

- `1.0.8-runtime`
- `1.0.8-sdk`
- `2.0.4-runtime`
- `2.0.4-sdk`
- `2.1.1-runtime`
- `2.1.1-sdk`

The SDK version is increased when the .NET Core CLI tools that are included in the SDK are fixed and reshipped with an existing Runtime, for example, when the version is increased from Version 2.1.1 to version 2.1.2. Also, it is important to note that the SDK tags are updated to represent the SDK version and not the Runtime. Based on this, the Runtime will catch up with the SDK version numbering the next time it ships, for example, both the SDK and Runtime will take Version number 2.1.3 in the next release.

Semantic Versioning

Semantic Versioning is used in .NET Core to provide descriptions of the type and and degree of change that occur in a version of .NET Core. **Semantic Versioning (SemVer)** uses the MAJOR.MINOR.PATCH versioning pattern:

```
MAJOR.MINOR.PATCH[-PRERELEASE-BUILDNUMBER]
```

The PRERELEASE and BUILDNUMBER parts of SemVer are optional and not part of supported releases. They are used specifically for nightly builds, local builds from source targets, and unsupported preview releases.

The MAJOR part of the versioning is incremented when an old version is not being supported anymore, there is an adoption of a newer MAJOR version of an existing dependency, or the setting of a compatibility quirk is toggled off. MINOR is incremented whenever there is a newer MINOR version of an existing dependency or there is a new dependency, a Public API surface area, or a new behavior is added. PATCH is incremented whenever there is a newer PATCH version of an existing dependency, support for a newer platform, or there are bug fixes.

When MAJOR is incremented, MINOR and PATCH are reset to zero. Similarly, when MINOR is incremented, PATCH is reset to zero while MAJOR is not affected. This implies that whenever there are multiple changes, the highest element affected by the resulting changes is incremented while the other parts are reset to zero.

Usually, preview versions have -preview[number]-([build]|"final") appended to the version, for example, 2.1.1-preview1-final. Developers can select the desired features and level of stability based on the two types of releases of .NET Core available, which are **Long-Term Support (LTS)** and **Current**.

The LTS version is a relatively more stable platform, supported for a longer period while new features are added less frequently. The Current version adds new features and APIs more frequently, but there is a shorter allowed duration to install updates with more frequent updates being made available and a shorter support period than for LTS.

.NET Core packages and metapackages

The .NET Core platform is shipped as a set of packages that are typically called metapackages. The platform is essentially made of NuGet packages, this contributes to it being lightweight and easily distributable. The packages in .NET Core provide both primitives and higher level data types and common utilities available in the platform. Also, each package directly maps to an assembly both with the same name; `System.IO.FileSystem.dll` assembly is the package for `System.IO.FileSystem`.

Packages in .NET Core are defined as fine-grained. This comes with great benefits as the resulting application developed on the platform has small print and only contains packages that are referenced and used in the project. Unreferenced packages are not shipped as part of the application distribution. Additionally, fine-grained packages can provide differing OS and CPU support as well as dependencies peculiar to only one library. .NET Core packages usually ship using the same schedule as the platform support. This allows fixes to be distributed and installed as lightweight package updates.

Some of the NuGet packages available for .NET Core are listed here:

- `System.Runtime`: This is the .NET Core package, which includes `Object`, `String`, `Array`, `Action`, and `IList<T>`.
- `System.Reflection`: This package contains the types for loading, inspecting, and activating types, including `Assembly`, `TypeInfo`, and `MethodInfo`.
- `System.Linq`: A set of types for querying objects, including `Enumerable` and `ILookup<TKey, TElement>`.
- `System.Collections`: Types for generic collections, including `List<T>` and `Dictionary<TKey, TValue>`.
- `System.Net.Http`: Types for HTTP network communication, including `HttpClient` and `HttpResponseMessage`.
- `System.IO.FileSystem`: Types for reading and writing to local or networked, disk-based storage, including **file** and **directory**.

Referencing a package in your .Net Core project is relatively easy. For example, if you include `System.Reflection` in your project, you can reference it in the project, as shown here:

```
<Project Sdk="Microsoft.NET.Sdk">
<PropertyGroup>
<TargetFramework>netstandard2.0</TargetFramework>
</PropertyGroup>
<ItemGroup>
```

```
<PackageReference Include="System.Reflection" Version="4.3.0" />
</ItemGroup>
</Project>
```

Metapackage

Metapackage is a reference or dependency that is added to a .NET Core project in addition to the already referenced target framework in the project. For example, you can add `Microsoft.NETCore.App` or `NetStandard.Library` to a .NET Core project.

At times, it is required to use a set of packages in a project. This is done through the use of metapackages. Metapackages are groups of packages that are often used together. Also, metapackages are NuGet packages that describe a group or set of packages. Metapackages can create a framework for the packages when the framework is specified.

When you reference a metapackage, essentially a reference is made to all the packages contained in the metapackage. In essence, this makes the libraries in the packages available for IntelliSense during project development with Visual Studio. Also, the libraries will be available when the project is being published.

In a .NET Core project, a metapackage is referenced by the framework targeted in the project, which implies that a metapackage is strongly associated or tied to a specific framework. Metapackages give access to groups of packages that have already been confirmed and tested to work together.

The .NET Standard metapackage is the `NETStandard.Library`, which constitutes a set of libaries in the .NET Standard. This is applicable to the different variants of the .NET platforms: .NET Core, .NET Framework and Mono framework.

`Microsoft.NETCore.App` and `Microsoft.NETCore.Portable.Compatibility` are the main .NET Core metapackages. `Microsoft.NETCore.App` describes the set of libraries that constitute the .NET Core distribution and depends on `NETStandard.Library`.

`Microsoft.NETCore.Portable.Compatibility` describes the set of facades that enable the mscorlib-based **Portable Class Libraries (PCLs)** to work on .NET Core.

Microsoft.AspNetCore.All metapackage

Microsoft.AspNetCore.All is the metapackage for ASP.NET Core. The metapackage comprises packages supported and maintained by the ASP.NET Core team, supported packages by Entity Framework Core, as well as the internal and third-party dependencies used by both ASP.NET Core and Entity Framework Core.

The available default project templates that target ASP.NET Core 2.0 use the Microsoft.AspNetCore.All package. The version numbers of ASP.NET Core version and Entity Framework Core are similar to that of the Microsoft.AspNetCore.All metapackage. All available features in ASP.NET Core 2.x and Entity Framework Core 2.x are included in the Microsoft.AspNetCore.All package.

When you create an ASP.NET Core application that references the Microsoft.AspNetCore.All metapackage, .NET Core Runtime Store is made available for your usage. .NET Core Runtime Store exposes the required runtime assets to run ASP.NET Core 2.x applications.

During deployment, assets from the referenced ASP.NET Core NuGet packages are not deployed together with the application, the assets are in the .NET Core Runtime Store. These assets are precompiled for performance gain, to speed up application startup time. Also, it is desirable to exclude packages that are not used. This is done by using the package-trimming process.

To use Microsoft.AspNetCore.All packages, it should be added as a reference to the .NET Core .csproj project file, like in the following XML config:

```xml
<Project Sdk="Microsoft.NET.Sdk.Web">

  <PropertyGroup>
    <TargetFramework>netcoreapp2.0</TargetFramework>
  </PropertyGroup>

  <ItemGroup>
    <PackageReference Include="Microsoft.AspNetCore.All" Version="2.0.0" />
  </ItemGroup>

</Project>
```

Packaging for NuGet distribution

.NET Core's flexibility is not only limited to the application's development, it extends to the deployment process. Deploying .NET Core applications can take two forms—**framework-dependent deployment (FDD)** and **self-contained deployment (SCD)**.

Using the FDD approach requires that there is a system-wide .NET Core installed on the machine where the application will be developed. The installed .NET Core runtime will be shared by your application and other applications deployed on the machine.

This allows your application to be portable between the versions or installations of the .NET Core framework. Also, with this approach, your deployment will be lightweight and only contain your application's code and the third-party libraries used. When using this approach, `.dll` files are created for your application, which allows it to be launched from the command line.

SCD allows you to package your application together with the .NET Core libraries and .NET Core runtime that are required to make it run. Essentially, your application does not rely on the presence of installed .NET Core on the deployment machine.

When using this approach, an executable file, which essentially is a renamed version of the platform-specific .NET Core host will be packaged as part of the application. This executable file is `app.exe` on Windows or `app` on Linux and macOS. Similar to when the application is deployed using the *framework-dependent approach*, `.dll` files are created for your application that allows it to be launched.

dotnet publish command

The `dotnet publish` command is used to compile the application, and to check the application's dependencies before copying the application and the dependencies into a folder in preparation for deployment. The execution of the command is the only officially supported way of preparing the .NET Core application for deployment. The synopsis is here:

```
dotnet publish [<PROJECT>] [-c|--configuration] [-f|--framework] [--force]
[--manifest] [--no-dependencies] [--no-restore] [-o|--output] [-r|--
runtime] [--self-contained] [-v|--verbosity] [--version-suffix]


dotnet publish [-h|--help]
```

When the command is run, the output will contain the **Intermediate Language** (IL) code contained in a `.dll` assembly, a `.deps.json` file that contains the project's dependencies, a `.runtime.config.json` file that specifies the expected shared runtime, and the application's dependencies copied from the NuGet cache into the output folder.

The command's argument and options are explained here:

- `PROJECT`: To specify the project to be compiled and published, it defaults to the current folder.
- `-c|--configuration`: This option is used to specify the build configuration, it takes the `Debug` and `Release` values, the default value is `Debug`.
- `-f|--framework <FRAMEWORK>`: The target framework option, when specified with the command, will publish the application for the target framework.
- `--force`: Used to force dependencies to be resolved, similar to deleting the `project.assets.json` file.
- `-h|--help`: Displays the help for the command.
- `--manifest <PATH_TO_MANIFEST_FILE>`: For specifying one or more target manifests to be used in trimming the packages published with the application.
- `--no-dependencies`: This option is used to ignore project-to-project references but restores the root project.
- `--no-restore`: This is to instruct the command not to perform an implicit restore.
- `-o|--output <OUTPUT_DIRECTORY>`: This is for specifying the path of the output directory. If the option is not specified, it defaults to `./bin/[configuration]/[framework]/` for an FDD or `./bin/[configuration]/[framework]/[runtime]` for an SCD.
- `-r|--runtime <RUNTIME_IDENTIFIER>`: The option is for publishing the application for a given runtime, used only when creating an SCD.
- `--self-contained`: Is for specifying an SCD. When a runtime identifier is specified, its default value is true.
- `-v|--verbosity <LEVEL>`: For specifying the verbosity level of the `dotnet publish` command. The allowed values are `q[uiet]`, `n[ormal]`, `m[inimal]`, `diag[nostic]`, and `d[etailed]`.
- `--version-suffix <VERSION_SUFFIX>`: For specifying the version suffix to be used when replacing the asterisk (*) in the version field of the project file.

An example of the command usage is running `dotnet publish` on the command line. This publishes the project in the current folder. To publish the `LoanApplication` project that was used in this book, you can run the `dotnet publish` command. This will publish the application using the framework specified in the project. The projects in the solution that the ASP.NET Core application depends on will be built alongside. See the following screenshot:

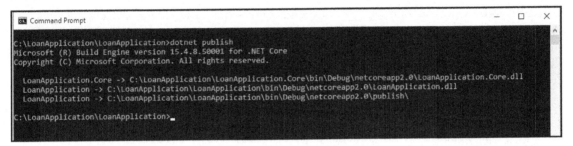

A `publish` folder is created in the `netcoreapp2.0` folder where all the compiled files and the dependencies will be copied to:

Name	Date modified	Type	Size
wwwroot	4/24/2018 1:20 PM	File folder	
appsettings.Development.json	12/21/2017 11:17 ...	JSON File	1 KB
appsettings.json	12/21/2017 11:17 ...	JSON File	1 KB
bower.json	12/21/2017 11:17 ...	JSON File	1 KB
bundleconfig.json	12/21/2017 11:17 ...	JSON File	1 KB
LoanApplication.Core.dll	4/24/2018 1:20 PM	Application extens...	5 KB
LoanApplication.Core.pdb	4/24/2018 1:20 PM	Program Debug D...	1 KB
LoanApplication.deps.json	4/24/2018 1:20 PM	JSON File	289 KB
LoanApplication.dll	4/24/2018 1:20 PM	Application extens...	9 KB
LoanApplication.pdb	4/24/2018 1:20 PM	Program Debug D...	2 KB
LoanApplication.PrecompiledViews.dll	4/24/2018 1:20 PM	Application extens...	74 KB
LoanApplication.PrecompiledViews.pdb	4/24/2018 1:20 PM	Program Debug D...	46 KB
LoanApplication.runtimeconfig.json	4/24/2018 1:20 PM	JSON File	1 KB
web.config	4/24/2018 1:20 PM	XML Configuratio...	1 KB

Creating a NuGet package

NuGet is the package manager for .NET, it is an open source package manager that provides an easier way of versioning and distributing libraries for applications built on both .NET Framework and the .NET Core platform. The NuGet gallery is the .NET central package repository for hosting all packages used by both package authors and consumers.

Using the .NET Core's `dotnet pack` command makes it easy to create NuGet packages. When this command is run, it builds a .NET Core project and creates a NuGet package from it. NuGet dependencies of a packed .NET Core project will be added to the `.nuspec` file, to ensure they're resolved when the package is installed. The following command synopsis is shown:

```
dotnet pack [<PROJECT>] [-c|--configuration] [--force] [--include-source]
[--include-symbols] [--no-build] [--no-dependencies]
    [--no-restore] [-o|--output] [--runtime] [-s|--serviceable] [-v|--
verbosity] [--version-suffix]
dotnet pack [-h|--help]
```

The command's argument and options are explained here:

- `PROJECT` is to specify the project to pack, which can be a path to a directory or a `.csproj` file. It defaults to the current folder.
- `c|--configuration`: This option is used to define the build configuration. It takes the `Debug` and `Release` values. The default value is `Debug`.
- `--force`: Used to force dependencies to be resolved similar to deleting the `project.assets.json` file.
- `-h|--help`: Displays the help for the command.
- `-include-source`: It's to specify that the source files be included in the `src` folder in the NuGet package.
- `--include-symbols`: To generate the `nupkg` symbols.
- `--no-build`: This is to instruct the command to not build the project before packing.
- `--no-dependencies`: This option is used to ignore project-to-project references but restores the root project.
- `--no-restore`: This is to instruct the command not to perform an implicit restore.
- `-o|--output <OUTPUT_DIRECTORY>`: This is for specifying the path of the output directory to place the built packages.

- `-r|--runtime <RUNTIME_IDENTIFIER>`: This option is to specify the target runtime to restore the packages for.
- `-s|--serviceable`: Is for setting the serviceable flag in the package.
- `-v|--verbosity <LEVEL>`: For specifying the verbosity level of the command. The allowed values are `q[uiet]`, `m[inimal]`, `n[ormal]`, `d[etailed]`, and `diag[nostic]`.
- `--version-suffix <VERSION_SUFFIX>`: For specifying the version suffix to be used when replacing the asterisk (*) in the version field of the project file.

Running the `dotnet pack` command will pack the project in the current directory. To pack the `LoanApplication.Core` project, we can run the following command:

```
dotnet pack
C:\LoanApplication\LoanApplication.Core\LoanApplication.Core.csproj --
output nupkgs
```

When the command is run, the `LoanApplication.Core` project will be built and packed into the `nupkgs` file in the project folder. The `LoanApplication.Core.1.0.0.nupkg` file will be created, which is an archive file containing the packed project's libraries:

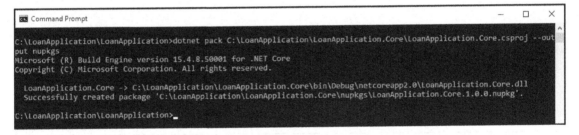

After the application has been packed, it can be published to the NuGet gallery by using the `dotnet nuget push` command. In order to be able to push packages to NuGet, you need to register for NuGet API keys. These keys are to be specified as options with the `dotnet nuget push` command when uploading packages to NuGet.

Run the `dotnet nuget push LoanApplication.Core.1.0.0.nupkg -k <api-key> -s https://www.nuget.org/` command to push the created NuGet package to the gallery, which will make it available for use by other developers. When the command is run, a connection will be established to the NuGet server to push the package under your account:

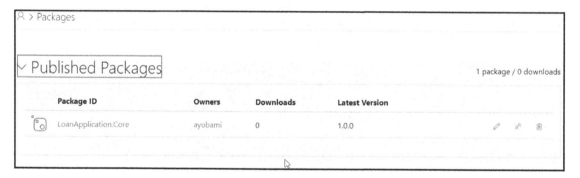

After the package has been pushed to NuGet gallery, when you log in to your account, you can find the pushed package in the list of published packages:

When you upload your package to the NuGet gallery, other programmers can search for your package directly from Visual Studio by using the NuGet package manager and add a reference to the libraries in their projects.

Summary

In this chapter, we started by executing the xUnit.net test with Cake. Also, we extensively discussed .NET Core versioning, the concepts, and how it affects application development on the .NET Core platform. Later, we packaged the `LoanApplication` project that was used in this book for NuGet distribution.

You have been taken through an exciting TDD journey in this book. Using the xUnit.net unit test framework, the concept of TDD was introduced and discussed extensively. Data-driven unit tests were covered, which allow you to test your code with data from different data sources.

The Moq framework was used to introduce and explain how to unit test code with dependencies. The TeamCity CI server was used to explain the concepts of CI. Cake, a cross-platform build system was explored and used to create build steps executed in TeamCity. Also, Microsoft VSTS, another CI tool, was used to execute Cake scripts.

Finally, effective use of TDD is greatly rewarding in terms of the quality of code and resulting application. With continuous practices, all the concepts explained in this book can become part of your day-to-day programming routine.

Other Books You May Enjoy

If you enjoyed this book, you may be interested in these other books by Packt:

.NET Core 2.0 By Example
Rishabh Verma, Neha Shrivastava

ISBN: 978-1-78839-509-0

- Build cross-platform applications with ASP.NET Core 2.0 and its tools
- Integrate, host, and deploy web apps with the cloud (Microsoft Azure)
- Leverage the ncurses native library to extend console capabilities in .NET Core on Linux and interop with native code
- Reuse existing .NET Framework and Mono assemblies from .NET Core 2.0 applications
- Develop real-time web applications using ASP.NET Core
- Learn the differences between SOA and microservices and get started with microservice development using ASP.NET Core 2.0
- Walk through functional programming with F# and .NET Core from scratch

.NET Standard 2.0 Cookbook
Fiqri Ismail

ISBN: 978-1-78883-466-7

- Create a .NET Standard 2.0 library
- Use System.IO within the .NET Standard 2.0
- Make use of your legacy .NET libraries with the new .NET Core standard
- Explore the thread support to create a multithreaded .NET Standard 2.0 library
- Create a .NET Standard 2.0 library and use it with an Android and iOS application
- Implement various Visual Studio 2017 diagnostics and debugging tools
- Create a NuGet Package and submit the package to the NuGet Package Manager
- Use Visual Studio 2017 azure tools to deploy the application to Azure
- Test and deliver a .NET Standard 2.0 library

Leave a review - let other readers know what you think

Please share your thoughts on this book with others by leaving a review on the site that you bought it from. If you purchased the book from Amazon, please leave us an honest review on this book's Amazon page. This is vital so that other potential readers can see and use your unbiased opinion to make purchasing decisions, we can understand what our customers think about our products, and our authors can see your feedback on the title that they have worked with Packt to create. It will only take a few minutes of your time, but is valuable to other potential customers, our authors, and Packt. Thank you!

Index

Made in the USA
Coppell, TX
08 July 2020